This is a comprehensive examination of Eliot's work
keeps in close
lations with
exegesis. Star
intellectual (
emotional) b
ative year
su

D0629176

considers this progress more in terms of the growth of the intellectual life . . . Both on the techniques and on the attitudes and beliefs of Mr. Eliot, Professor Smidt has much to say that, whether one is in agreement with it all or not, notably refreshes a well-worn subject."

—*The Times Literary Supplement*

" A professional job of work, which is also a pleasure to read."

POETRY AND BELIEF
IN THE WORK OF
T. S. ELIOT

POETRY AND BELIEF
IN THE WORK OF
T. S. ELIOT

by
KRISTIAN SMIDT

LONDON
ROUTLEDGE AND KEGAN PAUL

First published 1949
by the Norwegian Academy of Science and Letters

This completely revised edition
first published in England 1961
by Routledge & Kegan Paul Limited
Broadway House, 68–74, Carter Lane,
London, E.C.4

Reprinted 1967

Printed in Great Britain
by Lowe & Brydone (Printers) Ltd.
London

CONTENTS

Contents

ACKNOWLEDGEMENTS

THE Norwegian Academy of Science and Letters in Oslo, which brought out the first edition of this book, has generously given me a free hand in using it afresh, and I have been glad to take the opportunity for a thorough revision. The chapter on 'Point of View in Eliot's Poetry' originally appeared in a slightly different form in *Orbis Litterarum*, XIV, 1 (1959), and I am grateful to the editors for permission to incorporate it in the present work.

My thanks are due, as before, to Mr Eliot for granting me personal interviews in which he very kindly and patiently answered the questions I put to him. He is of course not responsible for any of my opinions or my interpretations of his statements. I am also obliged to Mr Eliot for permission to print quotations from *The Criterion* and from his address *On Poetry*; to Mr Eliot and Faber & Faber (and Harcourt, Brace in the U.S.A.) for quotations from *Murder in the Cathedral*, *Four Quartets*, *The Use of Poetry and the Use of Criticism* (Barnes and Noble in the U.S.A.), *Selected Essays* and minor quotations from other sources; to Mr Eliot and the Editor for quotations from the *New English Weekly*; and to Mr Eliot and the Editor for quotations from *The Listener*.

Finally, I wish to record my indebtedness to Mr Donald Gallup and his invaluable *T. S. Eliot: A Bibliography*, without which it would have been hard to find much of the material which has been drawn upon for this study.

'I am not eager to rehearse
My thought and theory which you have forgotten.
These things have served their purpose: let them be.'

(*Little Gidding*)

The various attempts to find the fundamental axioms behind both good literature and good life are among the most interesting 'experiments' of criticism in our time.

('Experiment in Criticism')

INTRODUCTION

M Y aim in this book is not to present a line-by-line elucidation
of Eliot's poetic works. This is a task which has already
been often and skilfully performed in respect of most of them. I
propose rather to explore the general background of attitudes,
beliefs and ideas from which the works have sprung. I do not, of
course, equate the philosophical sources with the finished product
of poetry, and to make this clear I shall include a consideration of
the creative process as described in Eliot's critical writings, as well
as a discussion of the kind and degree of belief which must be
assumed in the poet and required of the reader in relation to the
more or less explicit philosophy of the poems. Another problem
is the extent to which the poet is concerned with what he says and
the extent to which he concentrates on how to say it; a problem
which is forced upon us by the fact that both form and content
seem to clamour for special attention in Eliot's works and the fact
that his criticism has a good deal to say about their relationship.
In this connection, and because the poet in his later phase is a
professing Christian and uses religious themes for his works, we
shall have to ask whether an aesthetic view of poetry as an autonomous human activity can be reconciled with the absolute
demands of a religious belief.

It is hardly necessary for the present purpose to decipher Eliot's
poetry in terms of personal experiences. It would be useless labour
anyhow to attempt a reconstruction of all the memories, feelings
and thoughts which were in a poet's mind at the moment of
writing. Eliot quite understandably derides the biographical kind
of interpretation. And yet it is undeniable that poetry may have
its most significant sources in private experiences and that we are
curious to know their nature. Eliot has told us often enough that

such experiences have gone into the making of his own poems. The conception of a kind of impersonal core in the poet's soul whence his inspiration proceeds, though it may be a useful check to critics of the extreme biographical school, is a phantom and an illusion. A man does not'arrive at his opinions simply by deductions from abstract premisses, nor does he write poetry by a mechanical gestation of impersonal matter. Poetry is autobiographical.

'But,' says Eliot, 'this autobiography is written by a foreign man in a foreign tongue, which can never be translated.'[1] If this were strictly true we should be confined in the interpretation of poetry merely to the impressions of an indefinite number of different readers. We should have to believe that comparison and analysis, Eliot's favourite instruments of criticism, could yield us no understanding of the poet's intentions which could not be gained equally well by a sensitive reading of a poem. But although it may be true that a poem, as far as its meaning goes, is as much the reader's property as the writer's, we cannot content ourselves with this partial truth. We may give up gladly enough, since it must be so, a detailed knowledge of the poet's private experiences. I do not pretend that I can always tell what is fact in Eliot's poetry and what fiction. I do not expect that he should permanently believe all the statements that he makes in his poetry. Nor do I suppose that the poetry reveals his more particular views on particular subjects. But I do think it provides us with the terms of reference which we need to enable us to examine its outward and public significance. The poetry as a whole shows us the poet's general feelings and opinions, his view of life and his main philosophical positions. And far from having to resign ourselves to these generalities, we should be glad to be confined to them. They are precisely what should interest us: for it is the general attitudes and principles whose imaginative presentation produces the greatest repercussions, in individual minds and cultural life.

If we read thoughtfully, I think our interpretation will only come to rest in identifying itself with what we discover to be the poet's meaning. But I hasten to add that this only applies to one aspect of the poetry, that which, broadly speaking, can be labelled communication. In the total appreciation, the reader's background of private experiences must play such a large part that a

[1] *Nation and Athenæum*, Feb. 12, 1927.

complete identification of the significance of a given poem to the reader with its significance to the poet must remain forever unattainable.

In principle, then, we are not concerned with the poet's private life, nor is it our business to try to analyse and reconstruct his psychological make-up. But his life concerns us up to the point where we know enough to understand what he really wishes to convey and to avoid being held up in our enjoyment by his idiosyncrasies. If we wish to estimate the cognitive nature of T. S. Eliot's poetry it is necessary that we should know something about his geographical and cultural environments in successive periods, his main occupations and interests and the people with whom, as a writer, he has most significantly associated.

Eliot has used his personal experiences to create poetry, which in its nature is not personal so much as supra-personal; in fact, he once liked to think of it as *im*personal. He believes in the ability of the poetic mind to make comprehensive patterns out of scattered events, or, as he expressed it in a well-known essay, to amalgamate disparate experience, like falling in love and the smell of cooking. It is a main thesis of my book that such amalgamation is carried forward into the realm of ideas. And this does not merely produce a syncretism which from a philosophical or theological point of view might be a levelling-down of its component elements. It implies a whole which is in one sense more than its parts and in another sense different from them. I would ask the reader to bear in mind that this study is not primarily concerned with philosophy, but with poetry, and that poetry, like religion, is not averse to the accumulation of belief or beliefs, even in defiance of logic.

My attempt to present Eliot's views and my analysis of his works involves a rather abundant use of quotations, for which I would ask indulgence were it not that Eliot's own words are not only frequently needed but are so much more eloquent than mine. In prose quotations I have occasionally taken the liberty of substituting lower-case letters for initial capitals or vice-versa, depending on how the quotations are introduced; but I trust I have interfered in no other way with either phrasing or meaning.

ABBREVIATIONS
used in the footnotes

CR	*The Criterion*
EAM	T. S. Eliot, *Essays Ancient and Modern* (1945 edn.)
SE	T. S. Eliot, *Selected Essays* (1946 edn.)
UPC	T. S. Eliot, *The Use of Poetry and the Use of Criticism* (1945 edn.)

I

BACKGROUND AND INFLUENCES

I N the development of every man it is probably the first thirty years or so that count most. Knowledge and experience come to him with the greatest novelty in those years, his interests become clear to him and his profession is chosen or forced upon him. His opinions, tastes and attitudes have usually solidified in their main outlines by the time he is thirty. Afterwards comes a slower accretion of knowledge and experience, and, though sudden illuminations and changes occur, the rest is normally adaptation and modification on the existing basis, as well as the gradual strengthening or the gradual crumbling of that basis itself.

Eliot was still allowing himself to be guided quite extensively by the opinions of others when he was well over thirty, as is evident from his submission to Ezra Pound in the drafting of *The Waste Land*. His period of acknowledged Christianity did not begin till he was almost forty, and the process of freeing himself from outworn opinions and old prejudices can be traced to quite recent years. It may be asserted with some plausibility that Eliot only found himself in middle age. Nevertheless, the impressions and events of his early life have doubtless been of great significance. He recognises that 'The primary channel of transmission of culture is the family: no man wholly escapes from the kind, or wholly surpasses the degree, of culture which he acquired from his early environment.'[1]

[1] *Notes towards the Definition of Culture* (1948), p. 43.

Eliot spent the first sixteen years of his life in St Louis. And it may be considered surprising, in view of the relatively short time that he lived in and near Boston, that his New England background should be as frequently and as strongly stressed as it is. But we must accept the fact that the roots of old Yankee families clung with particular tenacity to their original soil when those families were transplanted to mid-western and western communities. It is natural enough that the Eliot children should have absorbed in their home something of the atmosphere of Massachusetts, where their mother had grown up, whence sprang their ancestors on both sides, and where the family still had its strongest connections.

Probably some of the pride of New England traditions lingered with the family and was imparted to the children. But at the time of Eliot's birth in 1888, New England culture was declining, and the Yankee spirit was not what it had been. 'The Boston mind,' says Mr Van Wyck Brooks, 'once so cheerful, was full of the sense of last things, as if it hoped for no resuscitation.' The literary tradition was exhausted, and the religious tradition, dissolving before the progress of Roman Catholicism, Jewry and Christian Science, was also in an advanced state of decay.[1] The fatigue may have communicated itself to some extent to the Bostonians settled in St Louis. At any rate, some of the pessimism which flourished in Eliot's early poetry may have derived from his closer contact with New England life in his youth.

The family background included the extreme form of Protestant rationalism known as Unitarianism, and the philosophies of Schleiermacher, Emerson, Channing and Herbert Spencer were held in high regard.[2] Unitarianism to Eliot seems intimately connected with what he calls 'the Boston doubt: a scepticism which is difficult to explain to those who are not born to it. This scepticism,' he goes on, 'is . . . not destructive, but it is dissolvent.'[3] In another context, however, he speaks of 'the best aspect of Unitarianism, a kind of emotional reserve and intellectual integrity'.[4] It is clear that in maturity he found much in this teaching that appealed to his temperament, whether or not the temperament

[1] Van Wyck Brooks, *New England: Indian Summer* (1946), pp. 409, 414.
[2] Cf. Eliot's introduction to *Savonarola* (1926) by Charlotte Eliot.
[3] 'A Sceptical Patrician', *Athenæum*, May 23, 1919.
[4] Book review, *CR*, May 1927.

itself had been gradually formed by the teaching. But a child, one supposes, may quite possibly have been irked by the austerity of Unitarianism. It lacked the picturesque elements of most Christian creeds. In fact it excluded itself from Christianity, as Eliot was aware: 'I was brought up outside the Christian Fold, in Unitarianism; and in the form of Unitarianism in which I was instructed, things were either black or white. The Son and the Holy Ghost were not believed in, certainly; but they were entitled to respect as entities in which many other people believed.'[1] This stern enlightenment must have been salutary in many respects. But children need at least as much nourishment for their senses and emotions as for their intellects. And they take it where they can find it, irrespective of creed. There can be no doubt, for instance, that an engraving of Murillo's Immaculate Conception, which as Mr Eliot has told me hung in his parents' house, made an enduring impression on his mind, and that the impression can be traced in some of his later work, particularly *Ash-Wednesday*. And who knows but that the Irish nursemaid Annie Dunne, to whom young Eliot was greatly attached, was the first to attract him in the direction of Catholicism. At least he still remembers an occasion on which she brought him along to her little Catholic church.[2]

Although Eliot's grandfather, one of the founders of Washington University, died before the poet was born, the family remained very much aware of his influence. When Eliot addressed members of Washington University at the centenary of its foundation in 1953, he began by telling them entertainingly about some of his childhood memories and about the general outlook that prevailed in his home:

> The standard of conduct was that which my grandfather had set; our moral judgements, our decisions between duty and self-indulgence, were taken as if, like Moses, he had brought down the tables of the Law, any deviation from which would be sinful. Not the least of these laws, which included injunctions still more than prohibitions, was the law of Public Service. . . . This original Law of Public Service operated especially in three areas: the Church, the City, and the University. . . . These were the symbols of Religion, the

---

[1] Book review, *CR*, July 1931.
[2] *American Literature and the American Language* (1953), Appendix, p. 29.

Community, and Education: and I think it is a very good beginning for any child, to be brought up to reverence such institutions, and to be taught that personal and selfish aims should be subordinated to the general good which they represent.[1]

The poet's father was in business and added the morality of the Puritan business man to the family ethos. T. S. Eliot wrote in later life that in the Puritan morality that he remembered, 'it was tacitly assumed that if one was thrifty, enterprising, intelligent, practical and prudent in not violating social conventions' success was assured.[2] He has come to see this morality as a 'secular heresy' but it is not improbable that his own adherence to it has contributed to his fair success in worldly affairs.

The boy's literary interests, one may assume, were stimulated by his mother, who was by way of being a writer herself, and whose dramatic poem *Savonarola* T. S. Eliot published with an introduction in 1926.

As for his geographical surroundings, we have Eliot's words to the effect that Missouri and the Mississippi have made a deeper impression on him than any other part of the world. 'I feel,' he wrote to a St Louis newspaper in 1930, 'that there is something in having passed one's childhood beside the big river, which is incommunicable to those who have not.'[3] However, the scenery of Massachusetts has entered into his poems as much as that of Missouri. He tells us that his family

> guarded jealously its connexions with New England; but it was not until years of maturity that I perceived that I myself had always been a New Englander in the South West, and a South Westerner in New England. . . . In New England I missed the long dark river, the ailanthus trees, the flaming cardinal birds, the high limestone bluffs where we searched for fossil shell-fish; in Missouri I missed the fir trees, the bay and goldenrod, the song-sparrows, the red granite and the blue sea of Massachusetts.[4]

The river and the sea, associated in the poet's mind with two such different places, were to become symbols of two planes of

[1] *American Literature and the American Language*, Appendix, pp. 4–5.
[2] Book review, *CR*, April 1937.
[3] Quoted in *American Literature and the American Language*, p. 29.
[4] Preface to E. A. Mowrer, *This American World* (1928).

existence, as in the first section of *The Dry Salvages*. There, the
river is 'a strong brown god':

> His rhythm was present in the nursery bedroom,
> In the rank ailanthus of the April dooryard,
> In the smell of grapes on the autumn table,
> And the evening circle in the winter gaslight.

And the sea has its

> beaches where it tosses
> Its hints of earlier and other creation:
> The starfish, the horseshoe crab, the whale's backbone;
> The pools where it offers to our curiosity
> The more delicate algae and the sea anemone.

These are boyhood observations put to a use undreamt-of when
they were first treasured up.

It is possible that feelings of ecstatic happiness are remembered
in connection with some of these observations. Sensitive children
may be almost overpowered by unaccustomed impressions of
colour and pattern, especially in natural objects. A friend of mine
has told me of his sense of mysterious exaltation on entering
a greenhouse for the first time as a boy. And Eliot speaks of 'the
experience of a child of ten, a small boy peering through sea-water
in a rock-pool, and finding a sea-anemone for the first time'. It
may be a simple experience, he says, but is 'not so simple, for an
exceptional child, as it looks'.[1]

There was enough for the eye in the landscapes in which Eliot
grew up, and enough that called upon the activity of a youngster.
What is clearly a memory from childhood which frequently
occurs in his poems is the image of children climbing an apple-
tree in an orchard. It has become a symbol of innocent bliss, and
is an instance of the poet's continual insistence on childhood as
the period of happiness. One becomes aware that he feels quite
strongly on this subject, and his childhood happiness fits well into
our general picture of his development. This development is
sketched—impersonally, but necessarily drawing upon much

---

[1] *UPC*, pp. 78–9.

personal matter—in *Animula,* where the child, in its first contacts
with the world, takes pleasure

> In the fragrant brilliance of the Christmas tree,
> Pleasure in the wind, the sunlight and the sea;
> Studies the sunlit pattern on the floor
> And running stags around a silver tray;
> Confounds the actual and the fanciful,
> Content with playing-cards and kings and queens,
> What the fairies do and what the servants say.

But this serenity did not last:

> The heavy burden of the growing soul
> Perplexes and offends more, day by day;
> Week by week, offends and perplexes more
> With the imperatives of 'is and seems'
> And may and may not, desire and control.
> The pain of living and the drug of dreams
> Curl up the small soul in the window seat
> Behind the *Encyclopaedia Britannica.*

Perhaps 'the drug of dreams' has a personal application, for as
boyhood turned into youth it looks as if real happiness dwindled.
'I am quite well aware,' said the poet in a broadcast talk, 'how unpleasant early youth can be or how few sensitive men were happy
in it.'[1] That young Eliot was more than usually sensitive we need
not doubt, and since he was intellectually wide-awake as well, his
experiences came to him in double guise. 'It is probable,' he wrote
when he was thirty, 'that men ripen best through experiences
which are at once sensuous and intellectual; certainly many men
will admit that their keenest ideas have come to them with the
quality of a sense-perception; and that their keenest sensuous experience has been "as if the body thought".'[2] It is possible that
Eliot's delicate sensibility, too often hurt in an insensitive world,
sought refuge in a certain aloofness. Mr Edmund Wilson suggests
that like Henry James and several other New England writers,
Eliot spent much of his maturity 'regretting an emotionally under-
nourished youth', the main cause of which was the Puritanism of
his environment and upbringing.[3] There may be some justice in

[1] *Listener,* April 6, 1932.
[2] 'A Sceptical Patrician', *Athenæum,* May 23, 1919.
[3] E. Wilson, *Axel's Castle* (1931), pp. 102, 105.

these words. But as for the 'situations unexplored' and the 'passions inhibited' that Mr Wilson darkly suggests, they must, if real, be left to the poet's privacy. We may speculate upon, but we must not infer too much from, what he has given us himself: namely the frequently recurring episode of an ecstasy of love broken and frustrated in some vague period of childhood and youth, a scene in an arbour during a shower of rain, a girl with brown hair holding flowers in her arms. The scene is glimpsed in a great number of poems and plays, in *La Figlia Che Piange*, *Dans le Restaurant*, *The Waste Land*, *Ash-Wednesday*, *The Family Reunion*, to mention the most conspicuous cases. However, the scene may have only a general application to the poet's feelings, itself being entirely imaginary, or it may simply have been suggested by Dante.

In his centenary address at Washington University, Eliot mentioned the education he had received 'in that preparatory department of the University which was named Smith Academy'—the most important part of his education as he thought. The subjects he was taught were 'the essentials: Latin and Greek, together with Greek and Roman history, English and American history, elementary mathematics, French and German. Also English!' And he was 'happy to remember that in those days English composition was still called *Rhetoric*'. He failed to pass his entrance examination in physics, but he was recommended warmly by his English master for his 'first poem, written as a class exercise'. On the whole, he said, his memories of Smith Academy were happy ones, though a certain amount of adolescent spleen seems to have crept into his life towards the end of his schooldays. In his last year he wrote his first published poems, which were printed in the school magazine.[1] He referred to them later as 'verses in the manner of *Don Juan*, tinged with that disillusion and cynicism only possible at the age of sixteen'.[2]

Up to now, his interest in literature had, by his own account, been sporadic. As a boy he had 'a liking for martial and sanguinary poetry' such as *Horatius*, *The Burial of Sir John Moore*, *Bannockburn*, Tennyson's *Revenge*. But Shakespeare left him cold. Then, he says,

my early liking for the sort of verse that small boys do like vanished at about the age of twelve, leaving me for a couple of years with no

---

[1] *A Fable for Feasters* and *A Lyric*.
[2] 'Byron' in B. Dobrée (ed.), *From Anne to Victoria* (1937), p. 602.

sort of interest in poetry at all. I can recall clearly enough the moment when, at the age of fourteen or so, I happened to pick up a copy of Fitzgerald's *Omar* which was lying about, and the almost overwhelming introduction to a new world of feeling which this poem was the occasion of giving me. It was like a sudden conversion; the world appeared anew, painted with bright, delicious and painful colours. Thereupon I took the usual adolescent course with Byron, Shelley, Keats, Rossetti, Swinburne.

This period he takes to have persisted until about his twenty-second year, and while it lasted his consciousness was from time to time completely under the sway of different poets, so that what mattered was not so much the actual poetry that he read as the 'new and delightful feelings' in which he was absorbed. The frequent result was 'an outburst of scribbling which we may call imitation, so long as we are aware of the meaning of the word "imitation" which we employ. It is not deliberate choice of a poet to mimic, but writing under a kind of daemonic possession by one poet.'[1] At school the boy was also introduced to the classic poets of Greece and Rome. He very much enjoyed reciting Homer or Virgil, he says, but in his own fashion, which meant that he ignored the metrical rules.[2] As for contemporary writers, or American writers, there were apparently none that made any impression whatsoever upon him. And this continued to be so after he had entered Harvard in 1906. Here are his own words:

> Whatever may have been the literary scene in America between the beginning of the century and the year 1914, it remains in my mind a complete blank. I cannot remember the name of a single poet of that period whose work I read: it was only in 1915, after I came to England, that I heard the name of Robert Frost. Undergraduates at Harvard in my time read the English poets of the '90s, who were dead; that was as near as we could get to any living tradition. Certainly I cannot remember any English poet then alive who contributed to my own education. Yeats was well-known, of course; but to me, at least, Yeats did not appear, until after 1917, to be anything but a minor survivor of the '90s. (After that date I saw him very differently . . .) . . . there was no poet, in either country, who could have been of use to a beginner in 1908. The only recourse was to poetry of another age and to poetry of another language.[3]

---

[1] *UPC*, pp. 33–4.   [2] *The Music of Poetry* (1942), p. 9.
[3] 'Ezra Pound', *New English Weekly*, Oct. 31, 1946. See also *CR*, Commentary, April 1934; and Note p. 33.

Background and Influences

About 1906 Eliot first read John Donne,[1] but it was his discovery of the French Symbolists that really launched him on his career. In 1908 he read Arthur Symons's *The Symbolist Movement in Literature*, which came to him 'as an introduction to wholly new feelings, as a revelation'.[2] 'But for having read his book,' he says, 'I should not, in the year 1908, have heard of Laforgue or Rimbaud; I should probably not have begun to read Verlaine; and but for reading Verlaine, I should not have heard of Corbière. So the Symons book is one of those which have affected the course of my life.'[3]

How deeply it must have affected the course of his life becomes evident on reading it. One feels that Eliot may have modelled himself, simultaneously or in turn, on each and all of the writers presented by Symons, *as* presented by Symons. Of Huysmans, for instance, Symons says that he has 'the air of one perfectly resigned to the boredom of life'. 'It is always the unpleasant aspect of things that he seizes, but the intensity of his revolt from that unpleasantness brings a touch of the sublime into the very expression of his disgust. . . . He speaks with an accent as of pained surprise, an amused look of contempt, so profound that it becomes almost pity, for human imbecility.'[4] We are also introduced to the fastidious Laforgue, to Maeterlinck the mystic, and a number of others whose dominant traits may be rediscovered, if we wish, in Eliot.

It was in the French Symbolists that Eliot found a hope for poetry, having failed to find it in what was being written in his own language. And it was chiefly to Jules Laforgue that he went for guidance. 'He was the first,' he says, 'to teach me how to speak, to teach me the poetic possibilities of my own idiom of speech. Such early influences, the influences which, so to speak, first introduce one to oneself, are, I think, due to an impression which is in one aspect, the recognition of a temperament akin to one's own. . . .'[5]

Laforgue was a poet of spleen and profound pessimism, and this may have attracted the young man, still in the grip of his

[1] Cf. 'Donne in Our Time' in T. Spencer (ed.), *A Garland for John Donne* (1931).
[2] *The Sacred Wood* (2nd edn. 1928), p. 5.
[3] Book review, *CR*, Jan. 1930.
[4] Op. cit. (1899), p. 193. Symons here quotes an earlier article by himself.
[5] 'Talk on Dante', *Adelphi*, 1951, p. 107.

Byronic cynicism. But above all he was intrigued by Laforgue's idiom and technique. Laforgue brought the modern world and its language into poetry, and he experimented with a great diversity of lines and broken sequences. Eliot was searching for some criterion of formal beauty which would enable him to master English verse technique. He had read the classics, but had never had a mind for the rules of prosody or even been 'able to retain the names of feet and metres'. So, he tells us, 'when it came to applying rules of scansion to English verse, with its very different stresses and variable syllabic values, I wanted to know why one line was good and another bad; and this, scansion could not tell me. The only way to learn to manipulate any kind of English verse seemed to be by . . . becoming so engrossed in the work of a particular poet that one could produce a recognisable derivative.'[1] It is something like an irony of fate that Eliot should have learnt English verse technique from a French poet, but the fact that he did learn from a Frenchman obviously helped to liberate him from the manners that had been exhausted by the Victorian poets, and enabled him to introduce a new sense of rhythm into English poetry. He now actually made a 'deliberate choice of a poet to mimic', and one of the nine poems which he published in the *Harvard Advocate* in the years 1907 to 1910 was *Humouresque* '(After J. Laforgue)'. Even one or two of the poems in his first printed collection, especially *Conversation Galante*, are clearly imitations of Laforgue. Laforgue's *vers libre* was analogous, he found, to the free verse of the later Shakespeare, and of Webster, Tourneur and their contemporaries, whom he also studied at this time.[2]

On the importance of Baudelaire to his development Eliot is quite specific:

> I think that from Baudelaire I learned first, a precedent for the poetical possibilities, never developed by any poet writing in my own language, of the more sordid aspects of the modern metropolis, of the possibility of fusion between the sordidly realistic and the phantasmagoric, the possibility of the juxtaposition of the matter-of-fact and the fantastic. From him, as from Laforgue, I learned that

---

[1] *The Music of Poetry*, pp. 9–10.
[2] Cf. Eliot's introduction to Pound's *Selected Poems* (1928), p. viii; and *Adelphi*, 1951, p. 108.

the sort of material that I had, the sort of experience that an adolescent had had, in an industrial city in America, could be the material for poetry; and that the source of new poetry might be found in what had been regarded hitherto as the impossible, the sterile, the intractably unpoetic . . . It may be that I am indebted to Baudelaire chiefly for half a dozen lines out of the whole of Fleurs du Mal; and that his significance for me is summed up in the lines:

> Fourmillante Cité, cité pleine de rêves,
> Où le spectre en plein jour raccroche le passant . . .[1]

Presumably Eliot in his Harvard years did not seriously contemplate giving himself up to poetry. For one thing, there was nobody of standing in the literary world to encourage him. He declares that 'at a time which may be symbolised by the figures 1910, there was literally no one to whom one would have dreamt of applying. One learnt something, no doubt, from Henry James, and might have learnt more. But Henry James was a novelist. . . .' As for such writers as Shaw and Wells, 'they lived in another world altogether. One did not read them.'[2]

He took his A.B. and M.A. degrees at Harvard in 1910, and after a year at the Sorbonne returned in 1911 to work for a Ph.D. in philosophy. It was at this time, apparently, that he began to read Dante, puzzling out the *Divine Comedy* at first with a prose translation beside him and steeping himself in Dante's poetry by committing long passages to memory and reciting them to himself 'lying in bed or on a railway journey'. It was only after some difficulty that he arrived at an acceptance of the *Divine Comedy* in its entirety. He was held back, he says, by two prejudices: 'one against Pre-Raphaelite imagery, which was natural to one of my generation', and the other against 'cheerfulness, optimism, and hopefulness', words which 'stood for a great deal of what one hated in the nineteenth century'.[3] But when he did accept Dante it was with enthusiasm. In 1951 his 'Talk on Dante' revealed that after forty years he still regarded Dante's poetry as 'the most persistent and deepest influence' upon his own verse. Dante enabled him to establish in his verse 'a relationship between the mediæval inferno and modern life' and taught him the importance of three things: developing and refining the language of his nation, seeking 'width of emotional range' and being 'European'.[4]

[1] *Adelphi*, 1951, p. 107. [2] *New English Weekly*, Sept. 12, 1935.
[3] 'Dante', *SE*, p. 262. [4] *Adelphi*, 1951, pp. 106–14.

It was probably Dante, though it may have been Laforgue, that Eliot had in mind when, in 1919, he wrote that 'There is a kind of stimulus for a writer which is more important than the stimulus of admiring another writer.' He defined it as

> a feeling of profound kinship, or rather of a peculiar personal intimacy, with another, probably a dead author. It may overcome us suddenly, on first or after long acquaintance; it is certainly a crisis; and when a young writer is seized with his first passion of this sort he may be changed, metamorphosed almost, within a few weeks even, from a bundle of second-hand sentiments into a person. The imperative intimacy arouses for the first time a real, an unshakeable confidence . . . we have not borrowed, we have been quickened, and we become bearers of a tradition.[1]

Meanwhile Eliot continued his studies, and in his third year of graduate school became an assistant in the philosophy department. Books apart, far and away the most important influence in his Harvard days seems to have been that of Professor Irving Babbitt. Eliot knew him first in 1909, when Babbitt was instructor in French and when, as Eliot says,

> his reputation was only amongst a few . . . his outspoken contempt for methods of teaching in vogue had given him a reputation for unpopularity which attracted to him some discerning graduates and undergraduates at Harvard University. . . . The lectures which I attended were, I believe, concerned with French Literary Criticism; but they had a great deal to do with Aristotle, Longinus and Dionysius of Halicarnassus; they touched frequently upon Buddhism, Confucius, Rousseau, and contemporary political and religious movements. Somehow or other one read a number of books, Aristotle's *Politics* or Lafontaine's *Fables*, just because Babbitt assumed that any educated man had already read them.

Eliot was also struck by 'the frankness with which he discussed the things that he disliked, and which his pupils came to dislike too'.[2] He found in Babbitt not merely a tutor, 'but a man who directed my interests, at a particular moment, in such a way that the marks of that direction are still evident'. He was to retain his affection for and admiration of the older man, though his views came to differ from Babbitt's, and he paid a tribute of gratitude

---

[1] 'Reflections on Contemporary Poetry', *Egoist*, July 1919.
[2] Commentary, *CR*, Oct. 1933.

when he wrote in an article on Paul Elmer More: 'These [Babbitt and More] seem to me the two *wisest* men that I have known.'[1] On another occasion Eliot wrote: 'Babbitt's motive was awareness of, alarm at, the ills of the modern secular world; and his work as a whole constitutes the most complete and thorough diagnosis of the malady, as it shows itself in literature, in education, in politics and philosophy, that has been made.'[2] The ills of the modern world, then, were being persuasively demonstrated at Harvard. Babbitt was an authoritarian in all the fields mentioned by Eliot, as well as in ethics. An anti-romanticist, he believed in classicism and tradition, in the suppression of sentiment and the control of emotion. He promulgated his opinions with a fierce conviction and allowed them to colour whatever subject he spoke upon. He would have constituted a movement all by himself, even apart from his friend Paul Elmer More and the discerning students who gathered around him. T. S. Eliot, at an age when he was making up his mind about things, was evidently fascinated by a man who did not hesitate to erect signposts; and for better or for worse his opinions remained stamped by most of the teachings of Babbitt. If Eliot had leanings towards authoritarianism and anti-romanticism, they were confirmed by Babbitt, and what the young man lacked in the way of dogma was supplied by his instructor. The main subject on which the disciple was later to differ from the master was that of humanism. Babbitt, for all his abhorrence of eccentric individualism or sloppy enthusiasms, was an idealistic believer in human nature, its power to keep itself under an 'inner check' and the possibility of creating a sound society by rational discipline. Eliot may have absorbed these views at first, but he later found them incompatible with Christian orthodoxy. He underwent a similar revulsion with regard to Babbitt's interest in primitive Buddhism. Writing about Babbitt in 1937, he declared: 'One of the reasons why Buddhism appeals to him is apparently his hostility to Platonic ideas, and his dislike of the Platonic influence upon Christian theology.'[3] Nevertheless, Buddhism was another interest which Babbitt imparted to his disciple enduringly.

A contemporary of Babbitt's was George Santayana, who, then in middle age, taught in the philosophy department at Harvard.

[1] *Princeton Alumni Weekly*, Feb. 5, 1937.
[2] J. Baillie and H. Martin (edd.), *Revelation*, (1937), p. 15.
[3] Ibid., pp. 16–17.

He was very unlike Babbitt in many respects. One has the impression of a very modest and unassuming personality. His philosophy, based on disillusion, was primarily that of an aesthete. His stoic religion, which he called naturalism, assumed that life had no meaning or metaphysical import, but that there was a unity in nature to which man belonged and that a relative purpose could be achieved by means of gratuitous good. 'There is no opposition in my mind,' he wrote, 'between materialism and a Platonic or even Indian discipline of the spirit.' He saw in his own philosophy a kind of pragmatism, though he could not stomach the William James of the later years, who gave himself up to 'romantic metaphysics'.[1]

Surprisingly enough, Santayana did accept 'a pure and radical transcendentalism', which recognised no facts (these being in a different sphere of perception), but only 'essences', corresponding to the Platonic ideas. The realm of essence was an eternal and infinite one, to be penetrated by a species of thinking akin to poetry. 'Many ideas,' he declared, 'may be convergent as poetry which would be divergent as dogmas.'[2]

It is hard to find consistency in some of Santayana's ideas on art, best expounded in *Reason in Art* (1905). He seems to have believed both in supernatural inspiration and in the human intelligence each as the only basis of art.[3] But it clearly emerges that he was a classicist, who had no use for speculative aesthetics; he believed 'that imitation is a fundamental principle in art' and that 'the specific values of art are technical values'. Art, he thought, should aim at universality, by rendering universal and primary experiences and by expressing ultimate truths. It must be incorporated in the life of reason, and recognised for what it is: a servant with a useful function in our lives. 'Romanticism, ritualism, aestheticism, symbolism' are names of diseases which tend to degrade art from its useful function. Santayana praises Virgil and Dante as classic poets,[4] and in a later work, *Three Philosophical Poets* (1910), declares that the poet is never greater than when he

---

[1] 'A Brief History of My Opinions' in I. Edman (ed.), *The Philosophy of Santayana* (1936), pp. 12, 14.

[2] Ibid., p. 18.

[3] 'The ideas come of themselves, . . . dropping in their sudden form from the blue.' (*The Philosophy of Santayana*, p. 220. Cp. also p. 250.)

[4] Ibid., pp. 231, 236–7, 241, 244, 247.

grasps and expresses the philosophic vision of his universe, as Lucretius, Dante and Goethe did for successive ages.[1]

Many of Santayana's ideas would naturally appeal to Eliot. The philosophy of naturalism and disillusion might well attract a sophisticated young man who was immersing himself in the French Symbolists. The defence of classicism in its various aspects chimed with what Babbitt was teaching, and no doubt fell on good ground. Virgil, Lucretius and Dante were poets whom Eliot was to admire highly, though he was more critical of Goethe.

Another of Eliot's masters at Harvard was 'that extraordinary philosopher Josiah Royce'.[2] Royce was one of the leading monists and post-Kantian idealists. He held the whole universe to be con-tained in an all-comprehensive Mind, the Logos, or the Absolute; and to be differentiated within that Mind into individuals, both human, organic and 'inanimate'. The successive moments in the life of an individual were held together by a common memory in a larger self. But a richer life could be attained by the self, accord-ing to 'the law of mediation', if it lost itself in devotion to other individuals and to common causes. In the ethical corollaries of Royce's philosophy, order and security were supreme goods, as with Babbitt. And loyalty was the greatest virtue of the in-dividual, taking him beyond himself, and thus redeeming him for the complete life of reality. Royce's philosophy was voluntaristic in that it stressed the ability of the individual to work out his salvation by an effort of the will. But this effort was only made efficacious by the grace afforded by the Community.

I think we may assume that it was Royce who led Eliot to take an interest in F. H. Bradley. In the field of philosophy, Bradley was incomparably the most important influence on Eliot. Eliot thoroughly assimilated his *Ethical Studies* (1876), *The Principles of Logic* (1883) and *Appearance and Reality* (1893), and wrote his doctoral dissertation on Bradley and Meinong. Bradley, who was partly inspired by Hegel and Lotze, was an exponent of the new idealism, an opponent of the Utilitarian philosophy of Bentham and Mill and a critic of the somewhat mechanistic psychology of Alexander Bain and others. *The Principles of Logic* is a closely-reasoned attempt at establishing the paramount importance of universal notions over particular perceptions in various modes of

---

[1] *The Philosophy of Santayana*, p. 342.
[2] Introduction to *Savonarola*, p. viii.

thinking. Again we have something that reminds us of Plato's ideas. In *Appearance and Reality* Bradley endeavours first to prove, by a penetrating epistemological criticism, that all our experiential knowledge is mere illusion and appearance. He then goes on to argue that even appearance exists in some sense, and must therefore form *part* of Reality. It only needs to be completed in a transcendent pattern to become fully real. Even pain and evil have their place in this pattern: being transmuted, they are submerged in good. Bradley is less of a voluntarist and more of an intellectualist than Royce. He does not believe in individual immortality, but thinks that individuality is only a passing phase of the final Reality, or the Absolute, as he calls it. During this life of Appearance, however, we are isolated each in his own mind. Bradley develops a theory of 'finite centres', according to which all consciousness is contained in closed units complete in themselves and yet united in the Absolute.

In the admirable essay on F. H. Bradley included in his *Selected Essays*, Eliot describes the philosopher in words which would be very applicable to himself,[1] and which reveal a strong congeniality in the two. He praises Bradley's style, for which he still has a great admiration. Eliot was probably captivated at an early date by this excellent and persuasive prose, but he was also struck by Bradley's dislike of extreme positions and by the 'catholic, civilized and universal' qualities of his philosophy compared with the 'crude and raw and provincial' philosophy of the Benthamites. Bradley, he writes in his essay, had a great deal of wisdom; 'wisdom consists largely of scepticism and uncynical disillusion; and of these Bradley had a large share. And scepticism and disillusion are a useful equipment for religious understanding; and of that Bradley had a share too.'[2]

For a time, Eliot seems to have been completely in sympathy with the ideas of Bradley. But he soon adopted a more critical attitude. In an essay printed in *The Monist* in 1916 he demonstrated the similarity between Leibniz's theory of monads and Bradley's theory of finite centres and found a weakness in both philosophies in that they had recourse to 'divine intervention' to explain the communication between the subjective units or atomic universes. Eliot's later conversion to Anglicanism only estranged him further from Bradley. But as we shall see, the idealistic

[1] *SE*, pp. 406–7.   [2] Ibid., pp. 411–12.

philosophies of Royce and Bradley never lost their hold on him.

Even in 1912, however, the Idealists did not go unchallenged. Their claims were disputed by the Realists, who apparently exercised a certain counter-attraction on Eliot, since he could later write of them as follows:

> The Six Realists whose co-operative work, 'The New Realism', made a considerable stir in the philosophical departments of American universities in that year [1912]—and I was then in the philosophical department of an American university—were animated by a missionary zeal against the Hegelian Idealism which was the orthodox doctrine of the philosophical departments of American universities at the time, and which had begun to turn manifestly mouldy. . . .
> The Six Realists were un-Teutonised, and on the whole anti-religious, which was refreshing; they were ascetically, even gloomily, scientific; and they professed considerable respect for Mr. Bertrand Russell and his Cambridge friends. All this was to the good; but it must be admitted that the New Realism, like most pre-War philosophies, seems now as demoded as ladies' hats of the same period.[1]

It is no exaggeration to say that Eliot was completely absorbed in his philosophical studies. He has said in conversation that they *were* him at the time. During his visit to Paris in 1910–11, he attended Bergson's lectures at the Sorbonne and underwent 'a temporary conversion to Bergsonism'—his only conversion, he declared in after life, 'by the deliberate influence of any individual'.[2] In a symposium on 'What France Means to You' printed in 1944, he said that he supposed there were still Bergsonians, 'mais pour avoir vraiment connu la ferveur bergsonienne, il faut être allé, régulièrement, chaque semaine, dans cette salle pleine à craquer où il faisait ses cours, au Collège de France.'[3] One pictures Eliot arriving an hour and a quarter before the lecture started, as he says one had to do. He did even then, according to Matthiessen, write an essay criticising Bergson's *durée réelle* as 'simply not final',[4] but it must have taken some little time before the Bergsonian fervour

---

[1] 'Views and Reviews', *New English Weekly*, June 6, 1935. The 'Six Realists' were E. B. Holt, W. T. Marvin, W. P. Montague, R. B. Perry, W. B. Pitkin and E. G. Spaulding.

[2] *A Sermon* (1948), p. 5.

[3] *La France Libre*, June 15, 1944, p. 94. Quoted by E. J. H. Greene in *T. S. Eliot et la France* (1951), p. 10.

[4] F. O. Matthiessen, *The Achievement of T. S. Eliot* (2nd edn. 1947), p. 183.

wore off, and it never, as a matter of fact, entirely left him, in spite of his ironical treatment of Bergson in *The Sacred Wood*.

Back at Harvard, he applied himself to the ancient philosophy of India, reading Sanskrit and Pali under the guidance of Charles Lanman and studying Patanjali's metaphysics under J. H. Woods. The philosophical gain from these latter studies was meagre, he has admitted. He was left 'in a state of enlightened mystification'.[1] But affectively he was deeply impressed. And he is well aware that his poetry 'shows the influence of Indian thought and sensibility'.[2]

Anthropology and psychology were subsidiary interests. Eliot shows familiarity with the works of Durkheim, Lévy-Bruhl, Frazer, etc. He wrote a paper for Royce on 'The Interpretation of Primitive Ritual'. Royce was also interested in psychological experiments and experiences, such as the use of ether to produce an 'anesthetic revelation' of metaphysical truth. William James's theories of mental associations were dominant at Harvard. And at the time when Eliot wrote *The Love Song of J. Alfred Prufrock*, the nature of schizophrenia was being investigated by Morton Prince and the 'Boston School' of psychologists.[3]

During his first years of study he kept up his interest in poetry and wrote a number of pieces, some of which were to be included in his first printed collection.[4] His Paris year must have been the realisation of a cherished dream fostered by his reading of the French Symbolists. At fifty-six he still remembered his feelings of rich discovery:

> Je crois que c'était une bonne fortune exceptionelle, pour un adolescent, de découvrir Paris en l'an 1910. La *Nouvelle Revue Française* était encore vraiment nouvelle: et les *Cahiers de la Quinzaine* paraissaient, sous leur austère couverture de papier gris. [Then follows the passage on Bergson quoted above, and he continues:]

---

[1] *After Strange Gods* (1934), p. 40.

[2] *Notes towards the Definition of Culture* (1948), p. 113.

[3] See Morgan and Wohlstetter, 'Observations on "Prufrock"', *Harvard Advocate*, Dec. 1938, pp. 28–9.

[4] The following poems of the *Prufrock* collection (1917) seem to have been composed before 1912: *Conversation Galante* (1909), *Portrait of a Lady* (1910), *Preludes* (1910), *Rhapsody on a Windy Night* (1910), *The Love Song of J. Alfred Prufrock* (1910–11), *La Figlia che Piange* (1911). The remaining poems of the collection would have been composed in 1915. Dates are given by John Hayward in Pierre Leyris' volume of French translations (*Poèmes 1910–1930*) and by E. J. H. Greene in *T. S. Eliot et la France*.

On avait toujours une chance d'apercevoir Anatole France, le long des quais: et on achetait le dernier livre de Gide ou de Claudel le jour même de sa parution. Tantôt Paris était tout le passé; tantôt tout l'avenir: et ces deux aspects se combinaient en un présent parfait.

Another vivid impression of Paris was provided by the reading of Charles-Louis Philippe's *Bubu de Montparnasse*, the story of sordid vanities and squalid loves, of deceitfulness and genuine emotions among the pimps and prostitutes of the French metropolis. In his preface to an English translation of this book, Eliot said that he first read it in 1910. 'Read at an impressionable age, and under the impressive conditions, the book has always been for me . . . a symbol of the Paris of that time.'

It was no accident that brought him to Paris, he says. 'Depuis plusieurs années, la France représentait surtout, à mes yeux, la *poésie*. . . .'[1] It may have been Eliot the poet rather than the philosopher who chiefly profited by the stay. He perfected his French so successfully that he was able to write French verse of some merit. And he made friends among French poets. Many years later, in a *Criterion* Commentary, Eliot wrote: 'I am willing to admit that my own retrospect is touched by a sentimental sunset, the memory of a friend coming across the Luxembourg Gardens in the late afternoon, waving a branch of lilac, a friend who was later (so far as I could find out) to be mixed with the mud of Gallipoli.'[2] This friend must be the poet Jean Verdenal, to whom Eliot inscribed his first volume of poems. He may even, with his branch of lilac, have entered into the composition of Eliot's favourite frustration image.

From 1911 to 1915, however, there seems to have been a lull in Eliot's poetic production. Philosophy engulfed him, and the need to make a career. He may not have thought that he had a future as a poet. And anyhow he could not, and probably would not, make his living from poetry.

A short stay in Germany in 1914 included the unforgettable experience of witnessing Professor Eucken, of Jena, pounding the table and declaiming 'Was ist Geist? Geist ist. . . .' The Great War supervened and Eliot studied for a year at Merton College, Oxford. He chose this college because of its associations with Bradley (whom, incidentally, he never met), and because there he

---

[1] See Greene, loc. cit.　　　　[2] *CR*, April 1934.

would sit under Professor Harold Joachim, who was not only a great authority on Aristotle, but also a disciple of Bradley. Together with Bradley's idealism, he continued his studies of the German phenomenologists Meinong and Husserl. But above all he devoted himself to Aristotle and deepened a familiarity with and an admiration of that philosopher which could not fail to colour his general outlook.

His finished doctoral dissertation[1] is dated 1916. But it was never published, nor was anything else by Eliot in the years from 1910 to 1915. The philosopher in him lingered on, as we can tell by the essays in *The Monist* and a number of reviews in the *International Journal of Ethics* of 1916 and 1917. But he was soon swallowed up by the poet and the literary critic. We may, however, discern many of the features of the philosopher in the physiognomy of the poet, and these I shall endeavour to trace in subsequent chapters.

His poetic interests were no doubt instrumental in deciding him to settle more or less permanently in England. The notion of settling there was not strange to him. As early as 1909, recognising 'the failure of American life' at that time, he wrote in a book review of the class of 'Americans retained to their native country by business relations or socialities or by a sense of duty—the last reason implying a real sacrifice—while their hearts are always in Europe.'[2] Henry James was a Londoner, and was soon to become a British subject. Pound, J. G. Fletcher, Aiken, H. D. and Robert Frost all lived in England in the years preceding and during the Great War. And Mr Tinckom-Fernandez tells us that while at college he and Eliot discussed the idea of emigrating to a milieu more congenial to a writer, as Ezra Pound had done.[3] When Tinckom-Fernandez did go to Europe, Eliot saw him off. And in the following year he took ship himself. As it happened, his departure was final. Eliot was not to see his childhood home again in the lifetime of his parents. He was not to see America again for eighteen years, by which time he was a British subject.

---

[1] 'Experience and the Objects of Knowledge, in the philosophy of F. H. Bradley.' The dissertation was accepted but Eliot never returned to Harvard to take his final examinations for the Ph.D. He now holds honorary doctorates from a number of European and American universities.

[2] *Harvard Advocate*, May 7, 1909.   [3] Ibid., Dec. 1938, pp. 47–8.

The most momentous event during his first years in England, was no doubt his meeting with Ezra Pound:

> I was introduced to *Personae* and *Exultations* in 1910, while still an undergraduate at Harvard. The poems did not then excite me, any more than did the poetry of Yeats: I was too much engrossed in working out the implications of Laforgue. I considered them, however, the only interesting poems by a contemporary that I had found. My indebtedness to Pound is of two kinds: first, in my literary criticism; . . . second, in his criticism of my poetry in our talk, and his indications of desirable territories to explore. This indebtedness extends from 1915 to 1922, after which period Mr. Pound left England, and our meetings became infrequent.[1]

After the Second World War, Eliot wrote two articles on Pound for the *New English Weekly*, and again loyally acknowledged his indebtedness to him: 'I had kept my early poems (including *Prufrock* and others eventually published) in my desk from 1911 to 1915—with the exception of a period when Conrad Aiken endeavoured, without success, to peddle them for me in London. In 1915 (and through Aiken) I met Pound. The result was that *Prufrock* appeared in *Poetry* in the summer of that year; and through Pound's efforts, my first volume was published by the Egoist Press in 1917.'

Pound was rather eccentric, Eliot admits, but very kind if he became interested in anybody. 'He was so passionately concerned about the works of art which he expected his protégés to produce, that he sometimes tended to regard the latter almost impersonally, as art or literature machines to be carefully tended and oiled, for the sake of their potential output.'

Of Pound's general influence he says:

> Whether the name and principles of imagism were Pound's invention or Hulme's, I do not know, and I am not very much interested. Imagism produced a few good poems—notably those of H. D.—but it was quickly absorbed into more comprehensive influences, including Pound's. Then, with *The Catholic Anthology*, *The Egoist*, *The Little Review*, Pound accomplished more than any other man could have done with anthologies and periodicals of such limited circulation. . . . Pound did not create the poets: but he created a situation in

---

[1] 'On a Recent Piece of Criticism', *Purpose*, Apr./June 1938.

which, for the first time, there was a 'modern movement in poetry' in which English and American poets collaborated, knew each other's works, and influenced each other.

Eliot considered Pound's critical writing 'to be almost the only contemporary writing on the Art of Poetry, that a young poet can study with profit.' 'I think,' he wrote,

> that Pound was original in insisting that poetry was an art, an art which demands the most arduous application and study; and in seeing that in our time it had to be a highly conscious art. He also saw that a poet who knows only the poetry of his own language is as poorly equipped as the painter or musician who knows only the painting or music of his own country. . . . Pound's great contribution to the work of other poets . . . is his insistence upon the immensity of the amount of *conscious* labour to be performed by the poet.[1]

Pound had read widely. The literatures of Italy, of Provence, of China and Japan were well known to him; and he extended the interests and educated the tastes of those who gathered about him. In poetry he favoured a hard, unsentimental precision of statement, and an expression so clipped as to become enigmatic. He taught the necessity of taking contemporary speech as a model of style, of choosing for subject-matter and imagery 'topics and objects related to the life of a modern man or woman' and of seeking material that in itself was non-poetic.[2] The results called down a good deal of abuse upon the heads of the innovators,[3] but they were undismayed.

Eliot particularly remembered the impression it made on him when Pound, who was Yeats's secretary for a time, took him to see 'the first performance of *The Hawk's Well*, in a London drawing room, with a celebrated Japanese dancer in the role of the hawk'.[4] *Sweeney Agonistes* and *Murder in the Cathedral* certainly owe something to such impressions. Pound it was who made Eliot see Yeats in a new light. He also induced him to study Gautier,[5] and he confirmed him in his admiration of Dante.

Some of the credit must undoubtedly go to Ezra Pound for the confidence which is apparent in Eliot's poetic manifesto of 1919,

[1] 'Ezra Pound', I–II, *New English Weekly*, Oct. 31 and Nov. 7, 1946.
[2] *Milton* (1947), pp. 18–19.
[3] One of the epithets was 'drunken helots'—see *UPC*, p. 71.
[4] *New English Weekly*, Oct. 31, 1946.   [5] Ibid., Nov. 7, 1946.

Background and Influences

'Tradition and the Individual Talent'. One almost hears the voice of Pound in the statements that tradition is necessary and must be appropriated by great labour, and that it involves 'the historical sense, which we may call nearly indispensable to anyone who would continue to be a poet beyond his twenty-fifth year'.

The Imagist movement, of which Eliot made passing mention in a passage quoted above, may not have been very important as a school. But its determined onslaught on the Georgians, and the general principles it enunciated were extremely favourable to the creation of a new style of poetry, and have been potent factors in the development of most poets for the last few decades. The movement, which included poets on both sides of the Atlantic, originated about 1912,[1] and aimed at restoring to poetry its direct appeal to the senses, chiefly to the sense of sight by the precise use of visual images. A poem was to be a presentation rather than a description, moods were to be inferred from situations rendered in concrete terms, unnecessary words, especially adjectives, were to be shorn away, etc. A model was found in the handful of poems written by T. E. Hulme.

Eliot never met Hulme. The latter enlisted at the beginning of the Great War, went to France in 1915 and was killed in 1917. But he had long been the centre of a group of philosophers, writers and artists, and his spirit and ideas lived on in the literary circles of London when Eliot came to the capital. Many of his views coincided with those of Irving Babbitt. He was a disciplinarian and a classicist. But unlike Babbitt, Hulme distrusted humanism and held only 'the religious conception of ultimate values to be right'.[2] He believed strongly in the reality of Original Sin and the inability of man to attain perfection by any human effort. His religious attitude was to mean something to Eliot later, especially after *Speculations* was published in 1924. But at first it was mainly his literary ideas that mattered.

A schism occurred in the Imagist group when Ezra Pound and some of the other members seceded to Vorticism, a movement which Wyndham Lewis started in 1913. To all intents and purposes, however, Vorticism in poetry was the same as Imagism. The concrete image was to serve as the form, or the 'VORTEX, from

[1] Eliot, in his Washington University address, says 1910 and adds 'I was not there'.
[2] Cf. *SE*, p. 452.

which, and through which, and into which, ideas are constantly rushing'.[1] Eliot was drawn into this Vorticist-Imagist group, and it may have meant something to him to have been associated, in the beginning of his career, with such a daring, even eccentric, experimenter as Wyndham Lewis.[2] It is curious now to reflect that Eliot earned his living in the prosaic capacity of a schoolmaster[3] while engaged in what many people deemed to be literary anarchy.

The war-time London in which he settled must have been an unpleasant place in many respects. But one doubtless had the feeling that things were happening there, and that, with courage and perseverance, much might be achieved. Eliot, at any rate, grew to like the huge, rambling city, in spite of many things that he detested, perhaps in part *because* of the things that he detested, for they gave him an outlet for the spleen that he was nursing and which craved an aesthetic release. He feels that he expressed great affection for the city in *The Waste Land*, and it is true that one finds a kind of pitying fondness for the ugly medley of streets, pubs, gashouses and barges that is pictured there. Eliot, having always been a town-dweller, confesses to ingrown urban habits,[4] and London has (or had) characteristics which make it, to him, 'preferable to any other metropolis in the world' that he knows: 'it is still to a great extent,' he wrote in 1932, 'a collection of villages the borders of which touch, each retaining a local character of its own.' He did not need to be told, he said, that a number of the London villages he had in mind were scandalously filthy and ought to be torn down; he knew that quite well, and was not simply indulging a taste for the picturesque slum. But there was something he abhorred, and perhaps rightly, more than the slum, and that was the 'endless line of houses along a ribbon road over which passes a ceaseless stream of cars'.[5]

---

[1] Pound, 'Vorticism', *Fortnightly Review*, Sept. 1, 1914, p. 469.

[2] Eliot and Wyndham Lewis met in Pound's London flat in 1915. See Lewis's contribution to March and Tambimuttu (edd.), *T. S. Eliot* (1948).

[3] He taught for one term at High Wycombe, Bucks., and for four terms at the Highgate School, London, until the summer of 1917. He then became a clerk in the Colonial and Foreign Department of Lloyds Bank and remained there for 'eight very satisfactory years' until 1925. He was commended for his weekly digests of foreign trade reports and his articles on foreign trade movements in the *Lloyd's Bank Economic Review*.

[4] Cf. Commentary, *CR*, April 1938.

[5] 'The Search for Moral Sanction', *Listener*, March 30, 1932.

Background and Influences

While Eliot was assistant editor of the progressive review called *The Egoist* from 1917 to 1919, he also contributed a great number of articles, mostly reviews of books, to other periodicals. In 1919, which was a year of considerable output, and in the following year, he wrote especially for the *Athenæum*, then being edited in its last, brilliant phase by Middleton Murry. Murry, like Eliot, was struggling to find a foothold in philosophy or faith, and for a time, it seems, they were able to harmonise their views and aspirations, though in the years to come they were to drift far apart. Eliot informs us that some of his essays of this early period were written directly at the suggestion of Murry.[1]

However, a stronger ascendancy than Middleton Murry's was exercised by the critical writings of Rémy de Gourmont, whose influence Eliot gratefully acknowledges in the 1928 Preface to *The Sacred Wood*. Gourmont, who died in 1915, was one of the first critics to do justice to the French Symbolists, particularly Mallarmé. He has been described as 'antireligieux, antirationaliste, amoraliste, sceptique, en un mot anarchiste, puisant dans son tempérament, voluptueux, sensuel et artiste, la loi même de ses curiosités, s'il est vrai, comme l'a remarqué son frère, que "rien ne soit entré dans son intelligence que caressé par sa sensibilité".'[2] Gourmont could hardly be an acceptable guide for a young man in search of anything but a hedonistic philosophy. But he realised the need of a cultural tradition in Europe transcending the boundaries of the nations; he also had a fine perception in matters of literary style, and it was in such matters that Eliot was principally interested at the time. What gives coherence to the essays of *The Sacred Wood*, says Eliot in his Preface, 'is the problem of the integrity of poetry, with the repeated assertion that when we are considering poetry we must consider it primarily as poetry and not another thing'. From Gourmont's writings Eliot took his title quotations for the essay on 'The Perfect Critic':

> 'Eriger en lois ses impressions personelles, c'est le grand effort d'un homme s'il est sincère.'—*Lettres à l'Amazone.*
>
> 'L'écrivain de style abstrait est presque toujours un sentimental, du moins un sensitif. L'écrivain artiste n'est presque jamais un sentimental, et très rarement un sensitif.'—*Le Problème du Style.*

---

[1] Cf. Preface to *The Sacred Wood*, p. viii.
[2] Lanson and Tuffrau, *Manuel illustré d'histoire de la littérature française* (1931), p. 751.

These may be taken as examples of the maxims and observations which stimulated Eliot in the early years of his career as a critic.

By 1920 a number of Eliot's poems had been printed in three or four separate collections. The modernist poets were advancing, but they had not yet established their position. Writing about this time, Aldous Huxley complained:

> We to-day are metaphysicals without our Donne. Theoretically we are free to make poetry of everything in the universe; in practice we are kept within the old limits, for the simple reason that no great man has appeared to show us how we can use our freedom. A certain amount of the life of the twentieth century is to be found in our poetry, but precious little of its mind. . . . The twentieth century still awaits its Lucretius, awaits its own philosophical Dante, its new Goethe, its Donne, even its up-to-date Laforgue. Will they appear?[1]

Many people hailed the appearance of the poet of the age, when *The Waste Land* was published in 1922. But it may be noted that many of the admirers of the poem were not guided by genuine appreciation. If Pound is to be trusted, 'the bearing of this poem was not over-estimated, nevertheless the immediate reception of it even by second rate reviewers was due to the purely fortuitous publication of the notes, and not to the text itself. Liveright wanted a longer volume and the notes were the only available unpublished matter.'[2]

In the actual shaping of *The Waste Land* Pound played a significant part. And as usual Eliot acknowledged his debt. 'It was in 1922,' he says, 'that I placed before him [Pound] in Paris the manuscript of a sprawling chaotic poem called *The Waste Land* which left his hands, reduced to about half its size, in the form in which it appears in print. I should like to think that the manuscript, with the suppressed passages, had disappeared irrecoverably: yet, on the other hand, I should wish the blue pencilling on it to be preserved as irrefutable evidence of Pound's critical genius.'[3] The history of *The Waste Land* is unromantic. It is nevertheless a masterpiece, and we need not grudge Pound some of the credit.

[1] 'Subject-Matter of Poetry', *On the Margin* (1923).
[2] See D. Gallup, *T. S. Eliot, A Bibliography* (1952), p. 7.
[3] 'Ezra Pound', I, *New English Weekly*, Oct. 31, 1946. Actually Pound must have seen the manuscript in 1921, judging by correspondence preserved in the Houghton Library at Harvard.

Pound had at an earlier time induced Eliot to destroy some verses which he did not consider to be original enough, and Eliot subsequently, it seems, came to regret the destruction. But we may assume that the pruning of *The Waste Land* was all to the good. The poem first appeared without the notes in the initial number of the *Criterion*, for October 1922. Eliot had just become editor of this review, which was to acquire considerable prestige. So the year 1922 was a very important one in his life.

His regular contributions to the *Criterion* consisted of the Commentaries, in which he ranged over a great number of subjects of topical interest: literary and artistic, philosophical, educational, economic, political, etc. He achieved excellence in many of these Commentaries, and enriched the discussions of the day with well-founded views and careful criticism. But the review was equally important in bringing together many of the best brains and pens not only of England, but of the whole of Europe, and of America too. About 1929 the editor was able to state with pride that the *Criterion* 'had been the first periodical in England to print the work of such writers as Marcel Proust, Paul Valéry, Jacques Rivière, Charles Maurras, Henri Massis, Wilhelm Worringer, Max Scheler, E. R. Curtius'.[1] Thus the *Criterion* was strongly instrumental in creating that sense of the unity of European culture which the editor always thought so important, but which was to be shattered, at least temporarily, by the impact of the Second World War and the events leading up to it.

The years spent with the *Criterion* were no doubt formative and fruitful to Eliot personally. Not least important were the many contacts that were made and the friendships that were sealed. Eliot's friendship with Paul Valéry was one of the major gains.

Gradually a change of interests, or perhaps rather an expansion of interests, took place. Possibly 1926 marks the beginning of a spiritual awakening and a growth of independence. 'Only from about the year 1926,' says Eliot, 'did the features of the post-war world begin clearly to emerge. . . . From about that date one began slowly to realize that the intellectual and artistic output of the previous seven years had been rather the last efforts of an old world, than the first struggles of a new.'[2]

Eliot was attracted to 'a larger and more difficult subject' than that of the integrity and autonomy of poetry. He passed on to the

---

[1] 'Last Words', *CR*, Jan. 1939, p. 271.   [2] Ibid.

problem 'of the relation of poetry to the spiritual and social life of its time and of other times'.[1] And this again was part of a larger movement of his mind which resulted in his entering the Anglican communion about the same time as he became a British subject in 1927. In his preface to *For Lancelot Andrewes*, he defined his position at the time (1928) as 'classicist in literature, royalist in politics, and anglo-catholic in religion'. The definition gave rise to a certain amount of misunderstanding, but it certainly mirrors a determined choice of allegiances. The 'neo-Thomist' revival of which Jacques Maritain was, in Eliot's words 'the most popular and influential exponent', may have had something to do with the colour of his views. In a review of Maritain's *Three Reformers* written for the *Times Literary Supplement* in November 1928, Eliot described contemporary French neo-Thomism as representing, 'beyond its strictly theological import, a reaction against such philosophies as that of Bergson, against Romanticism in literature and against democracy in government'.

Since the late twenties Eliot has followed religious and ecclesiastical affairs very closely, as witness his *Thoughts after Lambeth* and his collaboration in a report on *Catholicity*. And *The Rock* and *Murder in the Cathedral* have both a good deal of the convert's missionary zeal.

His conversion was not sudden. In a talk on 'Christianity and Communism' in 1932 he gave the following testimony:

> Towards any profound conviction one is borne gradually, perhaps insensibly over a long period of time, by what Newman called 'powerful and concurrent reasons' . . . At some moment or other, a kind of crystallisation occurs, in which appears an element of *faith* . . . In my own case, I believe that one of the reasons was that the Christian scheme seemed to me the only one which would work. . . . That was simply the removal of any reason for believing in anything else, the erasure of a prejudice, the arrival at the scepticism which is the preface to conversion. And when I say 'work', I am quite aware that I had my own notion of what the 'working' of a scheme comprehends. Among other things, the Christian scheme seemed the only possible scheme which found a place for values which I must maintain or perish (and belief comes first and practice second), the belief, for instance, in holy living and holy dying, in sanctity, chastity, humility, austerity. And it is in favour of the Christian

---

[1] *The Sacred Wood*, p. viii.

scheme, from the Christian point of view, that it never has, and never will, work perfectly. No perfect scheme can work perfectly with imperfect men;[1]

Eliot's declaration of faith became a subject of controversy in literary circles, especially when it became apparent that Christian themes were more and more invading his poetry. Some people thought that he had suddenly and deplorably arrested his progress, others were confident that the new inspiration would possess him of his full powers. Time has shown that there was no drying-up of the sources of poetry, whatever we may think of the philosophical value of the later poems compared with the early ones. But in the field of criticism, perhaps, the artistic interests suffered. Thus it became impossible for Eliot, with his own changed and changing outlook, and with the background of political developments in Europe, to continue editing the *Criterion*. In January 1939 he wrote his 'Last Words'. The 'European mind' which he had championed, had disappeared from view, he said, in the political turmoils of the thirties. He had introduced young British writers to replace the absentees from the Continent. But even so he found it impossible, in the long run, to continue:

> For myself, a right political philosophy came more and more to imply a right theology—and right economics to depend upon right ethics: leading to emphases which somewhat stretched the original framework of a literary review. . . .
> I have wondered whether it would not have been more profitable, instead of trying to maintain literary standards increasingly repudiated in the modern world, to have endeavoured to rally intellectual effort to affirm those principles of life and policy from the lack of which we are suffering disastrous consequences. But such a task, again, would be outside the scope of *The Criterion*. . . .
> In the present state of public affairs—which has induced in myself a depression of spirits so different from any other experience of fifty years as to be a new emotion—I no longer feel the enthusiasm necessary to make a literary review what it should be.

Eliot reluctantly came to the conclusion that the writer must take a direct interest in politics; and one of the signs of this new attitude was his book on *The Idea of a Christian Society*. Only a few years earlier, when the civil war in Spain was calling upon the

---

[1] 'Christianity and Communism', *Listener*, March 16, 1932.

enthusiasms of so many young British poets and authors, Eliot declared, 'While I am naturally sympathetic, I still feel convinced that it is best that at least a few men of letters should remain isolated, and take no part in these collective activities.'[1] Such pronouncements were liable to stamp him as a fascist and reactionary, but they were the signs of his persistent loyalty to the disinterestedness of the poet. Eliot did not leave England during the nightmare of 1939-45, except for lecture tours under the auspices of the British Council to Sweden and elsewhere. And he contributed to the war effort in his way, by labouring to keep alive the sense of perennial cultural values.

Eliot's dislike of facile optimism is very characteristic. He speaks in his essay on 'Dante' of 'the Catholic philosophy of disillusion', and this is clearly the philosophy that he has embraced. One of the things it teaches is 'to look to *death* for what life cannot give'.[2] 'We fight,' he says elsewhere, 'rather to keep something alive than in the expectation that anything will triumph.'[3] Accordingly he regards it as the highest stage that civilised man can attain 'to unite the profoundest scepticism with the deepest faith'.[4] In this latter statement we recognise the significant dimensions in his perspective of life: he is not the peevish recluse that some of his statements might be twisted to suggest. But he does go through life with an acute sense of its troubles and discomforts.

He is still a director of Faber and Faber—the firm which he joined in 1925 when it was Faber and Gwyer—and works regularly in his monastic publishing office in Russell Square. He is a hard-working man, who attempts to throw no glamour over his poetic career, which, on one occasion, he referred to as 'a mug's game'.[5] 'An artist,' he says, 'needs to live a commonplace life if he is to get his work done—a life far more of routine, and indeed less "inextricably strange" than that of a politician or a stockbroker.'[6] Elsewhere he declares that 'the compensations for being a poet are grossly exaggerated; and they dwindle as one becomes older, and the shadows lengthen, and the solitude becomes harder to endure.'[7] We have seen him accepting Pound's insistence on the amount of conscious labour to be performed by the poet. And he

[1] *Authors Take Sides on the Spanish War* (1937).   [2] *SE*, p. 275.
[3] Ibid., p. 411.   [4] *Listener*, Jan. 9, 1947.   [5] *UPC*, p. 154.
[6] Baillie and Martin (edd.), *Revelation*, p. 30.
[7] Critical note in *Collected Poems of Harold Monro* (1933), p. xvi.

finds the labour of composition painful rather than pleasant.[1] He admits that he is too sceptical of his own abilities to be able to make a whole-time job of writing poetry, even if he had the means.[2] He would rather have no career than pander to a debased taste for 'commercial literature'. In all this there is a certain aloofness, a sense of loneliness in which the poet is imprisoned. His scepticism regarding his own abilities might also be interpreted as an exaggerated self-consciousness or as being due to inhibitions which bar the way against his natural urge for self-expression. Only 'once in every five or ten years' does inspiration flood the barriers. The rest is practice and patience.[3]

Honours and rewards have come to him, notably the Order of Merit and the Nobel Prize, both in 1948. Of how it feels to be a great and famous poet he has himself given a description, which I cannot resist quoting at some length, because it tells us so much about his character:

> I have always been haunted by one or the other of two doubts. The first is, that nothing I have written is really of permanent value: and that makes it hard to believe in what one wants to do next. Neither one's inner feelings, nor public approval, is satisfactory assurance: for some men have been enthusiastic about their own poetry, and nobody has agreed with them; and other men have been acclaimed as great poets, and ridiculed by a later generation. But the second doubt is still more distressing. I sometimes feel that some, at least, of what I have written, is very good, but that I shall never again write anything good. Some imp always whispers to me, as I am struggling to get down to any new piece of work, that this is going to be lamentably bad, and that I won't know it. At least three times during my life, and for periods of some duration, I have been convinced that I shall never again be able to write anything worth reading. And perhaps this time it is true. Certainly ambition, or the desire to do something of permanent value, is of no help, but rather a hindrance. And the more you get success, that is to say the more your work is praised and talked about in the magazines, the more difficult it becomes to write the next thing so that it shall be the thing you have it in you to write, instead of the thing that you know people expect of you to do.

Whether this is true for all artists I cannot say: but I am sure that

---

[1] Private conversation; cf. also *UPC*, pp. 144–5.
[2] Commentary, *CR*, Jan. 1932.
[3] Cf. Introduction to Pound's *Selected Poems*, p. xviii.

for a poet humility is the most essential virtue. That means, not to be influenced by the desire for applause, not to be influenced by the desire to excel anybody else, not to be influenced by what your readers expect of you, not to write something merely because it is high time you wrote something, but to wait patiently, not caring how you compare with other poets, for the impulse which you cannot resist—or to accept the outside invitation just as a job to be done without worrying whether it is to be poetry or not. I wrote 'The Waste Land' simply to relieve my own feelings; I wrote 'Murder in the Cathedral' because I was asked to provide a play for a festival in Canterbury Cathedral, under certain conditions and by a certain date.[1]

No one who has met T. S. Eliot in private life or has looked into the hundreds of articles of various kinds that he has written, can doubt that he has gone a very long way in perfecting himself in accordance with his ideals. His self-discipline seems to have kindled in him a peculiar graciousness. Above all he is eminently sincere, and the conviction of his sincerity is of capital importance in judging his poetry.

His Christianity, which in his prose writings may seem lacking in enthusiasm, a matter of the head rather than of the heart, a matter of Church membership even, is apparently suspect to some people. But he never wraps it up in stock phrases to which he cannot give personal assent, nor does he affirm more than he safely may. On the contrary, one often feels that he understates his religious views, and is over-scrupulous in revealing the limitations of his religious sensibility. That he sometimes makes rather extravagant claims on behalf of the Church is another matter.

From Eliot's own point of view it is possible that the peaks of what seems a fairly humdrum life have been the 'kind of unexplainable experiences which many of us have had, once or twice in our lives, and been unable to put into words'.[2] To a mind naturally inclined towards the metaphysical, any mystical experience which seems to put him within reach of another plane of essence or existence must be something to treasure up. Eliot has no faith in dreams, and finds his 'night-mind' 'quite uninteresting'.[3]

[1] *On Poetry* (1947), pp. 8–10. This is the printed text of an address to a girls' school (Concord Academy, Mass.).
[2] *Listener*, Dec. 19, 1946, p. 895.
[3] *Transition*, Spring 1938.

But with memories there is some mystery at work.

Why, [he asks] for all of us, out of all that we have heard, seen, felt, in a lifetime, do certain images recur, charged with emotion, rather than others? The song of one bird, the leap of one fish, at a particular place and time, the scent of one flower, an old woman on a German mountain path, six ruffians seen through an open window playing cards at night at a small French railway junction where there was a water-mill: such memories may have symbolic value, but of what we cannot tell, for they come to represent the depths of feeling into which we cannot peer. We might just as well ask why, when we try to recall visually some period in the past, we find in our memory just the few meagre arbitrarily chosen set of snapshots that we do find there, the faded poor souvenirs of passionate moments.[1]

There is more in memory, however, than meets the eye of consciousness. Of all that happens to us, nothing is wholly lost. This may be particularly true of reticent people, who are often peculiarly sensitive to impressions. And intellectually impressionable people like Eliot store up a great mass of ideas which do not necessarily enter into or even agree with the opinions that they express in public. Those whom they have once listened to attentively, or whose works they have read with interest, continue to speak to them and to speak through them. 'No voice is wholly lost.' So the poet sings with more voices than one and in his poetry embraces more ideas and creeds than in cold and sober prose he recognises as his own.

[1] *UPC*, p. 148.

NOTE (*see page* 8). The recent appearance of a selection of John Davidson's poems with a Preface by T. S. Eliot makes it necessary to add a few words concerning Eliot's indebtedness to this Scottish poet, whose name he links with that of the author of *The City of Dreadful Night*. Eliot had earlier (*The Saltire Review*, 1957) spoken of Arthur Symons, Ernest Dowson and John Davidson as poets from whom, at an impressionable age, he 'got the idea that one could write poetry in an English such as one would speak oneself. A colloquial idiom.' And he particularly mentioned Davidson's poem *Thirty Bob a Week* as having made 'a terrific impact' on him. He now tells us that he also 'found inspiration in the content of the poem, and in the complete fitness of content and idiom: for I also had a good many dingy urban images to reveal.' 'The personage that Davidson created in this poem,' he says, 'has haunted me all my life.' Thus he did not find English poetry completely barren.

II

THE VIEWS OF THE CRITIC

E LIOT has repeatedly asserted that he has no capacity for abstruse thinking.[1] He is a modest man, but it is true that a lack
of definiteness is a frequent feature of his statements in prose, and
that he rarely hazards excursions into general theory or abstract
speculation. When his climbing is steep he likes to tie a rope
round some jutting quotation or detail of style and work around
from that to the end of his tether, being content with the view of
the landscape which he may obtain in this way. His treatment of
poets is comparative rather than dogmatic. And John Crowe Ransom finds him 'a practitioner of Arnold's "touchstone" method
of judging poetry, though with infinite refinements; he cites, not
the same handful of resounding lines for every purpose, but lines
similar to the given lines, with an easy perception of which lines
are best. No critic', says Professor Ransom, 'proceeds so regularly
by the technique of comparative quotation.'[2]

In spite of his appeal to tradition, Eliot usually seems to conform in his appreciation of literature to Gourmont's rule 'Eriger
en lois ses impressions personelles'. Accordingly we find no explicit code or system of thought in his writings, and though something like a body of opinion may be compounded from his
scattered pronouncements, the view of Eliot as a literary legislator
owes more to his disciples than to himself. One often finds sweep-
ing interpretations of such of his phrases as 'objective correla-

[1] E.g. in *CR*, Jan. 1932, p. 274. He certainly invalidates the assertion
somewhat by coupling himself with F. H. Bradley in this respect.

[2] J. C. Ransom, *The New Criticism* (1941), p. 146.

tive' and 'direct sensuous apprehension of thought', which may deserve a wide application but which were not originally coined for general currency. There is also a mistaken notion that Eliot uniformly exalts the minor Elizabethan dramatists and the Metaphysicals as if on general principle, though his praise and blame are apportioned with great nicety.

At the outset of his critical career Eliot did write a programmatic article of general scope, 'Tradition and the Individual Talent', but this probably worked up an expectation for more of the same kind, which in turn fostered the illusion that Eliot was actually providing it. Such books and articles as *The Use of Poetry*, 'Religion and Literature', *What is a Classic?* and *Poetry and Drama* are his nearest approach to a systematic treatise.

On one occasion Eliot suggested that he is by nature 'trop disposé à mesurer toutes choses selon les règles d'une conception dogmatique qui tendrait de plus en plus à devenir rigide et formelle',[1] and that he must consequently train his mind to a more flexible treatment of literary matters. This may be why he tries to avoid dogmatic assertions. He may also have inherited from Santayana a distrust of what the latter called 'treating artificial problems in a grammatical spirit'. Thus we find Eliot praising Machiavelli because his thoughts form no system: 'for a system almost inevitably requires slight distortions and omissions'.[2]

That there should be inconsistencies and contradictions in a critic who avoids general aesthetic theories is only to be expected. Eliot as a matter of fact admits to them[3] and thus takes the edge off any complaints. Still, the trend of his criticism is usually clearer and less ambiguous than some writers on Eliot, like Yvor Winters and more recently F. R. Leavis, will have it. It is more disappointing to find a certain prevalence of prejudice, which leads him to treat some authors in a rather captious spirit. In many cases he has had to change or modify his views because he began by being too intolerant. But it is certainly to his credit that he has publicly expressed regret for his depreciatory treatment of Arnold, Whitman and Milton. At an early date he took a stand against individualism in poetry. He has later come to accept it, even in such extreme cases as those of Milton and Kipling. He is

---

[1] 'Rencontre', *Nouvelle Revue Française*, April 1925.
[2] *For Lancelot Andrewes* (1928), p. 58.
[3] *The Music of Poetry*, p. 8.

somewhat specious in doing so, but manages to contradict himself with a fairly good grace.

It is part of Eliot's conception of criticism that it can never be final, but must change with the times.[1] Thus he has some theoretical justification for the fluctuations in his own opinions of poets and their works. But it is hard to avoid discovering a measure of diffidence in his views. They are usually presented with the utmost wariness and fenced about with qualifications:

> And his conversation so nicely
> Restricted to What Precisely
> And If and Perhaps and But.

This constant circumspection seeps into his very style, and at times may be a little irritating.

Professor Muriel Bradbrook, who has written an excellent appreciation of 'Eliot's Critical Method', is of the opinion that 'the influence of Mr Eliot as a critic must surely be noted rather in the history of taste than in the history of ideas,' and, further, that 'Mr Eliot employs criticism not to the communication of truths but to the co-operative delineation of the poetic experience'.[2] I think Miss Bradbrook is right. Eliot's limitations as a critic may have prevented him from becoming a theoretician of his art or a critic of the philosophical or purely scholarly type. But perhaps his limitations have made him all the greater as a connoisseur of poetry. His freedom from dogmatism, his attention to detail, his ability to change his ground and his mind, and his careful precision when formulating an opinion combine to make him one of the best arbiters of taste of our generation. It is extraordinarily enriching to have the beauties of Dante or Lancelot Andrewes pointed out by so discerning a judge. His sensibility may be counted on; and his prose style, though sometimes hesitant, has a remarkable finesse, which has enabled him more than once to invent memorable phrases for subtle relationships.

All this means that Eliot's best qualities as a critic are precisely those which make him a poet, and which would have made a poet of a lesser man than he. Sensibility and mastery of style may

[1] See 'Shakespearian Criticism: I. From Dryden to Coleridge' in Granville-Barker and Harrison (edd.), *A Companion to Shakespeare Studies* (1934).
[2] B. Rajan (ed.), *T. S. Eliot. A Study of His Writings by Several Hands* (1947), pp. 119, 123.

even be said to be attributes of the poetical *rather* than of the critical mind. And, on the other hand, the limitations which make themselves felt in Eliot's criticism impose no restrictions, or much less noticeable ones, on his verse. The 'incapacity for abstruse thought' does not matter so much in poetry, where truth may be expressed by other means than rational argument. Logical inconsistencies, even, if rightly managed, often lend depth to poetic speech. So Eliot's diffidence disappears in his poetry, at least in so far as expression is concerned—though he may write *about* the uncertainty that he feels, which is a different matter. In poetry he has also made a virtue of the unsystematic and fragmentary form of composition. And it may be argued that his later verse in particular is made all the more captivating by the latitude of dogma which it implies.

Nevertheless, the poet cannot be separated from the critic. The interest of Eliot's poetry is partly dependent on the extent to which it either illustrates the practicability of his critical views or, on the contrary, contradicts his theories. The verse cannot be fully appreciated without reference to the views expressed in the prose. And the views expressed in the prose writings, or many of them, may be legitimately looked for in the poetic works.

THE IMPERSONAL THEORY OF POETRY

The year 1921, when the three essays later collected in the volume called *Homage to John Dryden* were first published, may be said to close a distinct period in Eliot's criticism, the period of the young firebrand who was intent on making the *bourgeoisie* sit up and take notice. The attitude of the intellectual is marked in this early criticism, and we are not surprised to find, as one of its characteristic features, an insistence on the important role of the intellect in the processes of poetry. Eliot favoured the idea of the intellect merging, so to speak, with the senses of the poet. The intellectual poets (as distinct from reflective poets like Tennyson and Browning) were able to 'feel their thought as immediately as the odour of a rose'. Such poets were Jonson, Chapman and Donne. They were capable of a 'direct sensuous apprehension of thought, or a recreation of thought into feeling',[1] to quote one of his now famous phrases.

[1] 'The Metaphysical Poets', *SE*, pp. 286–7.

Thought ceases to be poetic not only if it is divorced from feeling but also if the poet begins to ruminate. There is hardly an opinion that Eliot laboured more to inculcate in this period than the undesirability of personal ideas and philosophies, in criticism as well as in poetry. What the creative writer needs, he asserted, is merely a point of view. Eliot uses superlatives in praising Henry James for avoiding ideas: 'James's critical genius comes out most tellingly in his mastery over, his baffling escape from, Ideas; a mastery and an escape which are perhaps the last test of a superior intelligence. He had a mind so fine that no idea could violate it.'[1] Similar praise is accorded elsewhere to Dante and Shakespeare, while Swinburne and Kipling are censured for having 'concepts (Liberty, Empire) and oratory'. William Blake was too busy philosophising on his own, to the detriment of his art, while 'the borrowed philosophy of Dante and Lucretius is perhaps not so interesting, but it injures their form less'. Goethe's *Faust* and Ibsen's *Peer Gynt* embody philosophies and 'a creation of art should not do that: he [the artist] should *replace* the philosophy'.[2]

Eliot at this point finds philosophies justifiable in poetry only if, as with Lucretius and Dante, they serve, not their own ends, but those of the poetry. Therefore it is safest for the poet to borrow his ideas, so as not to fall into the temptation of subordinating poetry to speculation. The Idea is dangerous, both when personal and when popularised. It is only compatible with art when it remains in its pure state; and 'it can remain pure only by being stated simply in the form of general truth, or by being transmuted, as the attitude of Flaubert toward the small bourgeois is transformed in *Education Sentimentale*. It has there become so identified with the reality that you can no longer say what the idea is.'[3]

To put it plainly, it is not the business of the poet to argue, persuade, teach or speculate; it is his business to *present* something. 'Permanent literature is always a presentation'[4]—a statement which immediately puts us in mind of the Imagist movement. Accordingly, 'the poet can deal with philosophical ideas,

---

[1] 'In Memory of Henry James', *Egoist*, Jan. 1918.
[2] 'Kipling Redivivus', *Athenæum*, May 1919; 'Blake', *SE*, p. 320; 'The Possibility of a Poetic Drama', *The Sacred Wood*, p. 66.
[3] *The Sacred Wood*, p. 68. [4] Ibid., p. 64.

not as matter for argument, but as matter for inspection'.[1] And for this purpose traditional ideas are better than original ones.

Eliot begins his essay on 'Tradition and the Individual Talent' by referring to the vague censure often implied when the term 'traditional' is used. He finds an undue prejudice in favour of originality in literature. 'Whereas if we approach a poet without this prejudice we shall often find that not only the best, but the most individual parts of his work may be those in which the dead poets, his ancestors, assert their immortality most vigorously.' Tradition is thus indispensable. The poet must 'be aware that the mind of Europe—the mind of his own country—a mind which he learns in time to be much more important than his own private mind—is a mind which changes, and that this change is a development which abandons nothing *en route*'. The poet must continue to develop his consciousness of the past throughout his career; and that implies 'a continual surrender of himself as he is at the moment to something which is more valuable. The progress of an artist is a continual self-sacrifice, a continual extinction of personality . . . It is in this depersonalization that art may be said to approach the condition of science.'[2]

He then goes on to study more closely the relation of a poem to its author, and in this connection uses the phrase 'the Impersonal theory of poetry'. The creative mind of the poet, he says, 'may partly or exclusively operate upon the experience of the man himself; but, the more perfect the artist, the more completely separate in him will be the man who suffers and the mind which creates'. 'It is not in his personal emotions, the emotions provoked by particular events in his life, that the poet is in any way remarkable or interesting.' And further, 'the business of the poet is not to find new emotions, but to use the ordinary ones and, in working them up into poetry, to express feelings which are not in actual emotions at all'. The original subject-matter must be transformed. In his slightly later essay on 'The Metaphysical Poets' Eliot even assumed that thought may be recreated into feeling or feeling into

---

[1] 'Dante', *The Sacred Wood*, p. 162.

[2] A comparison with some of Matthew Arnold's pronouncements may be recommended at this point; e.g. (from the 1853 Preface to *Poems*): 'he [the Poet] needs . . . to be perpetually reminded to prefer his action to everything else; so to treat this, as to permit its inherent excellences to develop themselves, without interruption from the intrusion of his personal peculiarities: most fortunate, when he most entirely succeeds in effacing himself . . .'

thought. In a similar way, minor subjects, he thought, may release major emotions,[1] and major emotions may appear, when objectified, as something of minor importance.

In the process by which personal emotion and feeling become impersonal the author again assigns a large place to the intellect. But at one stage in the creative process something mysterious seems to happen, which Eliot can only explain by means of a chemical comparison. The poet's mind, he says, is 'a receptacle for seizing and storing up numberless feelings, phrases, images, which remain there until all the particles which can unite to form a new compound are present together'. At which moment the mind acts as a catalyst and there occurs a spontaneous fusion with the effect of creating 'a new art emotion'. And 'it is not the "greatness", the intensity, of the emotions, the components, but the intensity of the artistic process, the pressure, so to speak, under which the fusion takes place, that counts'.[2]

Thus, though a poetic theme may appear quite simple it usually has complex sources. 'A love affair . . .,' says Eliot, writing on Shakespeare's sonnets, 'might cause a successful or bad investment; it cannot, without a great many other and alien experiences of which the ordinary man is incapable, cause good poetry.'[3] A fusion takes place between many disparate elements, and the results of the fusion may be very difficult indeed to analyse.

In introducing his notion of 'intensity of the artistic process' Eliot seems to approach a kind of aesthetic mysticism. The most important moment in the creation of a poem is removed from the sphere of reason and familiar emotions and transferred to a special artistic faculty which can only be known by its effects. It follows that poetry is not, as Babbitt would have it, a matter of conscious technique. 'It is a concentration which does not happen consciously or of deliberation.'[4] Eliot, it must be admitted, comes close to accepting the idea of supernatural inspiration.

But there are other ways of making personal experiences impersonal which anybody can understand and which Eliot obviously must have known. One simple way is that of treating a lyrical theme in a more or less dramatic way, as seems to have been

---

[1] Cf. Eliot's Introduction to Marianne Moore, *Selected Poems* (1935).
[2] 'Tradition and the Individual Talent', *SE*, p. 19.
[3] *Nation and Athenæum*, Feb. 12, 1927.
[4] *SE*, p. 21.

The Impersonal Theory of Poetry

done, for instance, in *The Love Song* and *Portrait of a Lady*. Another is the use of 'objective correlatives'.[1]

The original experiences which Eliot draws upon may be either the chance impressions of life, or carefully sought-for and selected events. In the former case one would expect that only the poet can find significance in them, and that his attempts to transmute them into something objectively 'rich and strange' must be foiled. Thus some of the scenes and people mentioned in *Gerontion* seem to represent private memories whose hidden meaning is fully apparent to the poet alone. The effort of objectification, therefore, must begin with the choice of subject-matter if the reader is to find a meaning. I do not say that the poet must perform a conscious labour of construction or *invent* his 'objective correlatives'. He is at liberty to *discover* them even in his chance experiences provided he recognises something inherent in those experiences (not something merely due to his accompanying moods and associations) which evokes the idea or the emotion he wishes to present. A 'correlative' or symbol of this kind can express an objective observation in terms of a subjective experience, and a general truth in terms of a subjective truth. The idea or emotion is made concrete, but in another context than that of the poet's original experience. Thus, as Eliot has told me, the phrase 'La figlia che piange' was the name given to an old relief preserved in a museum in Northern Italy. Eliot, travelling in Italy, was advised by a friend to go and see this piece of sculpture, but failed to find it. However, the name stuck in his mind, and he used it as a suggestive title for one of his poems. The fact that he only heard the phrase by accident does not make it less expressive, for we feel that he was struck by it precisely because it represented something personal to him whilst being generally evocative at the same time. A chance thing like the figlia phrase may be *found*, instead of being expressed from within, but it still expresses some inner experience, because it is found to correspond to that experience. The process of transmutation, then, is no arbitrary affair.

The objectification of meaning will sometimes appear to occur in three stages. There is first the original experience, then the attitude of the poet abstracted from that and similar experiences

---

[1] Eliot first used this phrase in his essay on *Hamlet* in 1919. According to Professor Harry Levin ('Criticism in Crisis', *Comparative Literature*, VII, 2 (1955)) it was originally formulated by Washington Allston.

and finally a common attitude or idea, which may be the expression of the spirit of the age. The first stage is not, on the whole, our concern, but the two next stages are. Where they both occur, they give the poems two strata of meaning. On the surface appears the completely objectified meaning, but on a deeper level the meaning which is generalised while still belonging to the poet. In *The Waste Land*, as we shall see, the objective idea or attitude which appears on the surface is that of the disillusion of modern humanity. Deeper down we find the poet's personal feelings and ideas, abstracted from his particular experiences. We must be aware all the time of both levels.

At the end of the essay on 'Tradition and the Individual Talent' the author declares that 'poetry is not a turning loose of emotion, but an escape from emotion; it is not the expression of personality, but an escape from personality. But, of course,' he says, 'only those who have personality and emotions know what it means to want to escape from these things.' It would seem that his impersonal theory at least partly originated in a revulsion from his own emotional freight at the time, and an intense distrust of the private and individual personality. Perhaps this distrust has something to do with doubt as to the spiritual nature of man. He certainly rejected a metaphysical belief in the human soul and in the personality as a definite entity. The point of view which he struggles to attack in his essay is perhaps related, he says, 'to the metaphysical theory of the substantial unity of the soul: for my meaning is, that the poet has, not a "personality" to express, but a particular medium, which is only a medium and not a personality, in which impressions and experiences combine in peculiar and unexpected ways.' If there is no individual soul it is obviously no irreparable loss to exclude from poetry what we are in the habit of calling personality. In that case it is clear that tradition, even if it represents the second-hand, is both more rich and more reliable than the private mind. And that an outside authority, such as is recognised in Classicism, is greatly to be desired.

In Eliot's later criticism the personal passions of the poet are still regarded as being the fundamental but transmuted material of poetry. He speaks of Shakespeare as being 'occupied with the struggle—which alone constitutes life for a poet—to transmute his personal and private agonies into something rich and strange, something universal and impersonal. The rage of Dante against

Florence, or Pistoia, or what not, the deep surge of Shakespeare's general cynicism and disillusionment, are merely gigantic attempts to metamorphose private failures and disappointments.'[1] And elsewhere he declares that 'we all have to choose whatever subject-matter allows us the most powerful and secret release; and that is a personal affair.'[2] An original impulse which is entirely personal is transformed into a correlative which is entirely impersonal.

Now, in so far as the poet can change his private agony into something rich and strange this will no doubt mean a gain to his art. The reader can hardly want to read simply the *journal intime* of the poet put into verse. But the 'new art emotion' or 'significant emotion' of which Eliot speaks can surely be only a part of the emotional content of a poem. A poem which uses words and deals with human beings or the world in which they live cannot fail to make its appeal to the common emotions of practical life. Nor does the poet do away with his private emotions by using them to produce an art emotion. The art emotion may be produced, but the private emotions will still be there if they are strong enough to need expressing.

The impersonal theory, therefore, must have been a difficult one to uphold consistently, and in several of the essays of the early period there are statements which appear to contradict it. Thus Ben Jonson's works, we are told, cannot be appreciated without 'knowledge of Jonson', which I take to mean knowledge of the life and private personality of Jonson.[3] And by the time Eliot was asked to lecture on W. B. Yeats in 1940 he had changed his position and was no longer interested even in elucidating his former views. He now thought that the kind of impersonality which was more than that of the mere skilful craftsman was achieved by the mature poet 'who, out of intense and personal experience, is able to express a general truth; retaining all the particularity of his experience, to make of it a general symbol'.[4] The words to be stressed here are 'retaining all the particularity of his experience'. They are a far cry from the theories of 1919.

Even a casual study of Eliot's poetry will make it clear that he

---

[1] 'Shakespeare and the Stoicism of Seneca', *SE*, p. 137.
[2] Introduction to Marianne Moore, *Selected Poems*, p. 9.
[3] 'Ben Jonson', *SE*, pp. 157, 159.
[4] *Selected Prose* (1953), p. 201.

is really an individualist as well as a traditionalist. And the ideal in literature must surely be a fusion of the particular and the common, the individual and the traditional. Only in such a fusion can literature subsist. The pleasure derived from reading consists to a large extent in a recognition of variations within a traditional framework. And any deviation from the central compromise between individuality and tradition can only be in degree. Eliot's early ideal of completely transcending the personality is an impossible one.

His views on the legitimacy of ideas in poetry also seem to have undergone a certain amount of change. It may be reasonably doubted whether he would still say that permanent literature is always a presentation. The *Four Quartets* are rather an exploration, and they were undoubtedly written for permanence. As for Dante and Lucretius, he has come to recognise them as unashamedly didactic.[1]

Eliot wants poetry to express the 'permanent and universal'.[2] And perhaps his ultimate views in the question of impersonality in poetry are determined by the sense of an Absolute beneath the changing phenomena which has become very insistent in his writings. 'All great art,' he wrote in 1932,

> is in a sense a document on its time; but great art is never merely a document, for mere documentation is not art. All great art has something permanent and universal about it, and reflects the permanent as well as the changing. . . . And as no great art is explicable simply by the society of its time, so it is not fully explicable simply by the personality of its author: in the greatest poetry there is always a hint of something behind, something impersonal, something in relation to which the author has been no more than the passive (if not always pure) medium.[3]

This 'hint of something behind' enables him to state that 'the essential advantage for a poet is not, to have a beautiful world with which to deal: it is to be able to see beneath both beauty and ugliness; to see the boredom, and the horror, and the glory'. The poet may even be groping for the inexpressible; he may be 'occupied with frontiers of consciousness beyond which words fail, though meanings still exist'. It is the truthfulness of his perception of reality that counts; and 'we cannot be *primarily* interested in any

[1] See *UPC*, pp. 95–6. [2] 'A Dialogue on Dramatic Poetry', *SE*, p. 46.
[3] Commentary, *CR*, Oct. 1932.

writer's nerves . . . or in any one's heredity except for the purpose
of knowing to what extent that writer's individuality distorts or
detracts from the objective truth which he perceives'.[1]

The 'hint of something behind' is actually a half-admission of
belief in the divine inspiration of the poet. Eliot has never been
very explicit on this subject. The unconscious creative process
described in 'Tradition and the Individual Talent' suggests a
possible approach to a theory of inspiration, but in an article
written about the same time as this essay Eliot made fun of 'the
British worship of inspiration, which in literature is merely an
avoidance of comparison with foreign literatures, a dodging of
standards'.[2] When I asked him point-blank whether he believed
in the possibility of divine inspiration in poetry, he did not re-
pudiate the idea, but neither did he positively assent to it. His
plainest commitment was probably made in a broadcast talk on
'Vergil and the Christian World' given in 1951. After discussing
Virgil as an unconscious prophet of Christianity he said:

> . . . if the word 'inspiration' is to have any meaning, it must mean
> just this, that the speaker or writer is uttering something which he
> does not wholly understand—or which he may even misinterpret
> when the inspiration has departed from him. This is certainly true
> of poetic inspiration. . . . A poet may believe that he is expressing
> only his private experience; his lines may be for him only a means of
> talking about himself without giving himself away; yet for his
> readers what he has written may come to be the expression both of
> their own secret feelings and of the exultation or despair of a
> generation.[3]

Other statements may be found in 'The *Pensées* of Pascal' and in
The Use of Poetry.[4] While it would be unwise to attach too much
importance to them, they do undoubtedly throw an interesting
light on Eliot's attitude to his own poetry and on the belief attitudes which he invites his readers to assume. The passage from
Eliot's broadcast talk is particularly relevant to an understanding
of *The Waste Land*.

From one point of view—that of language in its relation to

---

[1] *UPC*, p. 106; *The Music of Poetry*, p. 15; 'Baudelaire in Our Time',
EAM, p. 67.

[2] 'Professional, or . . .', *Egoist*, April 1918.

[3] *Listener*, Sept. 13, 1951.

[4] *EAM*, p. 142; *UPC*, pp. 144-5.

culture—Eliot has no doubts as to the function of poetry. In fact he has tended more and more to regard the poet's task as being primarily an objective one concerned with the cultural and social development of his community. Thus in 1945 he wrote that 'it is the business of the poet to express, and to criticise, the culture in which he lives and to which he belongs'[1]—and this holds good even if his conscious purpose is another. Particularly it has become a favourite idea that it is '*the* social rôle of the poet' to develop the language. The reason is that the life of a people is intimately bound up with, and its intelligence and feelings in part dependent upon 'the structure, the rhythms, the sounds, the idioms' of its language. Poetry is especially the most '*precise* medium' for emotion,[2] and therefore it may be useful in teaching us, as citizens, to be critical of what we read and hear, and to distinguish an appeal to the emotions from an appeal to the intellect.[3]

All this simply shows that there has been no stagnation in Eliot's concern with tradition and the individual talent, and that his aestheticism has not shut him up in an ivory tower.

FORM AND MATTER

It may be a common impression that Eliot tries to 'impose upon us a conception of poetry as some sort of pure and rare aesthetic essence'.[4] This 'essence', presumably, would have to be manifested in the formal elements of poetry. The impression is a very partial one, but it can be supported by numerous quotations from Eliot's prose. For instance: 'Not our feelings, but the pattern which we may make of our feelings, is the centre of value'; 'what is poetic about poetry is just the invention or discovery or elaboration of a new idiom in verse'; 'Poetry begins, I dare say, with a savage beating a drum in a jungle, and it retains that essential of percussion and rhythm'; '*If* poetry is a form of "communication", yet that which is to be communicated is the poem itself, and only incidentally the experience and the thought which have gone into it.' And Eliot considers that at least in some kinds of poetry 'the chief use of the "meaning" of a poem' may be 'to satisfy one habit of the reader, to keep his mind diverted and quiet, while the

---

[1] 'The Social Function of Poetry', *Adelphi*, July/Sept. 1945.
[2] Ibid.   [3] See *On Poetry*, pp. 12–15.
[4] Edmund Wilson, *Axel's Castle* (1931), p. 119.

poem does its work upon him: much as the imaginary burglar is always provided with a bit of nice meat for the house-dog'. We also have his assurance that there are passages in his poetry which he 'invented out of nothing because they sounded well', and that his interest in poetry is 'primarily a technical interest'.[1] Kipling, says Eliot, is a writer for whom poetry is an instrument. But, he goes on,

> Most of us are interested in the form for its own sake—not apart from the content, but because we aim at making something which shall first of all *be*, something which in consequence will have the capability of exciting, within a limited range, a considerable variety of responses from different readers. For Kipling the poem is something which is intended to *act*—and for the most part his poems are intended to elicit the same response from all readers. . . . For other poets—at least, for some other poets—the poem may begin to shape itself in fragments of musical rhythm, and its structure will first appear in terms of something analogous to musical form; and such poets find it expedient to occupy their conscious mind with the craftsman's problems, leaving the deeper meaning to emerge, if there, from a lower level.[2]

We must take poetry as we find it, he says, even if the poet perceives 'possibilities of intensity' through the elimination of meaning.[3]

It must not be inferred, however, that Eliot holds with the doctrine of 'art for art's sake' if by this is meant the belief in 'some illusory *pure* enjoyment'.[4] Pure enjoyment is impossible because poetry cannot divorce itself completely from meaning. And anyhow, 'the music of verse is strongest in poetry which has a definite meaning expressed in the properest words.'[5] With his eye on the outer influences affecting a poet, Eliot believes that the real, and not the formal, impulses are the original ones. Thus he declares that 'any radical change in poetic form is likely to be the symptom of some very much deeper change in society and in the individual'.[6] As for the relation of the formal elements to the private material

---

[1] Introduction to Valéry's *Le Serpent* (1924), p. 12; *Listener*, April 16, 1930; *UPC*, pp. 155, 30, 151; *SE*, p. 127; *Milton*, p. 6.
[2] *A Choice of Kipling's Verse* (1941), p. 18.
[3] *UPC*, p. 151.   [4] Ibid., p. 98.
[5] *Milton*, p. 19.   [6] *UPC*, p. 75.

employed by the poet, we learn that the purpose of complexity of form 'must be, first, the precise expression of finer shades of feeling and thought.'[1]

The last statement especially is hard to reconcile with the pronouncements asserting the primacy of form. But a more thorough examination will probably reveal an underlying consistency. Although the conscious attention of the poet may be fixed on the form, and the meaning may be left to emerge, if there, from a lower level, this is not to say that the meaning is quite unimportant to the inception of the poem. It may even be the prime factor, though unconscious. Eliot thinks that a poem may be prepared unconsciously and then suddenly come to eruption. And the fidelity of the expression to feeling and thought may be to feeling and thought *inherent* in the expression or created with it. If 'feelings, phrases and images' are stored up together and finally fused as he says in 'Tradition and the Individual Talent' that they are, this can only mean that form and matter are born together in a single creative act, and that they are equally important and valuable components of the poetry that is created. Thus we are led to an integral view of the relation between them.

Eliot himself leads us up to this integral view by means of a little equivocation; he speaks of the importance of 'the distinction between form and substance, and again between material and attitude. . . . In the perfect poet they . . . are the same thing; and in another sense they *always* are the same thing. So it is always true to say that form and content are the same thing, and always true to say that they are different things.'[2] This helps us over the stile and we can proceed to cull such statements as these: from the poetic processes a masterpiece now and then results, 'in which medium and material, form and content, are indistinguishable'; 'the music of poetry is not something which exists apart from the meaning. Otherwise, we could have poetry of great musical beauty which made no sense, and I have never come across such poetry'; 'the music of verse is strongest in poetry which has a definite meaning expressed in the properest words'; 'What matters, in short, is the whole poem.'[3]

After all, a word is indissolubly both a pattern of sound and a

[1] *What is a Classic?* (1945), p. 16.
[2] Introduction to Pound's *Selected Poems*, pp. ix–x.
[3] Ibid., p. xx; *The Music of Poetry*, pp. 13, 18; *Milton*, p. 19.

complex of meaning. And what enters into and makes the poetry, is a verbal combination of sound and sense.

As for the ways of responding to a poem, Eliot finds that 'the legitimate responses of the reader vary very widely' between two extremes. At one end of the scale are those who, with Montgomery Belgion, 'like poetry merely for what it has to say,' at the other end those who, with Dr Richards, 'like the poetry because the poet has manipulated his material into perfect art . . .'; 'between these extremes occurs a continuous range of appreciations, each of which has its limited validity.'[1]

Only this comprehensive and integral view is finally tenable, and Eliot is quite aware of its merits. But if it were possible to weigh his various statements in opposite scales, it is probable that a slight preponderance would be found in favour of the formal elements as the prime factors in poetry. And this must be because the formal elements, after all, are the truly dynamic ones. Eliot's basic idea seems to be that beauty of form provides a stimulus which, as far as emotional, sensual or intellectual content goes, is undifferentiated. And each reader is allowed to differentiate the meaning to himself by his particular responses, much as is commonly done in the case of music.

POETRY AND RELIGION

In Eliot's criticism after about 1921 the discussion of the creative process no longer predominates as it did before that time. He is more concerned with the actual subjects of poetry. And the eligible subjects are found to cover a wide range of possibilities. From the start the sordid and ugly were recognised. Now, as he strikingly demonstrates in the essay on Dante of 1929, he has come to see not only damnation, but purgation and beatitude as well, as fit subjects for a poet. Further, one learns from the *Purgatorio*, he says, 'that a straightforward philosophical statement can be great poetry'.[2]

Perhaps as a result of the general subordination of purely aesthetic interests to metaphysical, political and cultural which took place in his criticism after 1921, he attempted more

[1] 'Poetry and Propaganda' in M. D. Zabel (ed.), *Literary Opinion in America* (1951 edn.), p. 103.
[2] *SE*, pp. 252-3, 264.

systematically to relate his aesthetic opinions to his main beliefs and attitudes in other fields. He soon came to treat religion in a less cavalier fashion than at first, to see that it mattered to art more than he had thought, and, now and again, almost to change his ground by subordinating art to dogma.

Eliot had begun by declaring, in effect, that religion was of no importance to the artist. In a book review of 1916, he admitted that one's enjoyment of art must obviously be coloured by one's philosophy, but asserted for his own part that he saw no reason why a man's enjoyment of art 'should be atrophied by a naturalistic philosophy or stimulated by a theistic one'. 'The feeling and the belief,' he explained, 'are different things in different categories of value. We enjoy the feeling, and we cannot rest content unless we can justify it by exhibiting its relation to the other parts of our life. Having made this attempt, we then enjoy the theory we have made.'[1]

We are repeatedly told, throughout Eliot's critical writings, that art is independent and supreme in its own sphere. In 'The Function of Criticism' the author 'assumed as axiomatic that a creation, a work of art, is autotelic'. And in one of his Commentaries he observes that 'from the point of view of art, . . . Christianity was merely a change, a provision of a new world with new material; from the point of view of communism as of Christianity, art and literature are strictly irrelevant.'[2] A Christian, he says in the same article, is free to allow for inconsistencies in the affairs of this world, such as the appearance of good art even where there is a bad philosophy.

Again and again Eliot points to the difference between art and belief. Having read Maritain's *Situation de la Poésie*, and incidentally warned poets against the study of aesthetics, he goes on: 'I would make a distinction which Maritain has omitted to make: that between the possible interests of the poet at the times when he is not engaged in writing poetry, and the direction of his attention when writing. . . . Certainly, in the effort of composition . . . the poet can only properly be occupied with how to say it.'[3]

Eliot rejects the idea of literature 'as a means for eliciting truth or acquiring knowledge' or as 'the expression of philosophical or

---

[1] *International Journal of Ethics*, Jan. 1916, pp. 285–7.
[2] *CR*, Jan. 1933, p. 246.
[3] *New English Weekly*, April 27, 1939.

religious intuition', preferring to see it as 'a means of refined and intellectual pleasure'.[1] In a number of contexts we are told that poetry is essentially entertainment. In general, says Eliot, 'a poet wishes to give pleasure, to entertain or divert people.' Thus he adopts the conception of the use of poetry attributed by Jacques Rivière to the masters of the seventeenth century, such as Molière and Racine: 'If in the seventeenth century Molière or Racine had been asked why he wrote, no doubt he would have been able to find but one answer; that he wrote "for the entertainment of decent people" (*pour distraire les honnêtes gens*)'.[2] And very definitely Eliot tells us in *The Music of Poetry* that 'the end of understanding poetry is enjoyment, and . . . this enjoyment is gusto disciplined by taste'.

He is particularly emphatic in asserting that literature can be no *substitute* for religion or philosophy, or indeed for anything else that is not art, 'not merely because we need religion, but because we need literature as well as religion'.[3] He says the same thing repeatedly in *The Use of Poetry*, and stresses this point obviously because he finds that it is here that abuses have been most common ('Our literature is a substitute for religion, and so is our religion'[4]). He puts the chief blame on Matthew Arnold for propagating this heresy by his attitude to poetry, and by his definition of it as 'a criticism of life'. But in our secular age Arnold has had many followers.

Poetry and religion are in Eliot's opinion sovereign and autonomous in their different spheres; and they should be kept apart. A *confusion des genres* results in treating the Mass primarily as art or turning poetry into magic. 'You cannot take heaven by magic.' With religion may be grouped all beliefs and philosophies. 'I believe,' he says 'that for a poet to be also a philosopher he would have to be virtually two men.'[5] Even Coleridge, he declares, was able to exercise the one activity only at the expense of the other.

He admits, however, that there is a necessary connection between religion and philosophy on the one hand and poetry on the other. For one thing, we cannot 'distinguish, as people sometimes do, between the occasions on which a particular poet

---

[1] 'Experiment in Criticism' in *Tradition and Experiment in Present-Day Literature* (1929), p. 200.
[2] *UPC*, pp. 31, 128. [3] 'A Dialogue on Dramatic Poetry', *SE*, p. 48.
[4] Ibid., p. 44. [5] *UPC*, pp. 140, 98–9.

is "being a poet" and the occasions on which he is "being a preacher"'. Dr Richards thought *The Waste Land* effected 'a complete severance between poetry and *all* beliefs'. Eliot, with an unimportant reservation, thinks him wrong. At the same time he seems to suggest that a complete severance between poetry and all beliefs would have been a good thing for poetry if it had been possible: it would do 'what all poetry in the past would have been the better for doing'. In other words, the connection between poetry and belief is a practical, not an ideal, necessity. Therefore it should not artificially be made more pronounced than it actually is: 'Any theory which relates poetry very closely to a religious or a social scheme of things aims, probably, to *explain* poetry by discovering its natural laws; but it is in danger of *binding* poetry by legislation to be observed—and poetry can recognise no such laws.'[1]

On the other hand, as early as 1922 Eliot stated in an article on 'The Lesson of Baudelaire' that 'all first-rate poetry is occupied with morality' and that what matters to a poet is the problem of good and evil.[2] In *After Strange Gods* he apparently subjected art to the rule of religion by deliberately applying the criterion of Christian orthodoxy to a number of writers as the supreme test of the value of their works. In *The Use of Poetry* he gave it as his opinion (his 'eccentricity', he called it) that aesthetic studies should be 'guided by sound theology',[3] and his essay on 'Religion and Literature' exhorts all Christians to maintain consciously, in literature, 'certain standards and criteria of criticism over and above those applied by the rest of the world'. Is this a contradiction of the statements on the autonomy of poetry exemplified above? Or what does Eliot really mean?

Discussing 'The Modern Mind' in *The Use of Poetry*, he quotes the views of various authorities to show how wide is the disagreement in modern criticism as to the religious function of poetry. Thus I. A. Richards, allying himself with Arnold, thinks 'poetry is capable of saving us', i.e. that poetry has a cultural function to perform, a task of salvation for which men previously looked to religion. Jacques Maritain, on the contrary, thinks 'it is a deadly error to expect poetry to provide the super-substantial nourishment of man'. While Henri Bremond thinks of poetry as a mystical revelation, Dr Richards asserts that it is nothing of the kind.

[1] *UPC*, pp. 130, 139.   [2] *Tyro*, 1, 1922.   [3] *UPC*, p. 150.

On the whole, the 'later' Eliot would certainly accept Maritain's Thomistic aesthetics, as expounded particularly in *Art et scolastique*. Some of Maritain's views it may be useful to summarise at this point. What the intelligence apprehends in knowing beauty, says Maritain, is a glimmering of the Divine; and he takes his argument from Aquinas:

> *splendor formae*, disait saint Thomas . . .: car la *'forme'*, c'est-à-dire le principe qui fait la perfection propre de tout ce qui est, qui constitue et achève les choses dans leur essence et dans leurs qualités, qui est enfin, si l'on peut ainsi parler, le secret ontologique qu'elles portent en elles, leur être spirituel, leur mystère opérant, est avant tout le principe propre d'intelligibilité, la *clarté* propre de toute chose. Aussi bien toute forme est-elle un vestige ou un rayon de l'Intelligence créatrice imprimé au coeur de l'être créé.[1]

God is the fountain of beauty, and beauty belongs to the transcendental and metaphysical order. Therefore the fine arts, which are particularly ordered to beauty, have a special character among the other arts. They are like a horizon where matter comes into contact with spirit. They have a spiritual soul, and enable souls to communicate with each other and to contemplate, with delight, the reality of the spirit. The fine arts, therefore, are an end in themselves and completely disinterested—fruits, to be enjoyed as such. They can help us on the road to salvation, however, by the secondary effects of the emotions that they arouse in us if not as a fulfilment of their proper purpose. For the objects of art can be read as signs of a transcendent reality, the apprehension of which is the beginning of knowledge. And the purity of the artist, though it cannot save his soul, can reflect, and so prepare, moral purity. 'Inutiles par eux-mêmes à la vie éternelle, l'art et la poésie sont plus nécessaires que le pain à la race humaine. Ils la disposent à la vie de l'esprit.'[2]

The sole end of art itself is the work to be done and the beauty of the work. But in its human aspect, as residing in a person, art has a moral significance and is subordinate to the sanctification of man and to the human virtues. That is to say that 'l'art n'a aucun droit contre Dieu'.[3] If a conflict arises between the purposes of the

[1] *Art et scolastique* (3rd edn. 1935), p. 38.
[2] J. Maritain, *Réponse à Jean Cocteau* (1926), p. 29.
[3] *Art et scolastique*, p. 123.

artist creating his works of art and the needs of the man in his spiritual struggles towards the light, then the artist is in duty bound to give way. It is obvious that such conflicts will always arise in practical life, except perhaps in the case of the saint, whose every artistic impulse would be inspired by the love of God. In the ordinary course of things, the intrinsic perfection of art is marred by sin. But if saintliness is not within the reach of all, at least grace is possible, and makes possible a Christian art, which is the art of humanity redeemed and to which everything belongs, the profane as well as the sacred. The builders of cathedrals believed, and therefore their work 'révélait la vérité de Dieu'. Conversely, Maritain considers that 'partout, lorsque l'art a connu, égyptien, grec ou chinois, un certain degré de grandeur et de pureté, il est déjà chrétien, chrétien en espérance, parce que tout resplendissement spirituel est une promesse et une figure des équilibres divins de l'Évangile'.[1]

Implicit in Maritain's aesthetic is a fairly strong faith in the goodness of human nature and in the efficacy of human virtues, a faith which perhaps is natural to a Catholic. His views would have been unacceptable to a Protestant and Puritan philosopher like Søren Kierkegaard, who may be taken to represent an opposite extreme in Christian thought. Of art, or poetry, Kierkegaard has a poor opinion. There are poets who have reached the ethical and religious stages, but in general, he thinks, the 'existence' of a poet lies in the obscurity of indecision, refusing the ethical choice. And 'the poetic ideal is always a false ideal, for the true ideal is always real. When the spirit is prevented from soaring to the eternal realm of spirit, it dawdles on the way, gladdened by the images which are reflected in the clouds, and bemoaning their transience. Therefore a poet's existence is by its nature an unhappy existence—.'[2] Kierkegaard goes still further. He declares that 'from a Christian point of view . . . a poet's existence is one of sin, the sin of imagining instead of being, of approaching goodness and truth through the imagination instead of realising them, that is to say, of existentially striving to realise them'.[3]

Maritain and Kierkegaard do not differ greatly in their con-

[1] *Art et scolastique*, pp. 110, 114.
[2] Kierkegaard, *Enten-Eller*, *Samlede Værker* (1920), Vol. II, p. 227 (my translation).
[3] *Sygdommen til Døden*, *Samlede Værker*, Vol. IX, p. 213 (my translation).

cepts of beauty, which to both is chiefly the splendour, perceptible
to the intellect, of what is right and good, and derives ultimately
from God. But Maritain gives it a wider significance, including
the satisfaction of the senses which Kierkegaard condemns. And
the two philosophers are entirely at variance as to the function
and value of art.

Eliot does not entirely share Maritain's humanism. He has more
than a little of Kierkegaard's Puritan scepticism with regard to
human nature, derived perhaps from his own New England
heritage. But in other respects he seems to be at one with Maritain,
and certainly shares his attitude to art. In the ninth Chorus of *The
Rock* the poet speaks of the various branches of art, and asks:

> LORD, shall we not bring these gifts to Your service?
> Shall we not bring to Your service all our powers
> For life, for dignity, grace and order,
> And intellectual pleasures of the senses?
> The LORD who created must wish us to create
> And employ our creation again in His service
> Which is already His service in creating.

The creative activity in itself is here regarded both as a gift of God
and as service of God.

Form in poetry is the pattern of metre, sounds, images, ideas,
and the pattern of lines, colours, etc. in the images called up; it is
harmony, correspondence, symmetry, balance, in dynamic self-
assertion. Jacques Maritain by his emphasis on pure form suggests that these things can reach, or enable us to reach, the high
realms of the spirit. And Eliot seems to express a similar idea in
Burnt Norton:

> Only by the form, the pattern,
> Can words or music reach
> The stillness,

Geometry has a finality and perfection which may put us in
mind of the Absolute. And to a Romantic way of thinking the
apprehension of formal beauty may certainly be conducive to the
vision beatific. But perhaps the idea of a higher glory must have
entered our minds in other ways before we can see it reflected in a
formal pattern.

Our experience seems to tell us that what is already in our
minds is seized by the aesthetic emotions and lifted up to be

bathed in the light of beauty. And those emotions are not like a whirlwind which stirs up dead leaves. A work of art arranges and brings into harmony the contents of our minds, and so enables us to build them into new understanding and new intuitions.

If we could imagine contents which were morally or spiritually neutral, we could perhaps imagine also a kind of uplift caused by the pure beauty of form. Such contents, however, are a practical impossibility even in music, because the contents are not only given by the art but are also present in the minds of the listeners, just as in conversation the contents, or meanings, of the individual words spoken to us are present in our minds beforehand, together with a host of other things, and what we hear only presents them to us in a new order. Art, then, is clearly edifying in a spiritual sense only if it involves edifying contents, that is to say, either if it finds edifying contents (which may be the same thing as a mood of devotion) in the mind of the enjoyer, or if it puts such contents into that mind. In either case it is enough that there should be a general awareness of certain things, a general direction of interests, even scattered fragments of ideas or emotions—for art will integrate them. Not only is a didactic poem not art in its didactic aspect, but it is not necessary to the effect of edification that there should be a clear belief or purpose in the mind of the enjoyer or in the poem. Thus if the contents of a poem are such as merely to engage the mind on a religious plane the beauty of the poem will tend to create a sense of value on that plane, and hence edify.

Because art gives us the impetus, but not necessarily the contents and perhaps not the direction, it is powerless alone to provide our spiritual guidance. This is what most Christian thinkers have realised, and Eliot reminds us. But that does not mean that he entirely rejects the idea of the epistemological function of poetry. Poetry *may*, occasionally, be related to mystical apprehension. The poet may be groping for the inexpressible, he may be 'occupied with frontiers of consciousness beyond which words fail, though meanings still exist'.[1] Eliot is very wary and non-committal on this point, but when he says that 'there is a relation (not necessarily noetic, perhaps merely psychological) between mysticism and some kinds of poetry, or some of the kinds of state in which poetry is produced',[2] he at least admits the possibility of a noetic

---

[1] *The Music of Poetry*, p. 15.   [2] *UPC*, p. 139.

relation. I asked him in 1948 if he thought poetry had any significance as a means of approach to mystical knowledge, and he replied that he did not think it had any direct significance, but that poetry could help us to approach an understanding of an ultimate reality, and it could give a sensitive reader the assurance that there is this kind of reality.

Eliot insists on the close connection between 'religion and literature' in the essay of that name. Most modern literature, especially fiction, has become quite secularised, he says. We completely separate our literary from our religious judgments. Yet, he declares (somewhat illogically), 'the separation is not, and never can be complete.' He means that though it may be complete on the conscious plane it remains incomplete on the unconscious plane—assuming of course that there is religion. For there is a common ground between religion and fiction, that of behaviour, or ethics. Eliot examines the moral usefulness or harmfulness of literature and says that 'The fiction that we read affects our behaviour towards our fellow men, affects our patterns of ourselves.'

> And if we, as readers, keep our religious and moral convictions in one compartment, and take our reading merely for entertainment, or on a higher plane, for aesthetic pleasure, I would point out that the author, whatever his conscious intentions in writing, in practice recognizes no such distinctions. The author of a work of imagination is trying to affect us wholly, as human beings, whether he knows it or not; and we are affected by it, as human beings, whether we intend to be or not.

Our reading necessarily 'affects us as entire human beings; it affects our moral and religious existence'. The term 'religious existence' implies that the effects described are independent of the faith or lack of faith of the readers of literature. From Eliot's point of view even unbelievers have a religious existence, a relation in their lives of a positive or negative character to the absolute truths of religion, something that interpenetrates the entire personality, including the artistic sensibility. It follows that even a poet who on the conscious plane does away with all 'meaning' must nevertheless exercise some subtle influence which touches his own religious existence and that of others.

In later essays Eliot speaks of art as 'one of the essential constituents' of the soil in which religion flourishes; and finds that both aesthetic sensibility and spiritual perception can be so deepened and merged with each other that 'in the end, the judgment of a work of art by either religious or aesthetic standards will come to the same thing.'[1] The latter, however, is an idea which he does not further develop, though it would be interesting to see how far he could pursue it.

Eliot would not disparage a poem simply because it contained a 'message'. On the contrary, he considers it a gain if poetry serves other purposes *over and above* that of being poetry:

> Poetry is of course not to be defined by its uses. If it commemorates a public occasion, or celebrates a festival, or decorates a religious rite, or amuses a crowd, so much the better. It may effect revolutions in sensibility such as are periodically needed. . . . It may make us from time to time a little more aware of the deeper, unnamed feelings which form the substratum of our being, to which we rarely penetrate;[2]

The poet may even have some axe to grind, or a definite practical purpose in writing. Eliot admits that these things are compatible with the greatest poetry,[3] provided they comply with the conditions set by the work of art and do not intrude as foreign elements.

Great poets transcend the limitations which may be indicated for lesser craftsmen. They possess, or we expect them to possess, a 'general awareness', which enables them to move freely and securely, whatever subject-matter they choose or find. And if at the same time their awareness is coloured by Christian belief, then they will be 'great Christian religious poets', in the sense in which Dante and Corneille and Racine were such poets 'even in those of their plays which do not touch upon Christian themes'.[4] For Eliot apparently does not place specifically religious themes higher than others. He does not think poetry should set forth a belief; what poetry conveys 'is *what it feels like* to hold certain beliefs'.[5]

Altogether, what the author wants is 'a literature which should

---

[1] 'Notes toward a Definition of Culture', *New English Weekly*, Feb. 11, 1943; 'Cultural Forces in the Human Order', M. B. Reckitt (ed.), *Prospect for Christendom* (1945), p. 64. Cp. *Notes towards the Definition of Culture*, p. 30.

[2] *UPC*, p. 155.

[3] Cf. book review, *CR*, July 1931, and 'The Social Function of Poetry', *Adelphi*, July/Sept. 1945.

[4] *EAM*, pp. 97–105. [5] 'The Social Function of Poetry.'

be *un*consciously, rather than deliberately and defiantly, Christian.'[1] His wish in this matter is remote from Paul Claudel's desire for a clearly religious literature. But it is not far from Maritain's views. On occasion he explicitly suggests a compromise between the view of poetry as entertainment and the view of it as a vehicle for instruction or 'salvation': 'between the motive which Rivière attributed to Molière and Racine [*distraire les honnêtes gens*] and the motive of Matthew Arnold bearing on shoulders immense what he thought to be the orb of the poet's fate, there is a serious *via media*.'[2]

In his statements on religion and aesthetics Eliot speaks as a Christian, but as one for whom there is no need to emphasise his own faith. This partly accounts for his failure to completely clarify the relationship between art and religious belief. The practical connection between the two nobody can fail to recognise, and it does not need expatiating upon. Besides, too many people welcome Eliot's art as a contribution to Christian propaganda, or decry it for the same reason. It is natural that the poet should react from such partisan attitudes and that his reaction should colour his statements. But when we have allowed for these things there still seems to be a residue of aestheticism unaffected by the conversion to Christian orthodoxy, and perhaps a certain discrepancy at times between the beliefs of the man and the attitudes of the poet.

[1] *EAM*, p. 99.   [2] *UPC*, p. 137.

III

POETIC BELIEF

How seriously are we required to believe the statements we read in poetry, and how definitely must the poet believe what he writes? Is there any essential connection between belief and enjoyment? For the solution of such problems the kind of philosophical or didactic poetry whose purpose is primarily to instruct and teach offers no useful material; nor, on the other hand, do historical, narrative and descriptive poems where complete realism and veracity are clearly aimed at. In these cases the sincere poet believes what he says and the reader is asked to accept and assent in recognised ways. We may also disregard poems which are so obviously extravagant that belief in any usual sense is certainly not expected. That leaves us with poems which incorporate seemingly rational statements of various kinds, but which may be thought to aim chiefly at artistic effect. In the immediate focus of our interest we shall find philosophical poetry which does not aim directly at instruction, and our main problem is to know when and how belief is involved in it.

ELIOT'S VIEWS

Eliot frequently discusses these questions of belief and tells us that neither the poet nor the reader is obliged to believe in the ordinary way in the ideas which have been assimilated into the poetry or on which the poetry more or less tacitly rests. Very likely his own spiritual development partly accounts for his views. In his period of agnosticism he read Dante and found that Dante's ideas, his medieval theology and philosophy, would stand in the way of enjoyment if they had to be fully believed in. He could not fully believe in them, but nevertheless recognised the greatness of the poetry, helped, perhaps, by Santayana and Pound. So he not only decided that real belief was unnecessary but even that Dante need not have believed in these things himself. The theory of poetic belief which was thus indicated may not have originated with Eliot. But he probably found it congenial—as well as useful as a sort of defence around his own poetry, enabling him to conceal himself in his works.

Altogether, there seems to have been a constant sceptical and analytical tendency in Eliot's early speculations on belief and meaning. Later, when he was drawn into a discussion with I. A. Richards on the question of poetic belief, he somewhat modified his early views, but they were not fundamentally changed.

It is natural that his thoughts regarding this problem should have been brought to a focus about the time of his entering the Anglican communion. In 'A Note on Poetry and Belief' published in *The Enemy* for January 1927, the author is concerned with the nature of belief, which he finds to have 'been in constant mutation' throughout history. This is proved both by the history of poetry and by the history of Christian dogma, as he had earlier found it proved in primitive ritual. Belief was a number of different things to Dante, Crashaw, and Christina Rossetti; it is yet another thing to Eliot, for whom even 'doubt and uncertainty are merely a variety of belief'. And Christianity, he thinks, 'will probably continue to modify itself'. The author's point of view is psychological rather than dogmatic (actually he fails to distinguish between belief as personal conviction and belief as impersonal dogma), and from this point of view it is natural to regard matters of belief as being in a state of flux determined by individuality and historical climate. This way of looking at belief makes it a kind of constantly repeated interpretation of dogma in relation to the spirit of the age. And for such a task of interpretation the poet, we may conclude, is peculiarly fitted, for it demands a great deal of intuition and sympathetic imagination. Thus, by what he implies, perhaps, rather than by what he actually says, Eliot relates the psychological nature of belief much more closely than is usual to the nature of the poetic imagination.[1]

This, of course, only means that belief is made less fixed and static than usual; it does not reduce the poetic imagination into a technique for metaphysical speculation. Such speculation, as we have seen, is held to be no business of the poet's: 'a poet who is also a metaphysician . . . would be a monster.' Nor need the poet actually believe in the ideas which he uses. Dante's poetry certainly contains philosophy; but Eliot maintains that Dante's belief as a man is not identical with his belief as a poet for 'his private belief becomes a different thing in becoming poetry'.[2] Shakespeare is another poet whose philosophy must not be accepted too literally. In 'Shakespeare and the Stoicism of Seneca' the author gives it as his 'own frivolous opinion' 'that Shakespeare may have held in private life very different views from what we extract from his extremely varied published works; that there is no clue in his writings to the way in which he would have voted in the last or would vote in the next election; and that we are completely in the dark as to his attitude about prayer-book revision. I admit,' adds Eliot, 'that my own experience, as a minor poet, may have jaundiced my outlook; that I am used to having cosmic significances, which I never suspected, extracted from my work. . . .' In the same essay, the cases of Donne and Chapman are found to be similar to those of Dante and Shakespeare. In Donne, the author found only 'a vast jumble of incoherent erudition on which he drew for purely poetic effects'. And Professor Schoell had shown Chapman 'lifting long passages from the works of writers like Ficino and incorporating them in his poems completely out of their context'.[3]

In fine, Eliot doubts 'whether belief proper enters into the activity of a great poet, *qua* poet. That is, Dante, *qua* poet, did not believe or disbelieve the Thomist cosmology or theory of the soul: he merely made use of it, or a fusion took place between his initial emotional impulses and a theory, for the purpose of making

---

[1] It is interesting to note that the report on *Doctrine in the Church of England* made by the Commission on Christian Doctrine appointed by the Archbishops of Canterbury and York in 1922 and published in 1938, regarded the language of devotion as 'more nearly akin to poetry than to science', and both the language of devotion and that of poetry as presenting truth in a symbolical way (p. 35).

[2] 'Dante', *SE*, p. 258.   [3] *SE*, pp. 127, 139.

poetry.'[1] Indeed, as we have seen, Eliot thinks it a blemish if a personal belief is too apparent in poetry. 'With Goethe, for instance, I often feel too acutely "this is what Goethe the man believed", instead of merely entering into a world which Goethe has created.'[2]

Nevertheless there is, as we have also seen, a necessary connection between poetry and belief. In Eliot's words:

> we are forced to believe that there is a particular relation between the two, and that the poet 'means what he says'. If we learned, for instance, that *De Rerum Natura* was a Latin exercise which Dante had composed for relaxation after completing the *Divine Comedy*, and published under the name of one Lucretius, I am sure that our capacity for enjoying either poem would be mutilated. Mr Richards's statement (*Science and Poetry*, p. 76 footnote) that a certain writer has effected 'a complete severance between his poetry and *all* beliefs' is to me incomprehensible.[3]

(The last sentence refers to Richards's opinion of *The Waste Land*.)

The 'particular relation' between poetry and belief appears, on analysis, to fall under several heads. There is first the poetic use of philosophical ideas as a kind of game. This is how Donne used his chequered learning according to Eliot.[4] The game consists in making a kind of pattern of ideas, and for this purpose it is evident that borrowed ideas (and emotions) may serve the poet's turn as well as his own. Since everything is proffered in play, the question of sincerity does not arise.

Secondly, there is the emotional rendering of the poet's philosophy, which, as in the case of Lucretius or Dante, appears as a *fusion* between the philosophy and 'his natural feelings'.[5] Eliot thinks that poems in which such a fusion has taken place 'were not designed to persuade the readers to an intellectual assent, but to convey an emotional equivalent for the ideas. What Lucretius and Dante teach you, in fact, is *what it feels like* to hold certain beliefs; what Virgil teaches you [in his *Georgics*], is to feel yourself inside the agrarian life.'[6]

[1] *SE*, p. 138. [2] 'Dante', *SE*, p. 258.
[3] 'Dante', Note, *SE*, p. 269. Cf. also 'A Note on Poetry and Belief', *Enemy*, Jan. 1927.
[4] Cf. T. Spencer (ed.), *A Garland for John Donne* (1931), pp. 8, 12.
[5] *CR*, Jan. 1926, p. 37.
[6] 'The Social Function of Poetry'; cf. also *On Poetry*, p. 13 and *UPC*, p. 136.

The third possible and legitimate relation between poetry and belief is that of the poetic illustration of a philosophy which is already existent and moreover generally accepted, so as to need no rational presentation or justification. In this case it is not so much the poet's belief as the belief or ethos of the age in which he lives that is exploited poetically. 'When a poet has expressed successfully a philosophy we find that it is a philosophy which is already in existence, not one of his own invention.'[1] Eliot mentions Dante's ideas on the freedom of the will and the order of the seven deadly sins as things that Dante may have simply borrowed from Aquinas without personally vouching for them; and the theory of the soul in Dante as deriving from Aristotle's *De Anima*.[2] He admits that 'the "truest" philosophy is the best material for the greatest poet',[3] but he considers Dante and Lucretius fully justified in using 'other men's philosophies cheerfully without bothering too much about verifying them for themselves'.[4]

In fact, 'a philosophical theory which has entered into poetry is established, for its truth or falsity in one sense ceases to matter, and its truth in another sense is proved'.[5] This is Eliot's version of 'Beauty is truth, truth beauty'. The sense in which he thinks that poetry can prove the truth of a philosophy is primarily aesthetic. A Christian, he says, will not think of Dante as proving Christianity, or a materialist of Lucretius as proving materialism or atomism. 'What he will find in Dante or Lucretius is the *esthetic* sanction: that is the partial justification of these views of life by the art to which they give rise . . . what poetry proves about any philosophy is merely its possibility for being lived—for life includes both philosophy and art.' It is a very limited sanction that poetry gives to the ideas it successfully embodies, if we understand the author to say that philosophy in art merely proves that philosophy can be used in art. But he also means, no doubt, that art, by its imaginative testing and illustration of a philosophy enables us to realise more fully the practical implications of that philosophy. Poetry, he says, 'is not the assertion that something is true, but the making that truth more fully real to us'.[6]

---

[1] 'The Social Function of Poetry.'   [2] 'Dante', *SE*, p. 259.
[3] 'Poetry and Propaganda', *Literary Opinion in America*, p. 106.
[4] Introduction to Valéry's *Le Serpent*.
[5] 'The Metaphysical Poets', *SE*, pp. 288–9.
[6] 'Poetry and Propaganda', *Literary Opinion in America*, p. 106.

Whatever the poet's motives for using philosophical ideas, Eliot, while recognising a wide variety of responses to the poetry, warns us against extremes. It is wrong to think 'that it is simply the value of the *ideas* expressed in a poem which gives the value to the poetry; or that it is the *truth* of [the poet's] view of life—by which we ordinarily mean its congruity with our own view—that matters'. And it is also wrong to think 'that the ideas, the beliefs of the poet do not matter at all; that they are rather like some alloy, necessary for the poet in order to manipulate his true material, which is refined out of the poetry in the course of time'. He comes to the conclusion that a *good* poet presents a certain ambiguity. 'At moments,' he says, 'I feel that his language is merely the perfect instrument for what he has to say; at other moments I feel that he is simply making use of, even exploiting, his beliefs for the sake of the verbal beauty in which he can express them. He appears to be both inside and outside of his beliefs and interests. Where this doubt about the attitude of the poet cannot arise, one is tempted to suspect the poetry.'[1]

A poem, as Eliot acknowledges, is a different thing to the reader from what it is to the poet. This is inevitably so, though one may strive to make the difference between the poet's and the reader's experiences as small as possible. Theoretically it is tenable that the reader would derive the greatest enjoyment from poetry if he were able to recapture the emotions and thoughts of the author and the state of tension in which he created the poem. Eliot, however, does not think the writing of poetry in itself enjoyable, and apparently would hardly think it desirable for the reader to recapture the poet's labour pains. He is perfectly content to let the reader enjoy poetry in his own way, provided his appreciation is not too one-sided.

Eliot is generally sceptical of all 'interpretation', though he regards it as unavoidable, because we are urged to it by a restless instinct.[2] This being so, one does well to recognise that a poet is as much in the dark as anybody else about many things that go to the making of a poem, and that 'what a poem means is as much what it means to others as what it means to the author'.[3] The reader, therefore, has a certain scope for finding his own beliefs

[1] 'The Social Function of Poetry.'
[2] Cf. Introduction to G. W. Knight, *The Wheel of Fire* (1930), p. xiv.
[3] *UPC*, p. 130.

in what he reads and colouring it with his own view of life. But in many cases he comes up against ideas or beliefs which are obstinately explicit, and which he must either accept, or pretend to accept, or reject. And this brings us to the centre of the problem of the reader's poetic assent.

'There is a difference,' asserts the author in his essay on Dante, 'between philosophical *belief* and poetic *assent*'.[1] And in the Note to Section II of this essay, he explains his position as follows:

> *If* there is 'literature', *if* there is 'poetry', then it must be possible to have full literary or poetic appreciation without sharing the beliefs of the poet. That is as far as my thesis goes in the present essay. . . .
>
> If you deny the theory that full poetic appreciation is possible without belief in what the poet believed, you deny the existence of 'poetry' as well as 'criticism'; and if you push this denial to its conclusion, you will be forced to admit that there is very little poetry that you can appreciate, and that your appreciation of it will be a function of your philosophy or theology or something else. If, on the other hand, I push *my* theory to the extreme, I find myself in as great a difficulty. I am quite aware of the ambiguity of the word 'understand'. In one sense, it means to understand without believing, for unless you can understand a view of life (let us say) without believing in it, the word 'understand' loses all meaning, and the act of choice between one view and another is reduced to caprice. But if you yourself are convinced of a certain view of life, then you irresistibly and inevitably believe that if anyone else comes to 'understand' it fully, his understanding *must* terminate in belief. It is possible, and sometimes necessary, to argue that full understanding must identify itself with full belief. A good deal, it thus turns out, hangs on the meaning, if any, of this short word *full*.
>
> In short, both the view I have taken in this essay, and the view which contradicts it, are, if pushed to the end, what I call heresies (not, of course, in the theological, but in a more general sense).

After considering a number of literary examples, in which he finds that his understanding and acceptance of the propositions they enunciate, or his lack of understanding and acceptance, affect his poetic appreciation, Eliot continues:

> So I can only conclude that I cannot, in practice, wholly separate my poetic appreciation from my personal beliefs. Also that the distinction between a statement and a pseudo-statement is not always, in particular instances, possible to establish . . .

---

[1] *SE*, p. 257.

. . . Actually, one probably has more pleasure in the poetry when one shares the beliefs of the poet. On the other hand there is a distinct pleasure in enjoying poetry as poetry when one does *not* share the beliefs, analogous to the pleasure of 'mastering' other men's philosophical systems. It would appear that 'literary appreciation' is an abstraction, and pure poetry a phantom; and that both in creation and enjoyment much always enters which is, from the point of view of 'Art', irrelevant.

We see that in Eliot's opinion it is not only pleasant, but necessary too, sometimes, to entertain beliefs that one does not actually hold. He finds the use of poetry in this respect similar to that of philosophy. We study different philosophies 'largely for the exercise in assumption or entertaining ideas', and 'only by the exercise of understanding without believing, so far as that is possible, can we come in full consciousness to some point where we believe *and* understand. Similarly with the experience of poetry. We aim ideally to come to rest in some poetry which shall realize poetically what we ourselves believe; but we have no contact with poetry unless we can pass in and out freely, among the various worlds of poetic creation.'[1]

Eliot here makes an important point. He does not think, however, that *any* philosophy should be acceptable to the reader, as he tells us in *The Use of Poetry*:

We may be permitted to infer, in so far as the distaste of a person like myself for Shelley's poetry is not attributable to irrelevant prejudices or to a simple blind spot, but is due to a peculiarity in the poetry and not in the reader, that it is not the presentation of beliefs which I do not hold, or—to put the case as extremely as possible—of beliefs that excite my abhorrence, that makes the difficulty. Still less is it that Shelley is deliberately making use of his poetic gifts to propagate a doctrine; for Dante and Lucretius did the same thing. I suggest that the position is somewhat as follows. When the doctrine, theory, belief, or 'view of life' presented in a poem is one which the mind of the reader can accept as coherent, mature, and founded on the facts of experience, it interposes no obstacle to the reader's enjoyment, whether it be one that he accept or deny, approve or deprecate. When it is one which the reader rejects as childish or feeble, it may, for a reader of well-developed mind, set up an almost complete check.[2]

---

[1] 'Poetry and Propaganda.'   [2] *UPC*, p. 96.

Poetic Belief

Eliot is not doctrinaire or one-sided in this matter. He does not think 'culture' requires us to make 'a deliberate effort to put out of mind all our convictions and passionate beliefs about life when we sit down to read poetry'.[1] As usual, he brings a number of qualifications to bear on his main position. But it remains true that he does definitely advocate a suspension of belief or disagreement and the adoption of a poetic assent as a condition of poetic enjoyment. Of Dante he says that

> It is wrong to think that there are parts of the *Divine Comedy* which are of interest only to Catholics or to mediaevalists. . . . You are not called upon to believe what Dante believed, for your belief will not give you a groat's worth more of understanding and appreciation; but you are called upon more and more to understand it. If you can read poetry as poetry, you will 'believe' in Dante's theology exactly as you believe in the physical reality of his journey; that is, you suspend both belief and disbelief. I will not deny that it may be in practice easier for a Catholic to grasp the meaning, in many places, than for the ordinary agnostic; but that is not because the Catholic believes, but because he has been instructed.[2]

He repeats this opinion in *The Use of Poetry* (where he calls Dante 'about as thoroughgoing a didacticst as one could find'). It is a cardinal opinion in his critical writings, and has a general application: 'some of the early Buddhist scriptures affect me as parts of the Old Testament do; I can still enjoy Fitzgerald's *Omar*, though I do not hold that rather smart and shallow view of life.'[3] Eliot regards it as a personal prejudice of his that he takes the greatest pleasure in 'poetry with a clear philosophical pattern'. But though he prefers a 'Christian and Catholic' philosophy, he is quite prepared to enjoy 'that of Epicurus or of the Forest Philosophers of India' as well.[4]

The theory of poetic assent is applicable not only to the thought contained in poetry, but also to the feelings. Thus Eliot declares that he enjoys Shakespeare's poetry to the full extent of his capacity for enjoying poetry. 'But,' he adds, 'I have not the slightest approach to certainty that I share Shakespeare's feelings.'[5]

Altogether, Eliot's views on poetic belief are more definite and consistent than his opinions on a great many other matters, and this makes it particularly important to discuss and assess them in a more general context.

[1] *UPC*, p. 97.   [2] *SE*, pp. 257–8.   [3] *UPC*, p. 91.
[4] Introduction to *The Wheel of Fire*, p. xiv.   [5] *UPC*, p. 115.

GENERAL DISCUSSION

I. A. Richards agrees with Eliot in thinking that strict belief need not be accorded to the ideas or philosophy employed by a poet. But Richards goes a step further than Eliot in repudiating the rational meaning of poetry, which makes Eliot accuse him of wanting poets to create in a vacuum.[1] What Richards contends is briefly this: 'It is never what a poem *says* which matters, but what it *is*. The poet is not writing as a scientist.' Poetry is produced by and in turn acts on an intricate system of interests in the mind, and its worth is a matter of the degree to which it moves the mind 'towards a wider equilibrium'. Now the human mind cannot find equilibrium and order unless it believes in something. We may believe in true statements, which to Richards are scientific statements, or in false statements, which he calls 'pseudo-statements'.

> On the whole true statements are of more service to us than false ones. None the less we do not and, at present, cannot order our emotions and attitudes by true statements alone. . . . This is one of the great new dangers to which civilization is exposed. Countless pseudo-statements—about God, about the universe, about human nature, the relations of mind to mind, about the soul, its rank and destiny—pseudo-statements which are pivotal points in the organization of the mind, vital to its well-being, have suddenly become . . . impossible to believe as for centuries they have been believed.

Only scientific knowledge can now command belief in anything like the old sense, but this knowledge is not sufficient for a fine organisation of the mind. It cannot be trusted 'to give support to our lives—a support we now recognise as largely emotional'. The only remedy, therefore, 'is to cut our pseudo-statements free from that kind of belief which is appropriate to verified statements'. We must distinguish between different modes of belief if we are to survive morally.[2] Accordingly, Richards distinguishes between 'intellectual belief' and 'emotional belief'.

> In primitive man . . . any idea which opens a ready outlet to emotion or points to a line of action in conformity with custom is quickly believed. . . . This acceptance, this use of the idea—by our

---

[1] See 'Poetry and Propaganda', *Literary Opinion in America*, p. 102; and 'A Note on Poetry and Belief'.

[2] I. A. Richards, *Science and Poetry* (2nd edn. 1935), pp. 31–90.

interests, desires, feelings, attitudes, tendencies to action and what not—is emotional belief. So far as the idea is useful to them it is believed, and the sense of attachment, of adhesion, of conviction, which we feel, and to which we give the name of belief, is the result of this implication of the idea in our activities.

'An emotional belief is not justified through any logical relations between its idea and other ideas. Its only justification is its success in meeting our needs.' Emotional belief can be accorded—and actually is accorded, if we will only recognise it—to pseudo-statements, thus enabling us to benefit by such statements without coming into conflict with our knowledge of scientific truth. But emotional belief must be 'kept from interfering with the intellectual system. And poetry is an extraordinarily successful device for preventing these interferences from arising,' because it charms us into something more than Coleridge's willing suspension of disbelief: 'the question of belief or disbelief, in the intellectual sense, never arises when we are reading well.'[1] Poetry, therefore, is 'capable of saving us'. And 'the tradition of poetry is the guardian of the suprascientific myths',[2] which are necessary to our mental well-being.

Whereas Richards distinguishes between intellectual belief and emotional belief, Eliot does not reject intellectual belief in poetry, but distinguishes instead between what we may call genuine belief and assumed, or temporary belief. He repudiates Richards's idea of separating sensibility and intellect and finds his division of belief into two kinds both unnatural and unhistorical. Belief is not just a matter of two distinct categories, but of infinite gradations from doubt to assent. And irrespective of the rise of modern science, it 'has been in constant mutation . . . from the beginning of civilisation' and will continue to change in the future. Richards's distinctions cannot help anyone to believe, since 'it takes application, and a kind of genius, to believe anything.' For belief, I understand Eliot to mean, is something that concerns all activities of life at a given time, including both science and poetry.[3]

The distinction between intellectual and emotional belief cer-

---

[1] Richards, *Practical Criticism* (1929), pp. 275-7.
[2] *Science and Poetry*, p. 90.
[3] Cf. 'A Note on Poetry and Belief' and 'Poetry and Propaganda'.

tainly seems rather factitious.[1] The actual movement of belief is always an affair of the emotions, as even Richards recognises when he defines belief as 'the sense of attachment, of adhesion, of conviction, which we feel'. What he calls 'intellectual belief' is really an emotional belief caused by the perception of cohesion, completeness and harmony in ideas. This perception is related to the perception of beauty in art; in one case the intellect is primarily instrumental in arranging the matter for our understanding, whilst in the other case the senses are also at work. 'Intellectual' or 'scientific belief' has, in the last analysis, nothing more certain about it than any other kind of belief, certainty, too, being an affair of the emotions. It is true that the material of scientific belief belongs to a closed system of thought distinct from, let us say, the material of religious belief. But the whole system of thought may, for all we know, be as mythical in the case of science as in the case of religion, or, conversely, as absolutely valid in the case of religion as in the case of science.

Belief must be conceived of more or less on the same lines as F. H. Bradley conceives of thought. Real thought to Bradley is 'different from thought discursive and rational'. It does not predicate, it gets beyond mere relations and reaches something other than truth. It is 'absorbed into a fuller experience' which also comprises feeling and will.[2] In the same way we must regard belief as different from rational assent; it comprises thought, feeling and will in a higher emotional experience which reaches something other than truth.

Eliot sometimes approaches a conception of belief similar to the one I am trying to define. Thus in *The Music of Poetry* he regards the reader's emotion as the criterion of the significance of a poem: 'If we are moved by a poem, it has meant something, perhaps something important, to us; if we are not moved, then it is, as poetry, meaningless.'[3] He almost says here that understanding is dependent on emotion. It would probably have covered his intention as well, if he had said that belief is dependent on emotion.

---

[1] One is rather surprised to find that Richards makes this distinction, since, in his *Principles of Literary Criticism*, he insists so strongly on the similarity between aesthetic experiences and experiences of any other kind, and on the essential oneness of all psychic or, as he prefers to call it, neural activity.

[2] F. H. Bradley, *Appearance and Reality* (2nd edn. 1906), p. 171.

[3] *The Music of Poetry*, p. 15.

In his 'Note on Poetry and Belief' he holds, as we have seen, that belief as a psychological phenomenon varies with times and individuals, and implies that it is a matter of sympathetic understanding, not of mere rational demonstrability. He even includes a wider range of attitudes in the concept of belief than I am prepared to do, by classing doubt and uncertainty as a variety of belief, just as the phenomenologists class the non-existent as a variety of Reality.

We may now return to Richards, who, in *Mencius on the Mind*, tells us that we must acquire the habit 'of regarding all thinking— even the most seemingly autonomous—as purposive; and of expecting the form of the thinking to be not independent of the purpose'.[1] Now this leads to a different train of thought from that induced by the distinction between intellectual and emotional belief. It leads us to think of all statements as appealing equally to the same kind of belief (which, we have determined, is emotional) but by a great number of different ways, or, to use another concept of Richards's, in a great number of different tones. 'Tone', with Richards, is one of the ways in which the meaning of a poem is conveyed, and it includes the many different devices and clues by which the author reveals his attitude to his subject-matter and to his readers. Clearly tone can be shaded off into almost infinite modifications, which the mind can register correctly, but which language can describe only approximately. And the same applies to what Richards calls purpose, or intention, which is the general plan and aim of the poet when writing a poem, and the organising principle of the other kinds of meaning (sense, feeling and tone).

To the spectrum of 'tone' there corresponds a spectrum of belief. To acquire the habit of mind of regarding all thinking as purposive means to modify our belief indefinitely in accordance with the sort of thinking we come up against. Or rather, since belief is essentially the same thing in all cases, it means modifying the mental machinery by which belief is operated, so as to make belief more or less permanent, more or less temporary, more or less intermittent, and to regulate its strength through all degrees from complete disbelief to intense belief. The mental machinery by which this is done is primarily judgment, which may be either an abstract ability to recognise perfection (intelligence) or a more concrete ability to find satisfaction (the senses). Of course, in a poem the

[1] Op. cit. (1932), p. 91.

poet has already judged for us to a certain extent, as he shows by his tone, and he wishes us to accept his judgment. This we generally do; and it is one of the pleasures of reading poetry to escape the necessity of judging. But a good reader will know directly, or any reader will know from habit, that the poet's judgments have not been tested, and very likely would not stand testing from the point of view of scientific reliability. Therefore he accepts them in a kind of holiday spirit. And this may be why poetic belief *seems* different from other belief.

Our common scientific attitude is really no more than a tacit social convention by which we agree to discriminate between 'truths' to which we can accord a strong belief because they are supported by a great deal of 'evidence', and other kinds of truth or falsehood. When Blake was asked whether, when the sun arose, he did not see a round disc of fire somewhat like a guinea, he replied, 'O, no, no, I see an innumerable company of the Heavenly host crying, "Holy! Holy! Holy! is the Lord God Almighty!"' There may be a stronger, but not necessarily a better reason for the questioner's view than for the poet's. And, in the final analysis, as F. H. Bradley forcibly demonstrates in the first part of his *Appearance and Reality*, scientific truth is based on an illusory, or as we might say, imaginative, apprehension of Reality, and we recognise it as emotional in its movement of assent. Thus scientific belief is only one mode of belief among many others.

Belief in relation to its object is essentially one thing and indivisible. But as with the sense of beauty, to which it is obviously akin, it can appear in the company of many strange and mixed emotions. In relation to the person who believes, it is modally qualified. Perhaps Eliot had some such idea at the back of his mind when he used the expression '*belief attitude*' in his essay on Dante.

In theory there is an infinite modality of beliefs. In practice we find systems, or clusters, of modal beliefs. Thus we hold one cluster of beliefs when in 'intellectual' or 'scientific mood', another when in fairy-tale mood, etc.[1] In this sense, then, we may

[1] If one mode of belief, the religious mode, is more appropriate to religious knowledge than the others, it is neither completely distinct from the others, nor does it deny them. I have tried to define the modes of belief from a human, psychological point of view. This does not mean that what we believe or try to comprehend is inherent in our faculties of belief and comprehension. There may be a transcendent reality which remains unaffected by our efforts to define the ways in which we attain to belief in that reality.

speak of 'intellectual belief'; but not as opposed to 'emotional belief'. The latter expression is indeed something of a pleonasm, since all beliefs, i.e. all value-attachments, are ultimately emotional.

The tone of a poem is an indication of the system of beliefs into which we may incorporate the statements of the poem. If the tone fails to put us right at once, our judgment will have to function all the more actively. This will always be a disturbing element as long as it operates, but having keyed us to the right mood, it will enable us to appreciate a poem all the better. Much poetry, especially modern poetry, only reveals its beauty after quite intensive study.

Eliot is right, from an historical point of view, to speak of mutations of belief. The common moods of thought and belief change with the times. In former ages, before rational and scientific thought became a well-defined convention, the ideal of exact and truthful thinking was subtly different from what it is to us, and must have been applied very differently to many everyday statements which involved strong emotions or perhaps stock responses. It is only because our thinking to-day is governed so rigidly by reason that we are tempted to look upon rational belief as fundamentally distinct from poetic belief or religious belief. All this is part of a general movement of thought. It is typical, perhaps, that people nowadays ask of poetry: *what* does it say? *what* does it mean? and often forget, because they feel these rational questions to be so urgent, to attune themselves to the right mood of appreciation.

The philosophy of a poem, even if it functionally serves only the structure, is no matter of indifference to the consciousness of the reader. It is there for him to believe or refuse to believe, and the tone and purpose of the poem must lead him to do this in the right mood. We must also remember that thought has a tendency to move in images. The language of poetry therefore represents no deviation from normal thought processes, as we sometimes imagine. Rather it corresponds to a natural habit of thought. This may be one reason why we often pass over statements in poetry without 'noticing' them as statements. We have not been lulled to sleep, we have not suspended belief and disbelief, but we have been persuaded more easily than in ordinary discourse. For the language of images that poetry employs is very convincing. An image can frequently explain things better than a statement or an argument, so that it is more precise in its correspondence to the ideal meaning.

The convincing quality of poetic language makes it all the more incumbent upon us to believe poetic statements in the right mood. Only thus can we co-operate with the poet to complete the poem. A drama is not complete till the actors perform it on the stage. In a much lesser degree the reader is asked to bring a poem to completion. He has to contribute by his associations something which is elicited not just by the poetry, but by the words themselves, and the words, it must be remembered, are everybody's property. Poetic belief in what the poet has to say will make the reader pull out the appropriate stops for his associations, whereas disbelief will make him pull the wrong stops and produce discord.

For practical appreciation and criticism of poetry we must find the tone and purpose in each particular case and adjust our attitude accordingly. Richards says as much in his *Principles*. And Eliot advocates a similar idea when he says that we must be able to 'pass in and out freely among the various worlds of poetic creation'. Consequently, when we apply ourselves to reading a poem, the whole personality must be made responsive to begin with. We must open our minds as wide as possible, like a big target, to receive the still unknown communication. Only thus can the impact of the poem be fully registered, whereas if we sit down with the distinction between intellectual and emotional belief in mind, we may miss the impact altogether. After one or two readings the proper mood is given, through which belief is regulated. And the consequent crystallisation of an attitude within us is largely unconscious. In this sense it is right to say with Eliot and Richards that when we read poetry in the right way the question of belief simply does not arise. Belief is enjoyment.

As for the poet, it will be clear from the above that whatever he can feel attached to is an object of belief with him, and accordingly something he may write poetry about. And if we define belief in this wide sense, we must demand of the poet that he should be undeviatingly sincere. He cannot write good poetry by pretending to like things that he dislikes. At least he must transpose himself for a moment into a mood of liking them. But since such transposition is constantly possible thanks to the imagination, what it all amounts to is that the poet must be faithful to the feelings of the moment. I emphasise that this is all that can be positively demanded of him. The deeper his personality and his thought, and the more dependent his moods on his basic view of life, the deeper, too, will be his sincerity and the more constant his loyalty to what is permanent in his belief. Also the bigger, in length and scope, the poem that he composes, the more must it be governed by his permanent attitudes. But a short lyric may be governed by nothing more permanent than a caprice and yet be beautiful poetry.

There is one thing in Eliot's general views that helps to justify his claim that the poet should not be held responsible for belief in his poetic ideas—namely the notion that poetry may be created by an unconscious process. If this notion is valid, the final result of the creative process is something which is almost as new to the poet as to the reader,[1] so that the former may be excused for feeling that ideas contained in the poetry are not his own in the same way as ideas to which he has given his conscious assent. But this again raises an interesting problem: cannot the emanations from the subconscious be regarded as equally appropriated or believed in as are consciously accepted ideas and attitudes? Are they not even more thoroughly assimilated and a more genuine expression of the artist's mind than the superficial thoughts? And if the poet cannot be held responsible for everything that surges from his subconscious, must he not at least recognise it as forming part of his belief? Surely if the theory of unconscious creation is valid so much the better for poetry; for poetry in which unconscious inspiration plays a large part is likely to be particularly sincere.

I have not been using the word sincerity in Richards's sense of a general harmony of the personality. I doubt whether this kind of sincerity can be more than a striving, a goal to be aimed at. In order that such harmony should be complete, the subconscious would have to be something which merely duplicated conscious beliefs, perhaps in terms of symbols rather than of ideas. But for such a correspondence to subsist between the conscious and the subconscious, a person would have to be spiritually integrated and undivided to an extent which only saints, maniacs and possibly geniuses can be imagined as achieving. Ideally one might demand of a poet that he should be such a person, and probably he would write the best poetry if he were (A. E. Housman says that the four men whom he recognises as true poets in the eight-

[1] Cp. *UPC*, p. 126.

eenth century—Collins, Smart, Cowper, Blake—were all mad). But under more average circumstances, a poet usually has the choice between discarding his inhibitions and revealing the 'inner truth' about himself and his outlook, or else working under intellectual control and embroidering his surface reactions. He can perhaps do both at the same time; but he cannot completely fuse the two; and the inevitable tension that will arise is far from detrimental to his work.

Of course, there will always be certain areas of behaviour or belief, varying with various persons, in which the whole personality is integrated. It might be demanded that the poet should limit himself to such areas. If he did we might expect poetry of a serene and confident type when introspective, of a panegyric, indignant or elegiac, but none the less unified kind, when directed outwards to the environment. One would not expect such an integrated attitude to be common in the area of religion. Human nature is probably too divided—some would say too sinful—to reach this perfect wholeness in a main sphere of belief. Hence the tormentedness of much religious poetry and of much poetry of a religious nature, and, on the other hand, the banality and lack of deep genuineness of another great mass of devotional poetry. Perhaps it would not be wrong to say that good, genuine, even happy religious poetry at least presupposes a background of unhappiness. T. S. Eliot speaks of Dante using beatitude as a theme. He could hardly have done so in *Paradiso* if he had not been able to describe despair and suffering in *Inferno*.

APPLICATION TO ELIOT'S POETRY

Eliot was at one time doubtful concerning Dante's belief in what he wrote. Yet a poem of the scope of the *Divine Comedy* could hardly have been written unless it was governed fairly consistently by a philosophy which was part of the poet's permanent beliefs.

In the same way, I am prepared to find in Eliot's longer poems the impress of permanently held ideas or a settled attitude to life, especially when the same or similar ideas or moods recur in various poems (and, of course, in the prose writings); while I am also prepared to find a good many incidental views held with less settled conviction and employed for their poetic worth. As for the shorter poems, it is fairly easy to tell whether they agree in outlook with the longer ones. Eliot, as we have seen, sets the belief of the poet in the ideas that he uses at a discount. But, for reasons which I hope have been made clear, we must not let his opinion in this matter deter us from seeking his own beliefs in his poems. They may not make up an organised philosophy, and they may have been very much changed from their original state in the process of composition. But they are there. The poet's views and attitudes must colour what he writes, and they cannot be so much changed as to affect their general direction.

Eliot shows in his poetry, he says, what it feels like to believe in something. But precisely that is the belief, or at least the degree and mood of the belief. We believe in so far as we *feel positively*. And when Eliot defines behaviour as belief, as he does in his *Notes towards the Definition of Culture*,[1] he must be understood to include emotional attitudes in his concept of behaviour. He must also be understood to include the behaviour of a poet *qua* poet; for the way in which a poet writes is an aspect of his beliefs.

Eliot may hold certain beliefs primarily for their value to his poetry. They may even form a system or cluster of intellectual attachments more or less distinct from the beliefs which he ordinarily adheres to. But they are none the less beliefs. It matters little how consciously Eliot has used them. The main thing is that they do inform his poetry. He may have been consciously interested primarily in the technique of composition. But years of philosophical and theological studies are not sloughed off for the sake of pure poetry. And the fact that these beliefs are determined by a poetic mood does not prevent them from affecting his readers in other ways besides poetic enjoyment.

In order to enjoy Eliot's poetry—or that of any other poet—it is not necessary for the reader to trace minutely what the poet in various ways has believed in, or what statements and attitudes the poetry presents in a more or less recondite fashion. Nor is it necessary for the reader, in the ordinary course of things, to believe scientifically, religiously or in any other specific way the statements and attitudes that the poetry presents to him, except in such a degree and with such permanence as the particular poem requires in order to be enjoyed. I find it hard to believe that the reader can enjoy poetry, as Eliot suggests, without at least for a

[1] Op. cit., p. 32.

time sharing the feelings of the poet. But this does not mean that the reader can or should recapture the whole of the poet's experience, nor does it make it any less necessary to the reader to add his own interpretation to what the poetry gives him.

Ordinarily, I repeat, the reader need not speculate about the poet's ideas or try to find a philosophy in his poetry. But when poetry has become as influential as Eliot's, both in inspiring other poets and perhaps in affecting our general view of life, it is time to enquire what ideas and moods it incorporates, and where it will lead us if those ideas and moods, coming as they do in the convincing language of poetic imagery, should affect our deep attitudes. And for the sake of poetry itself, it is necessary from time to time to examine successful poetry to see what ideas and views can receive the sanction of art.

IV

POINT OF VIEW
IN ELIOT'S POETRY

S INCE most of Eliot's poems are in the first person, the problem
of poetic belief is bound up with the problem of point of
view, which we will now briefly consider before going on to the
relation between the more purely technical aspects of the poems
and their 'contents'. As I shall use the term here, 'point of view'
has to do with the identity of the 'I', or the supposed speaker of
the poem, and of the 'you', or the person who is addressed by the
speaker. The choice of the grammatical first and second persons
rather than the third is itself a choice of point of view. But the use
of the first person does not necessarily mean that the poet is
speaking in his own voice—he may have wanted to write a monologue for an imaginary character.

The point of view can only in part be determined by the use of
pronouns. And sometimes there are no pronouns to indicate the
speaker and the person or persons spoken to at all. The point of
view must be inferred, from verb forms or by other means. Imperatives like 'Look!' and 'Listen!' presuppose someone speaking
to somebody else. And even the progressive form of the verb
suggests an observer describing a present experience. Thus in
Eliot's lines

> In this decayed hole among the mountains
> In the faint moonlight, the grass is singing

there are both the demonstrative pronoun 'this' and the progressive form 'is singing' to argue an observer present at the scene described.

There are usually enough of these signs in a poem to give a sufficient indication of the point of view. And generally there is no need for the poet to preface his poem with an explanation of the degree of subjectivity or objectivity to be found in it. If no other indication is given the 'I' is naturally assumed to be that of the poet himself and the 'you' to refer to the reader. Our use of language for communication makes this normal: one person is understood to be uttering his thoughts in poetic form to another person reading or listening to his words. This is what T. S. Eliot has called the second voice of poetry, that of the poet speaking to an audience (the first voice being that of the poet talking to himself). But whereas communications in the first person are generally expected to be truthful, in poetic communications this does not strictly apply. No one expects the poet to be completely accurate with regard to details and actual facts, especially autobiographical facts. There is such a thing as *the poet's first person*, which is a universally accepted thing, and which may be defined as the identity of the poet as he chooses to reveal it in his works. It is quite understood that the poet may be speaking his own mind even though he may be using symbols or imagined happenings to do so.

In many cases, however, it is not absolutely clear whether the poet is addressing us or we are listening to a piece of drama. It is hard to decide, for instance, who the 'I' is in Tennyson's *Locksley Hall* or in Browning's *The Last Ride Together*. And the problem is no less evident in modern poetry than in that of the nineteenth century. In fact I wonder whether the blurring of the point of view may not be the chief reason for much of the obscurity that is complained of in our time.

In the whole body of Eliot's lyrical output, there is, as I said, a preponderance of poems in the first person. But they occur with somewhat varying frequency in his different collections.

Thus in the *Prufrock* collection of 1917, the 'I' is very much in the centre of the stage, both in the fairly long poems and in the short ones like *Morning at the Window* and *Conversation Galante*. Longish monologues like *The Love Song*, *Portrait of a Lady* and the slightly later *Gerontion* offer a special difficulty of personal reference. How, for instance, is one to interpret the following lines in *Gerontion*?:

> I would meet you upon this honestly.
> I that was near your heart was removed therefrom
> To lose beauty in terror, terror in inquisition.

If the reader thinks the characterisation of the old man is sufficient to give him an identity, then who is the 'you'? Most readers will probably be left guessing.

In the 1920 *Poems*, apart from *Gerontion* and one or two more, the focus is much more frequently on people described from the outside and presented in the third person: Burbank and Bleistein, Sweeney, the honeymooning couple of *Lune de Miel*. This change is accompanied by a formal change, from the irregular metrics and confidential, conversational tone of the early collection (which includes even a short piece printed as prose—*Hysteria*) to the regular, rhymed, tetrameter stanzas of the 1920 *Poems*.

The change may have something to do with the substitution of Gautier for Laforgue as a model. It also, perhaps, had something to do with the influence of Imagism on Eliot when he composed the poems of the later collection. But mainly I think it has to do with Eliot's own critical ideas as he developed them about 1919, especially his 'Impersonal theory of poetry'. The *Poems* of 1920 may have been written in pursuance of a deliberate policy of depersonalisation.

After 1920 there is on the whole a return both to the freer prosody and to the predominant use of the first person which we found in the *Prufrock* volume. The longer poems mostly alternate between passages of direct speech and passages of impersonal reflection and description. I refer to *The Waste Land*, *The Hollow Men*, *Ash-Wednesday* and the *Four Quartets*. Of these, *The Waste Land* is surely most difficult. And the difficulty is largely inherent in the point of view.

The *Ariel Poems* and *Coriolan* are mainly dramatic monologues presenting historical or legendary individuals identified by means of names or titles. Even these monologues, however, are not always completely and historically objective. The 'I' of *Marina* is only very vaguely the Pericles of Shakespeare's play who lost and found his daughter. And in *Journey of the Magi* the landscape is not only Oriental to suit the ostensible characters, but is also that of countries more familiar to the poet:

> Then at dawn we came down to a temperate valley,
> Wet, below the snow line, smelling of vegetation;
> With a running stream and a water-mill beating the darkness,
> And three trees on the low sky,
> And an old white horse galloped away in the meadow.

A passage in *The Use of Poetry* helps us to recognise some of Eliot's personal memories in the 'water-mill beating the darkness' and the 'Six hands at an open door dicing for pieces of silver'. His own point of view therefore seems to merge with that of the Magus, making it indeterminate.

We will look more closely at three poems in which the indeterminate point of view is very evident and which at the same time are particularly captivating.

The Love Song of J. Alfred Prufrock uses the pronouns 'I', 'you', 'we' and 'one' for the persons directly involved. There is a speaker and a person addressed by him, and they both occur in the first line—'Let us go then, you and I'. The 'you' is addressed explicitly quite often in the first part, and though it looks like an impersonal 'you' in places, the context seems to indicate a real companion:

> And time for all the works and days of hands
> That lift and drop a question on your plate;

This sounds like a completely generalised 'you'. But the next line makes the other person quite definite:

> Time for you and time for me,

Then there is a change. The 'you' almost disappears and the 'I' seems to fill the stage alone:

> And indeed there will be time
> To wonder, 'Do I dare?' and, 'Do I dare?'

Prufrock describes himself—'a bald spot in the middle of my hair', 'my morning coat', 'my necktie'—and continues to worry and waver:

> I have measured out my life with coffee spoons;
> I know the voices dying with a dying fall
> Beneath the music from a farther room.
>   So how should I presume?

'I should have been a pair of ragged claws', 'I was afraid', 'I grow old . . . I grow old . . .', 'I have heard the mermaids singing'—thus it goes on, until we are abruptly switched back to 'we' again right at the end.

We must suppose all along, however, that the 'I' goes on addressing the 'you' and that his many questions are not merely rhetorical but directed to his unheard interlocutor. We are reminded of the latter in just two instances in the middle part of the poem:

> Stretched on the floor, here beside you and me.

And a bit further on:

> Among the porcelain, among some talk of you and me,

Who are these two? The title tells us that the speaker is a certain J. Alfred Prufrock. And since the poem is called a love song, it is natural to suppose that the shadowy 'you', at least after the first verse paragraph, is a woman, the object of Prufock's hesitant and timorous desire.

If we look more closely, however, we discover that the woman of the poem appears under another pronoun, the indefinite 'one' which Prufrock chooses instead of 'she':

> If one, settling a pillow by her head,
>   Should say: 'That is not what I meant at all.
>   That is not it, at all.'

And again:

> If one, settling a pillow or throwing off a shawl,
>   And turning toward the window, should say:
>   'That is not it at all,
>   That is not what I meant, at all.'

This use of 'one' is so unconventional that it tends to be confusing. The reader's first impulse is probably to refer it to Prufrock. When the necessary mental adjustment has been made, however, the pronoun is recognised as a characteristic indirection of Prufrock's thought. He is imagining, and fearing, what her reaction may be to any advance on his part, and he thinks of her as 'one' rather than 'she' out of sheer timidity. The indefinite pronoun generalises and desexualises the situation and so renders it less dangerous to him.

The 'you' in the main part of the poem may conceivably be another pronoun for the same woman. But since in the beginning of the poem Prufock asks a companion to join him for the visit, and since it is natural to look for consistency in the use of pronouns unless there are strong reasons not to do so, it is far more likely that 'you' refers to one and the same person throughout the poem. And this person is not the object of Prufrock's inhibited passion.

Various attempts have been made to solve the riddle of Prufrock's interlocutor. The simplest and probably the most satisfactory explanation is that he is merely the confidant who is needed to make the monologue a dramatic one, one of the minor *dramatis personae*, intrinsically unimportant but useful in giving the main character an opportunity to speak. And this interpretation is supported by Mr Eliot in a letter to the present writer:

> As for THE LOVE SONG OF J. ALFRED PRUFROCK anything I say now must be somewhat conjectural, as it was written so long ago that my memory may deceive me; but I am prepared to assert that the 'you' in THE LOVE SONG is merely some friend or companion, presumably of the male sex, whom the speaker is at that moment addressing, and that it has no emotional content whatever.

This is a timely reminder that we tend nowadays to make even the complex seem much more complicated than necessary by our search for cryptic meanings. Eliot's explanation cannot be ignored. But it does not, of course, preclude associations which would give Prufrock's companion certain recognisable features, and Eliot would be the last person to discount such associations.

Thus, the reader can hardly help associating the person addressed with himself, or for that matter, herself, simply because he is addressed all the time. And having identified himself with the interlocutor he becomes to some extent concerned with the events of the poem. He cannot help feeling that the 'you' is something more than a sympathetic listener. He is involved with Prufrock in the latter's quandary. Prufrock even seems to make a point of this common involvement: 'Time for you and time for me', he declares at one point; and, at the end of the poem:

We have lingered in the chambers of the sea
By sea-girls wreathed with seaweed red and brown
Till human voices wake us, and we drown.

In these important concluding lines where 'we' replaces 'I' it seems clear that the companion also has a universalising function, making the experience no longer merely an individual experience, but raising it to a level at which it symbolises something common enough to be recognised by any reader capable of a positive response to the poem.

As for the Prufrock figure, it can hardly be considered irrelevant to our understanding of the poem to feel that Eliot is present in this creature of his imagination. The epigraph to *The Love Song*, from Guido's confession to Dante in the *Inferno*, would in any case prepare us for confidential matters. Certainly our familiarity with the rest of Eliot's poetry will help us to build up an image of a unique personality, which, as Eliot has said of Yeats, 'makes one sit up in excitement and eagerness to learn more about the author's mind and feelings'. We gradually learn to distinguish this personality in all or most of Eliot's works and we can hardly avoid recognising some of the author's features under the mask of Prufrock.

Prufrock represents, so to speak, a doubling of the personality, the poet and his fictitious character in one person. This may have something to do with the influence of Laforgue. Writing years later in a *Criterion* Commentary[1] about the functions of irony, Eliot mentioned its 'use (as by Jules Laforgue) to express a *dédoublement* of the personality against which the subject struggles'. That kind of ironic struggle is precisely what I find in *The Love Song of J. Alfred Prufrock*.

There is no need, however, to find the doubling of the personality objectified in the two interlocutors of the poem, the 'I' and the 'you'. To interpret them as the poet and his Psyche in the manner of Poe's *Ulalume* or as two attitudes of mind in the manner of Tennyson's *The Two Voices* is gratuitous and really quite uninteresting.

Turning now to *La Figlia Che Piange*, we find in the first section a somebody addressing a somebody else, apparently a young man talking to a girl in a garden. In the first part the 'I', or speaker, is

[1] *CR*, April 1933.

understood to belong to the scene because of the imperative verbs which he must be supposed to be uttering or thinking:

> Weave, weave the sunlight in your hair—
> Clasp your flowers to you with a pained surprise—

In the next part a 'he' and a 'she' also make their appearance:

> So I would have had him leave,
> So I would have had her stand and grieve,

It looks as if an observer—a poet or an artist to judge by his attitude—takes over in this section, having recorded the thoughts of the young man in the first part and now taking an objective and aesthetic view of the whole situation. But then comes a puzzling twist: the 'I' of the second section, the observer, includes himself in a 'we both', as if he had all the time been the girl's companion in the garden:

> I should find
> Some way incomparably light and deft,
> Some way we both should understand,

And in the final section the artist-observer again seems personally involved in the scene he remembers:

> She turned away, but with the autumn weather
> Compelled my imagination many days,

There can be no doubt after this that the speakers of the various sections are really the same person, that the artist (or poet) and the young man in the garden are identical, and that he is speaking of himself as 'he' and 'him' in the middle section. The revelation of this identity is made in the 'we both' and is confirmed in the last section. Again there is a *dédoublement* of the personality, still ironical in spite of the dominant lyricism of this poem. But the technical detachment of one character or attitude from the other, the observer from the agent-sufferer, is incomplete. And there is little attempt at disguise, unless it is disguise to suggest that the observer may be a painter rather than a poet. The general effect, therefore, is of something intermediate between objective description and personal confession. Certainly we have the effect of something far more significant to the poet than 'a gesture and a pose', the understatement by which he sums up the experience. We need only call to mind the loaded significance of the girl-in-the-flower-garden image in a great number of Eliot's poems and plays.

The Waste Land begins in the first person plural, with an 'us' in the fifth line which seems to comprise all humanity:

> Winter kept us warm, covering
> Earth in forgetful snow,

Immediately after that, the words 'Summer surprised us . . .' introduce the episode of the Hofgarten, in which 'us' and 'we' refer to two individuals, apparently a man and a woman striking up acquaintance in Munich. That episode is in turn followed by an unidentified voice addressing somebody as 'Son of man' and telling him:

> (Come in under the shadow of this red rock),
> And I will show you something different from either
> Your shadow at morning striding behind you
> Or your shadow at evening rising to meet you;

Then another voice, from Wagner:

> *Mein Irisch Kind,*
> *Wo weilest du?*

followed by the 'hyacinth girl' and somebody—again we do not know who—speaking to her:

> —Yet when we came back, late, from the Hyacinth garden,
> Your arms full and your hair wet, I could not
> Speak, and my eyes failed,

Madame Sosostris of the next section stands out clearly, but her client is unknown. And in the final section of 'The Burial of the Dead' there is again an anonymous speaker, one who watches the early morning crowd flowing over London Bridge and reflects, with Dante, 'I had not thought death had undone so many.' He meets and speaks to a man called Stetson and ends by calling him 'You! hypocrite lecteur!—mon semblable,—mon frère!'— which perhaps offers a hint of an explanation.

In 'A Game of Chess', after the initial description of the luxurious dressing-room, there is a dialogue between an anonymous woman and an anonymous man. Her words are given in quotation marks,[1] whereas his are not, which seems to indicate that he is the narrator of the incident and that we are invited to share his prescient and seemingly despairing point of view:

> And we shall play a game of chess,
> Pressing lidless eyes and waiting for a knock upon the door.

After that comes a dramatic monologue in a pub, with the female speaker sufficiently identified both by what she says and the way in which she says it.

Then 'The Fire Sermon', beginning with a mosaic of quotations from the Psalms, Spenser, Marvell and Shakespeare, each introducing a speaker, and all the speakers fused in the same 'I' by the juxtaposition of the quotations:

> By the waters of Leman I sat down and wept . . .
> Sweet Thames, run softly till I end my song,
>
> .   .   .   .
>
> But at my back in a cold blast I hear
>
> .   .   .   .
>
> Musing upon the king my brother's wreck

After the invitation from the Smyrna merchant, again reported by an (or the?) anonymous narrator, the poem introduces Tiresias, the ancient hermaphrodite and prophet:

> I Tiresias, old man with wrinkled dugs
> Perceived the scene, and foretold the rest—

And Tiresias having witnessed the episode of the typist and the 'young man carbuncular', the voice is once more that of the observer of life in the city of London.

The short part, called 'Death by Water', concludes with an exhortation to a universal audience, introducing a 'you' which has been absent since the 'Son of man' section in 'The Burial of the Dead':

> Gentile or Jew
> O you who turn the wheel and look to windward,
> Consider Phlebas, who was once handsome and tall as you.

---

[1] Many editions print a closing quotation mark at the end of the line 'What shall I do now? What shall I do?', thus apparently giving the succeeding lines to a different speaker. Mr Eliot has confirmed my supposition that there should be no quotation mark in this place.

And a 'we' which has also been virtually absent since 'The Burial of the Dead' is reintroduced in 'What the Thunder Said', where it assumes a great deal of importance: 'We who were living are now dying', 'If there were water we should stop and drink', 'We think of the key, each in his prison'. Mingled with this there is the voice of the single speaker, or of the same speaker using the singular pronoun, frequently addressing an unnamed companion: 'Who is the third who walks always beside you?', 'My friend, blood shaking my heart . . .', 'The sea was calm, your heart would have responded'. And last of all another mosaic of quotations and original lines, mostly in the first person singular.

With all this seeming fluctuation in point of view it is surely no exaggeration to say that much of the obscurity of the poem is due to the use of pronouns without reference to distinct persons. We have the impression at first of a hubbub of voices all heard in the dark in a strange room. Occasionally the characters take distinct shapes, in bits of narrative or in dramatic monologues and even dialogues. But more often we are left in doubt as to who the speakers are and to whom they are talking. Our natural tendency to identify the speaker with the poet and the persons addressed with ourselves, the readers, is disturbed by the frequency with which the speaker seems to assume imaginary personalities, that of Ferdinand in *The Tempest*, or the Fisher King in the Grail legends, or Tiresias the old prophet of Thebes.

The explanatory note on Tiresias appended to the poem by the author may give us a certain amount of help:

> Tiresias, although a mere spectator and not indeed a 'character', is yet the most important personage in the poem, uniting all the rest. Just as the one-eyed merchant, seller of currants, melts into the Phoenician Sailor, and the latter is not wholly distinct from Ferdinand Prince of Naples, so all the women are one woman, and the two sexes meet in Tiresias. What Tiresias *sees*, in fact, is the substance of the poem.

I am not sure how literally we should take this explanation or exactly how much it is capable of explaining. Certainly many of the voices in *The Waste Land* can easily be reduced to one voice, or at least one chorus, that of humanity, conscious of its emptiness and sterility but unable to define it and unable to cope with it. There is no voice in *The Waste Land* entirely non-human except that of the

Thunder, rumbling the words *Datta, Dayadhvam, Damyata,* and what I take to be the final sound of the rain, 'Shantih shantih shantih'. But there is the voice of an individual who is fully conscious of the plight of humanity and of the nature of that plight, one who has seen 'fear in a handful of dust' and has looked 'into the heart of light, the silence', who has grown old with Tiresias and 'passed the stages of his age and youth' with Phlebas the Phoenician, one who shares the common lot but who sees and knows more than the rest. And I cannot see that anything is gained by completely merging his voice with the others. On the contrary, there is a great loss in dramatic tension.

On the one hand, then, there is the observer-prophet and on the other the bewildered and unhappy inhabitants of the Waste Land.

The hint that was found at the end of 'The Burial of the Dead' may now be reconsidered: 'You! hypocrite lecteur!—mon semblable,—mon frère!' This would seem to indicate that Eliot is putting both himself and his readers into the poem, identifying them in the immediate context with 'Stetson' and more indirectly with humanity in general. We do indeed recognise the prophetic voice of the poem as that of the poet. In other words, it appears that the poet is partly speaking to us and partly to himself in so far as he shares the common dilemma. But he chooses to embody himself in various shapes in order to do so: Baudelaire, the Fisher King, Tiresias, Saint Augustine and so on. Thus the first and second voices of poetry structurally carry the whole poem and constantly emerge on the surface, but they are submerged at times by the third voice, that of the dramatically conceived characters like Madame Sosostris and the speakers in the pub.

So it remains true, it seems to me, that in many of his early poems Eliot wished to portray a common dilemma, a fact which helps to account for the great number of characters in his poetry, particularly in *The Waste Land.* But at the same time the dilemma must undoubtedly have been a private one, judging by the distinctness with which we recognise the ironic voice of the author in the poems we have analysed.

Eliot needed to explore his own mind, it must be legitimate to infer, because he found uncertainty and vacillation there. In 'Tradition and the Individual Talent' he also admitted that private emotions might be intense or painful enough to make it seem necessary to escape from them. 'Escape from' in this context may be taken to mean 'express'. In other words the early impersonal theory seems to indicate a strong—and, for that matter, quite reasonable—disinclination to reveal private emotions, which needed expressing but the full understanding of which was not for the general reader. And this in turn necessitated a technique by which the private could be made public.

We cannot, nor would Eliot now himself, adopt the mystico-chemical transmutation theory of 'Tradition and the Individual Talent' as the only explanation of the creative process. Such transmutation of private material into art belongs, if it has any reality, to the achievement of the mature artist. And it is fair to judge at least some of Eliot's early poetry as mainly that of the 'skilful craftsman' whom he spoke of in his lecture on Yeats. On that level, then, if there is a strong private emotion which the poet does not wish to reveal as such, a simple and obvious way to depersonalise it is to use some kind of mask or disguise, introducing a speaker whose attributes are not immediately recognisable as those of the poet, or presenting a character in the third person. Such ludicrous attributes of J. Alfred Prufrock as his name, his age and his baldness may be regarded under the aspect of depersonalisation, as a mask covering the poet's own features. Especially the use of an old or oldish speaker is frequent in Eliot's poetry, and in his early poems it is obviously an effective means of making the speaker outwardly unlike himself.

Eliot reminds us in *The Three Voices of Poetry* that Ezra Pound was the disciple of Robert Browning, who called some of his poems *Dramatis Personae*. Pound chose the title of *Personae*, which literally means 'masks', for a large collection of his own poetry. And Eliot, as we know, was at one time the disciple of Pound.

Even before that discipleship, however, he had written his *Portrait of a Lady*, which contains the lines:

> And I must borrow every changing shape
> To find expression . . . dance, dance
> Like a dancing bear,
> Cry like a parrot, chatter like an ape.

And perhaps there is a similar feeling in the following lines from *The Hollow Men*, of a somewhat later date:

Point of View in Eliot's Poetry

Let me also wear
Such deliberate disguises
Rat's coat, crowskin, crossed staves
In a field
Behaving as the wind behaves

The many 'I's of Eliot's early poems are to some extent deliberate disguises. This no doubt makes the obscurity of point of view at times excessive, and it is further increased by the poet's effort to fuse the private experience and the general observation, as in *The Waste Land*. But there is a special approach to this kind of poetry which helps to justify the indefiniteness. I mean the approach of the reader who is willing to co-operate with the poet in finding a meaning for himself. This approach Eliot not only allows but actively encourages, since his impersonal theory makes the meaning of a poem and its 'art emotion' as much the property of the reader as that of the poet. Eliot, who is more of an Arnoldian than I think he has ever admitted, has carried Matthew Arnold's idea of a special kind of poetic truth one step further by saying in effect that not only truth but meaning, too, is pragmatic—the meaning of a poem to a particular reader is whatever satisfies that reader most.

Many readers, no doubt, will welcome this attitude, since the richness of suggestion which is produced by the indeterminate point of view makes for poetic gain. They will be content to leave the puzzles unsolved, recognising mainly the comic and satirical abandon of the poet, which makes his verse vigorous and fresh in spite of the despondency which often seems to be at the bottom of it. But considering the state of mental pressure in which poetry is usually created and the amount of hard work that goes to its making, it seems probable that the fullest satisfaction must be derived when the reader's understanding approaches as close as possible to the poet's meaning. And though in his ironic and playful exuberance Eliot may at times have introduced lines and passages simply to tease the reader or jolt him out of his complacency, the earnestness which pervades even his comic effects will prevent one from putting them down to mere chance or caprice.

Almost all the time there is the serious philosophical preoccupation on Eliot's part with the question of identity and individuality. This is apparent in his plays no less than in his poems.

Thus the question of individual identity is a central one both in
The Dry Salvages and in *The Confidential Clerk.*

A typical attitude in some—if not all—of the plays is the conception of the central character as representative of a family or a
community and therefore as embodying their failings and their
hopes. This is particularly conspicuous in *Murder in the Cathedral,*
The Family Reunion and *The Cocktail Party.* In *The Family Reunion*
Agatha is able to enlighten Harry about his destiny:

> It is possible
> You are the consciousness of your unhappy family,
> Its bird sent flying through the purgatorial flame.

It is not fortuitous, therefore, that the general pattern of the play
should show us at the beginning a bewildered family group, then
individuals fighting out their conflicts and primarily one individual doing so, and finally the group again, now with the
promise of a new integration by the self-sacrifice of the protagonist. In the same way *Murder in the Cathedral* begins and ends
with the Chorus and has in the centre the sermon of the individual
Thomas Becket.

What the plays do dramatically the poems do mainly grammatically. We noticed both in *The Love Song of J. Alfred Prufrock*
and in *The Waste Land* something like a progression from 'we' to
'I' and back to 'we'. The same progression may be found in another
poem of indeterminate point of view, *The Hollow Men.* This may
have something to do with the habitual pattern of Eliot's thinking
or with a tendency to manipulate the speakers of his poems in a
certain dramatic rhythm. In either case what is suggested is a
drama of the individual identifying himself with a group and
vicariously acting or atoning for it. Naturally the point of view
cannot in such cases be fixed with precision. It fluctuates all the
time as the process of identification advances and recedes, or is
welcomed and repudiated by those concerned. And it is in the
living flux of his feelings as a distinct individual and as a representative of humanity that Eliot wrote his poetry.

It is interesting to note that as his philosophical certainty increased the point of view in his poetry became correspondingly
stable. Thus in *Ash-Wednesday* the point of view is still a little
ambiguous, but the features of the poet are definitely emerging
more distinctly than in the earlier poems. And the *Four Quartets,*

difficult as they may be in their use of imagery and in the development of their thought, do seem to have a quite simple poet–reader relationship, which is of course revealed most clearly in prosaic passages like:

> You say I am repeating
> Something I have said before. I shall say it again.
> Shall I say it again?

Thus, in the most recent phase of his poetic career, Eliot appears to have given up his impersonal theory and his technique of concealment almost entirely. When the private predicament ceased his poetry changed. Now that he has a governing point of view in private life he distinguishes clearly between the three voices of poetry, speaking distinctly in his own character in his poems and (with some exceptions, notably in *The Cocktail Party*) creating clear-cut dramatic characters in his plays.

In his early work, on the other hand, the mingling of lyrical and dramatic elements is one aspect of the lack of clarity in point of view. But nevertheless lyricism and drama have been combined into an exciting union. And since we are dealing with poetry and not confession or history, it would be invidious to complain that the cost in clarity is too great.

V

TECHNIQUE AND THOUGHT

T HERE are one or two pitfalls that we must avoid if we wish to examine Eliot's poetic technique in relation to his thought. The first is that of taking a too superficial view of the relation of form and matter, particularly of seeing in the broken structure of a poem a way of expressing the broken appearance of our civilisation. This is a view which Eliot has encouraged by his much-abused words about poetry having to be difficult to-day because of the complexity of modern life.[1] If Eliot meant simply that the difficulty of living must be symbolised by the difficulty of construing a poem, I think his opinion was rash and unmeditated. But he probably meant something more and different. Language, he said, has to be dislocated if necessary to fit the poet's *meaning*. The difficulty, in other words, is one of thought, not one inherent in modern civilisation and reflected mechanically by the poet from his environment to his poetic form. Yet we find so acute a critic as Paul Elmer More presenting Eliot as a 'lyric prophet of chaos' by whom 'the confusion of life' is 'reflected in the disorganized flux of images; its lack of clear meaning in the obscurity of language'; in whom there is 'something fundamentally amiss' since he can employ 'for an experience born of Anglo-Catholic faith a metrical form and a freakishness of punctuation suitable for the presentation of life regarded as without form and void.'[2] Mr Yvor Winters, who is inclined to blame the influence of Henry Adams, takes up the cry. Eliot, he says, 'surrenders his

[1] 'The Metaphysical Poets', *SE*, p. 289.
[2] 'The Cleft Eliot', *Saturday Review of Literature*, Nov. 12, 1932.

form to his subject', making it chaotic in order to express chaos.[1]

Now there is obviously some justice in such pronouncements, though it is hard to see why they should be so accusatory. A confused or fragmentary reality will tend to produce a confused or fragmentary representation of it. An ordered reality will tend to produce a neat representation. Eliot's early poetry describes a fragmentary world and a fragmentary view of life. But there is an immense difference between the description of reality and the organisation of a poem. Paul Elmer More and Winters, one feels, have not taken the mind of the poet and the creative process into account. More's objection to the form of *Ash-Wednesday*, for instance, would be valid if the poem were intended to be an ordered exposition of Anglo-Catholic doctrines. But the poem is obviously something quite different: it is the moulding of the poet's mind into patterns of sound and meaning. And I can see no reason why even a firm Christian faith should not be expressed poetically in fragments. We may make allowance for a certain amount of direct imitation of actual life in the form of the poetry and suggestion *of* actual life *by* the form of the poetry, but as an explanation of the relation between form and matter this view is altogether inadequate.

The second pitfall we must avoid is the temptation to make sharp distinctions between the 'prosy' parts of the poems and the 'poetical' parts. In the *Quartets* and the plays there are passages in which the poet modulates into the language of discourse. Eliot's poetry certainly moves on many different levels, and the directness with which ideas are expressed varies considerably. We can recognise the prosy passages quite easily, but it would not do to tear them from their contexts, or, on the other hand, to read the lyrical passages alone. Since the general purpose is poetic, all the parts of the poems must be included in our examination of technique and thought. Coleridge declared that 'a poem of any length neither can be, nor ought to be, all poetry. Yet,' he goes on, 'if an harmonious whole is to be produced, the remaining parts must be preserved in keeping with the poetry.'[2]

Eliot's poetic development shows a struggle towards the conditions of drama on the one hand and music on the other. It was

---

[1] L. Unger, *T. S. Eliot: A Selected Critique* (1948), p. 110.
[2] *Biographia Literaria*, ch. XIV.

the possibilities of drama, including the dramatic monologue, that he chiefly explored in his early poetry. The theoretical side of this interest is exemplified in such essays as '"Rhetoric" and Poetic Drama', 'A Dialogue on Poetic Drama' and the *Elizabethan Essays*. The poetry of his 'dramatic' phase has a strong descriptive element, usually combined with the critical expression of attitude. The dramatic presentation seems at first to have been employed chiefly to give objectivity to description and attitude, to allow the poet to escape from his own person and speak with the tongues of the old and experienced. Gradually he became interested in the opportunities which drama afforded to appeal to members of an audience at different levels of understanding. He also came to see that 'the most direct means of social "usefulness" for poetry, is the theatre'.[1] And though he did not mean that the theatre was the best means of 'getting a message across', the plays that he wrote soon after he made this statement, namely *The Rock* and *Murder in the Cathedral*, suggest that the idea of communicating a message was in his mind as well. At any rate, the dramatic form of poetry is the form that can least dispense with a sustained paraphrasable meaning.

To teach, however, was never Eliot's desire as a poet; and it may have been a feeling that the dramatic form tended to be too didactic that made him turn more resolutely to the exploration of musical form. The *Four Quartets* and the lecture on *The Music of Poetry* are symptomatic of this new emphasis. It was intimately accompanied by a contemplative tendency, which is more marked in the *Quartets* than ever before. The *Quartets* are definitely musical rather than dramatic in structure and quality, and contemplative rather than descriptive.

Eliot was long in two minds about musicality. It was pro-claimed by the French Symbolists, echoing Poe. 'De la musique avant toute chose,' said Verlaine. And Pound repeated: 'it is the musical phrase that matters.' But there were Tennyson, the Pre-Raphaelites, Swinburne and the early Yeats to show that what could be done with music in English apparently had been done, even to excess. So in his early compositions Eliot avoided, if not musicality, at least melodiousness, as much as he was able to without resorting to Whitmanesque prose-poetry. He was con-firmed in this avoidance by such writers as Julien Benda, who,

[1] *UPC*, p. 153.

in his *Belphégor*, indignantly denounced the effeminate cult of music.

There is no doubt, however, that Eliot has a fine ear for musical cadence and for musical composition, though he says he is ignorant of the technical subtleties of music. A poem, he states, often begins in his mind as a fragment of rhythm. So it was not surprising that his sensibility and his poetic antecedents should soon reassert themselves in a wholehearted surrender to the music of poetry.

The influence of music, one might think, would make for a poetry as purified of ideas and conceptual meaning as possible, or a poetry in which sound and meaning were kept in two compartments. Speaking of Milton's 'rhetorical style', Eliot complains of the dislocation that 'takes place, through the hypertrophy of the auditory imagination at the expense of the visual and tactile, so that the inner meaning is separated from the surface, and tends to become something occult, or at least without effect upon the reader until fully understood'. He thinks sense and sound can be appreciated at once in Dante and Shakespeare, but there seems 'to be a division, in Milton, between the philosopher or theologian and the poet'.[1]

Sometimes one feels the same division in Eliot. The incantatory passages are an example. And the systematic way in which the different sensations are evoked in sections of *Murder in the Cathedral* and the *Quartets* are another. The consistent appeal to the sense of smell in *Prufrock* and to the musical sense in the 1920 *Poems* are further indications of deliberate workmanship aiming perhaps chiefly at technical effects. But generally, in Eliot's view, the music of a word or a poem has at least as much to do with the structure of meanings and associations as with the structure of sounds:

> What matters . . . is the whole poem. . . . The music of a word is, so to speak, at a point of intersection: it arises from its relation first to the words immediately preceding and following it, and indefinitely to the rest of its context; and from another relation, that of its immediate meaning in that context to all the other meanings which it has had in other contexts, to its greater or less wealth of association

---

[1] 'A Note on the Verse of John Milton', *Essays and Studies*, XXI (1936), p. 38.

. . . a 'musical poem' is a poem which has a musical pattern of sound and a musical pattern of the secondary meanings of the words which compose it, and . . . these two patterns are indissoluble and one . . . the sound of a poem is as much an abstraction from the poem as is the sense.[1]

In the combination of music and contemplation which we find in the *Four Quartets* there is a reaching out beyond the limits of ordinary meaning to a transcendent reality which by its very existence implies a teleology even for the purest art.

> Words move, music moves
> Only in time; but that which is only living
> Can only die. Words, after speech, reach
> Into the silence. Only by the form, the pattern,
> Can words or music reach
> The stillness . . .
>
> (*Burnt Norton*, V)

This seems to indicate an unusually intimate combination of form and meaning. But only a close analysis of the poetic technique can establish the nature and reality of this combination.

TEXTURE, RHYME AND RHYTHM

There are no purely formal elements in poetry. Sound must be pitched and intoned according to its sense, and rhythm is rhythm of meaning as well as of stress, length and tone. This is probably why Eliot doubts 'whether, from the point of view of *sound* alone, any word is more or less beautiful than another—within its own language'.[2] I find it difficult to accept his opinion without demur: from the point of view of *sound* alone, the word 'spiteful' is no doubt more pleasing than the word 'gracious'. But as one might expect, the words in Eliot's poems rarely seem to be chosen from any obvious considerations of phonetic harmony, such as variations of vowel and consonant sounds, assonance and alliteration. If I may illustrate from the art of painting, his texture rarely has the startling coloristic *naïveté* of a Rousseau, the lushness of a Rubens or the limpidity of a Reynolds. But it has something of the blurredness of a Turner, the sullenness of a Gauguin or the asceticism of a Manet. He can produce a beauty of texture that is

---

[1] *The Music of Poetry*, pp. 18–19.   [2] Ibid., p. 18.

something apart and relies more on effects of shading within a
monochrome medium than on richness of contrast. For particular
purposes he can create lush and limpid textures as well. But the
general impression is one of sobriety, even of prosiness. I have
verified this impression by careful comparisons of Eliot's poetry
with passages from a number of other poets, ancient and modern:
Spenser, Shakespeare, Keats, Tennyson, Browning, Lawrence,
Auden. It would take up too much space to repeat these comparisons here. But a confrontation of a few typical lines by Eliot
with a few of Shakespeare's may be useful as an example:

> —Yet I'll not shed her blood,
> Nor scar that whiter skin of hers than snow,
> And smooth as monumental alabaster.
>
> > (*Othello*, V, ii, 3–5)

> So I would have had him leave,
> So I would have had her stand and grieve,
> So he would have left
> As the soul leaves the body torn and bruised,
> As the mind deserts the body it has used.
> I should find
> Some way incomparably light and deft,
> Some way we both should understand,
> Simple and faithless as a smile and shake of the hand.
>
> > (*La Figlia Che Piange*)

It is not Eliot's monotonous repetitions that mark the chief
difference (I do not mean 'monotonous' in a disparaging sense).
Shakespeare has similar repetitions (giving an all but monotonous
effect) in the lines before and after those I have quoted. But there
is a great difference in the patterns of sound. Shakespeare has
especially an almost incomparable variety of vowels. In the above
lines from *Othello* the stressed or half-stressed vowels are these:

[e], [ai], [ɔ], [e], [ə], [ʌ], [ɔ], [aː], [æ], [ai], [i], [ɔː], [ou], [uː], [ɔ], [e], [æ], [aː]

The consonants, too, show a fair variety, and when the complete
words are read out the effect is marvellously melodious.

In Eliot's lines, there is a preponderance, at first, of unstressed
and neutral vowels. The words 'would have' are in each case unstressed, and the following 'had' only weakly stressed. Full stress
only occurs on the 'so' and the last words of the first three lines.

In the last four lines the vowel scheme (apart from the unstressed vowels) is as follows:

[ai], [ai], [ʌ], [ei], [ɔ], [ai], [e], [ʌ], [ei], [ou], [ʌ], [æ], [i], [ei], [ai], [ei], [æ].

Thus in twenty-seven syllables of Shakespeare's lines there are eleven different vowel sounds; in thirty-four of Eliot's poem there are eight different vowel sounds (excluding unstressed vowels in both cases). But more important than this mathematical difference, which I do no take too seriously, is the difference of audible patterns obtained by the arrangement of the sounds.

A comparison of Eliot's texture with that of leading poets of the seventeenth century proper and the eighteenth century, reveals a far greater similarity. This may be due to Eliot's conscious admiration of the Metaphysical poets and the classicists. But it may also be due to a certain parallelism of talent, temperament and purpose. In the matter of texture these poets have in common a general finish and in some cases polish, which makes the sound music reliable and serviceable but not very differentiated, and not very highly exploited for particular effects. Vowel and consonant sounds are neat and orderly, submitting to the sound patterns of the verse lines and allowing the words to run on unimpeded.

Milton is famed for his sonority, but the texture of his verse often closely resembles that of Eliot's:

> Come, come; no time for lamentation now,
> Nor much more cause. Samson hath quit himself
> Like Samson, and heroicly hath finished
> A life heroic, on his enemies
> Fully revenged—hath left them years of mourning
> And lamentation to the sons of Caphtor
> Through all Philistian bounds; to Israel
> Honour hath left and freedom, let but them
> Find courage to lay hold on this occasion;
> To himself and father's house eternal fame;
> And, which is best and happiest yet, all this
> With God not parted from him, as was feared,
> But favouring and assisting to the end.
> Nothing is here for tears, nothing to wail
> Or knock the breast; no weakness, no contempt,
> Dispraise or blame; nothing but well and fair,
> And what may quiet us in a death so noble.
>
> (*Samson Agonistes*, ll. 1708 ff.)

No. For the Church is stronger for this action,
Triumphant in adversity. It is fortified
By persecution: supreme, so long as men will die for it.
Go, weak sad men, lost erring souls, homeless in earth or heaven.
Go where the sunset reddens the last grey rock
Of Brittany, or the Gates of Hercules.
Go venture shipwreck on the sullen coasts
Where blackamoors make captive Christian men;
Go to the northern seas confined with ice
Where the dead breath makes numb the hand, makes dull the brain;
Find an oasis in the desert sun,
Go seek alliance with the heathen Saracen,
To share his filthy rites, and try to snatch
Forgetfulness in his libidinous courts,
Oblivion in the fountain by the date-tree;
Or sit and bite your nails in Aquitaine.

(Murder in the Cathedral, pp. 83–4)

It may be partly because *Samson Agonistes* has very free rhythms
and because *Murder in the Cathedral* is deliberately archaic in some
respects that the similarity of tone in these poems is often so striking. But, in spite of the coolness which Eliot felt for Milton for a
long time, the two poets seem to be united by a certain similarity
of temperament, of acoustic sensibility—and of purpose.

That Eliot masters his sound effects is proved abundantly by the
many passages in which the texture, for some reason, is specially
rich or elaborate, for instance at the end of *The Love Song* and in
the *Landscapes*. A line in *Mr. Apollinax* contains what is probably
the most concentrated word music that he has composed:

Where worried bodies of drowned men drift down in the green silence,

Do Eliot's natural genius and inclination lie in the direction of
a musicality of sound pattern that he usually denies, or does he
have to put himself out purposely to attend to the sound pattern?
The truth probably lies somewhere between these explanations.
But it seems to me that the poet's sense of phonetic values is
critical rather than creative. His ear is generally (though not
always) too fine to allow him to write anything so unpleasing,
from a phonetic point of view, as Wordsworth's *Ode to Duty*; but
on the other hand, his imagination does not work with individual
sounds, so that they are often left to take care of themselves.

Eliot's use of rhyme follows no definite rules. Sometimes he

employs very exacting rhyme schemes, but more often he re-
nounces rhyme altogether. The most diverse schemes can jostle
each other in one and the same poem. The characteristic device,
however, is the apparently fortuitous rhymes, which occur
sporadically, interspersed among unrhymed lines. We find them
in large parts of *The Waste Land*, in *The Hollow Men* and in *Ash-
Wednesday*. Everything considered, it seems that he employs rhyme
opportunistically. But this is no sign of carelessness or lack of
ability. It is his achievement to have liberated rhyme so as to
decorate suitable points of a poem, instead of conforming to a
mechanical arrangement. 'Rhyme,' he says, 'is neither an essential
nor a superfluity.' Thus he restores to rhyme its aesthetic dignity.
When necessary he jingles, as in *A Cooking Egg* ('sitting—knitting,
Sidney—kidney, instruct me—conduct me'). At other times he
repeats words to rhyme with themselves, or he muffles the effect
by using only half-rhymes and consonances.

In the matter of rhythm, he is no more dogmatic than in the
matter of texture and rhyme. He thinks sensibility and practice are
more important than theory and that the imitation of recognised
models is the best schooling. His indebtedness to French poetry
helps to explain his independence of English prosody and the fact
that he was able to free himself from regular accentual rhythms.

All poetry can be scanned in two ways: according to the rhythm
of natural speech, and according to a systematic metre. In poems
of an artificial or solemn diction, one will tend to give preference
to the systematic metre. In poems of a conversational style one will
give preference to the natural speech rhythm. In both cases a contrapuntal effect is obtained by the simultaneous beat of both
rhythms.

The style of Eliot's poems favours the natural speech rhythm.
The systematic accompaniment tends to became very faint, and,
besides, it constantly changes from iambic to dactylic, etc. But it is
important that it should be there, for poetry must have some
regularity, however approximate. Fortunately, our consciousness
is able to act as an amplifier for whatever it is directed to. If we
look for redness in a mixture of colours, the red tint, if it is there
at all, *saute aux yeux*. A usual device for directing our attention
to rhythm is the typographical arrangement. If one takes a piece
of prose and divides it into short lines, its rhythmical qualities will
immediately become more marked. And, vice versa, much modern

poetry will apparently lose its rhythmical distinction if printed as prose. The difference between verse and prose can therefore be infinitesimal. Eliot's prose poem *Hysteria* might well have been printed as follows:

> As she laughed I was aware
> Of becoming involved in her laughter
> And being part of it, until her teeth
> Were only accidental stars
> With a talent for squad-drill.

Conversely, some of the lines from *The Dry Salvages* would look perfectly plausible as prose:

> It seems, as one becomes older, that the past has another pattern, and ceases to be a mere sequence—or even development: the latter a partial fallacy encouraged by superficial notions of evolution.

It is one of the criteria of verse as distinct from prose that the stressed syllables are relatively frequent. The proportion of stressed syllables to weak syllables we may call 'stress frequency'. Now a number of experiments, which anyone may carry out for himself, have shown me that the stress frequency in an average selection of Eliot's poetry is exactly intermediate between the stress frequency in a representative selection of English poetry of the kind tending towards prosodic regularity, and that of a representative selection of English prose (mostly recent). The 'free verse' of such as Whitman, Lawrence, Edith Sitwell and Auden, on the other hand, has a mean stress frequency which is exactly the same as that of prose, if the latter is divided into verse lines before counting the stresses. The highest stress frequency, as is to be expected, is found in regular verse (43 per cent in my analysis), then comes Eliot's verse (39 per cent), 'free verse' and prose (both 36 per cent), and lastly Eliot's prose (29 per cent). (The low stress frequency of Eliot's prose is probably due to its discursive nature.)

There would seem to be more variation (from poem to poem and passage to passage) in the stress frequency of Eliot's verse than in the free verse of most other poets. Eliot, it is evident, has a wide rhythmic range, and great flexibility. But this again means that he does not once and for all take up an extreme position in the neighbourhood of prose, as do the thoroughgoing *vers-libristes*. His poems often seem prosy. He himself thinks that 'moments of prosiness' are necessary for contrast and variety and because the poet cannot always stay on the lyrical plane. But rhythmically his verse generally comes somewhere between 'romantic' poetry and prose, between Tennyson's *Song of the Lotos-Eaters* and Shaw's *Candida*. Analysis confirms the impression that Eliot has restored the connection between the rhythm of poetry and the rhythm of ordinary speech. His task has been analogous to that of Dryden and Wordsworth, with which he expressly compares it in his essay on Milton. 'It was one of our tenets,' he says there, speaking of the young poets of the beginning of the century, 'that verse should have the virtues of prose, that diction should become assimilated to cultivated contemporary speech, before aspiring to the elevation of poetry.' Though he speaks of diction, his statement also has application to rhythm. And though he may personally have regarded the reform of diction as the more important, his practical reform of rhythm has been at least equally significant.

Our examination of texture, rhyme and rhythm leaves us with a general impression of *moderation*. None of these formal factors would draw our attention from the contents and meaning of the poems; on the contrary, by their approach to prose they tend to reassure us as to the significance and the seriousness of the contents. From the poet's point of view these things may look rather different. Eliot may have worked hard to achieve precisely that effect of unelaborateness and moderation which we admire, and this concern may have completely overshadowed the concern for the thought he was expressing. But if he had given an excessive amount of systematic and conscious attention to purely formal factors it hardly seems likely that he would have achieved the kind of balanced, undogmatic free verse that is peculiarly his.

The closeness of Eliot's poetic diction to prose was programmatical, as we know, and cannot be taken as an indication of his subjection of form to meaning, except perhaps in the prosy passages of his latest poetry. And form and meaning are served alike by his play on words, such as 'World not world, but that which is not world' in the third movement of *Burnt Norton*. The sound repetition here makes a formal impact, while the homonymy gives one that sense of secret, meaningful relationships which Émile Cailliet and Jean-Albert Bédé demonstrated in the use of 'homonymes, onomatopées et calembours' in primitive tabus.[1]

---

[1] Cailliet et Bédé, 'Le Symbolisme et l'âme primitive', *Revue de littérature comparée*, avril–juin 1932, p. 376.

VERSE STRUCTURE

Structure in Eliot's poetry is frequently determined by regular patterns of line and stanza and section. But more typically it resembles the accentual rhythm of the poems in being liberated from all narrowing rules.

There is one thing that strikes us at once in Eliot's technique of construction, both formal and logical: the abrupt breaks and veerings, in the division of the lines as well as in the longer sequences. The division of lines is determined, I suppose, largely by rhythmical considerations. It has usually nothing to do with syntax, and there is frequent enjambment of a very noticeable kind, as in the following lines from *Gerontion*:

Guides us by vanities. Think now
She gives when our attention is distracted
And what she gives, gives with such supple confusions
That the giving famishes the craving. Gives too late
What's not believed in, or if still believed,
In memory only, reconsidered passion. Gives too soon
Into weak hands, what's thought can be dispensed with
Till the refusal propagates a fear. Think
Neither fear nor courage saves us. Unnatural vices
Are fathered by our heroism. Virtues
Are forced upon us by our impudent crimes.

The line division seems to be determined by a kind of logical rhyming: 'Think now' with 'think', 'gives too late' with 'gives too soon', 'vices' with 'virtues'. There is in this something belonging to Eliot's 'music of ideas'. The sense is served by the emphasis given to the words that 'rhyme', and the formal pattern is equally well served.

Mr Eliot has told me that the division of lines in *The Family Reunion* was meant as a kind of punctuation, i.e. as a device to clarify or modify the meanings of the words. I assume that the line division has the same function in varying degrees in the remainder of his poetry. What usually happens, of course, is that a faint ambiguity is given to the meaning. When part of a sentence is retarded by a pause, this also means that part of the sense is withheld for a time while the reader's thought is engaged with the first part. When Harry says

One thinks to escape
By violence, but one is still alone

the words 'one thinks to escape' have at first a wider suggestiveness than when the qualification of the next line is added. However, the line division is often factitious from the point of view of sense, and there is a tendency to ignore it in reading, just as one commonly ignores the pauses between Shakespeare's blank verse lines in cases of enjambment. In a broadcast performance of *The Family Reunion* given by the BBC in the spring of 1948, the actors generally adhered to the grammatical rather than the prosodic pauses. But this was contrary to Eliot's intention. He means the line structure to serve both statement and cadence, sense and sound.

Usually what look like stanzas in his poetry simply correspond to the paragraphs of prose in that a space is left when a break in meaning requires it; and the breaks in meaning come at irregular intervals. But they are often much more absolute than in prose. In *The Waste Land*, especially, the transitions from one 'paragraph' to another are abrupt. Thus we skip straight from the hyacinth girl to Madame Sosostris, and only reflection shows us the connection and the contrast between them, as between timelessness and time, between the true and the false. Elsewhere, especially in the later works like *Ash-Wednesday* and *Four Quartets*, the transitions are easier. The prosy 'commentaries' in the *Quartets* indicate the nature of the suppressed links in *The Waste Land*: in the latter poem, as well as in *The Love Song*, *Gerontion* and elsewhere, parts of the poet's trains of thought have been left out. But this very fact invites reflection on the reader's part. The broken sequence, far from being a denial of thought and meaning, may be regarded as a negative way of emphasising these things.

Sometimes the division into stanza-paragraphs is as surprising as the division into lines. In some cases the spacing has been altered in later editions of the poems to conform more closely to the logical sequence. Other examples of apparently unnatural spacing remain. In some of these the intention is obviously to create pleasing proportions in the formal composition. In other examples definite effects of sense and emotion are primarily aimed at. This, I think, applies to the following two lines from *Ash-Wednesday*, which belong to the same sentence, but to different stanza-paragraphs:

One who moves in the time between sleep and waking, wearing

White light folded, sheathed about her, folded.

The 'white light', coming as it does in an initial position, becomes doubly impressive. The space in the middle of this sentence actually gives a feeling of dazzlement.

The wish to create contrasts is at the bottom of much of the broken sequence, and here again it is both the formal and the ideal contrasts that count. Eliot's usual device is to set off passages that may be immediately recognised as poetry by passages which are close to prose. If we read his poems with the preconceived idea that everything must be equally 'poetical' we are likely to be shocked. If, on the other hand, we read them in an unprejudiced frame of mind, we shall be willing to accept both the poetical and the prosy parts for what they are: different movements of a symphony, and different approaches to thought apprehended in emotion.

Altogether, the salient features of structure point no more conclusively to the supremacy of either thought or technique alone than do the other formal elements that we have considered.

IMAGERY AND SYMBOLS

Eliot's poetry rarely tells us directly what the poet thinks or feels. It relies to an unusually great extent on images and symbols.

The precision of many of the images gives clearness of outline and a formal, objective beauty independent of the intrinsic importance of the objects:

> The showers beat
> On broken blinds and chimney-pots,
> And at the corner of the street
> A lonely cab-horse steams and stamps.
>
> (*Preludes*, I)

The complementary *im*precision of much of the imagery cannot be said to have the same formal value. The charm of the indefinite in art lies rather in its spiritual effect; or, as Poe said, 'I *know* that indefiniteness is an element of the true music [of poetry]—I mean of the true musical expression . . . a suggestive indefiniteness of vague and therefore spiritual *effect*.' This suggestive indefiniteness I think we may find in the *Landscapes*, especially if we compare them with the *Preludes*:

> Children's voices in the orchard
> Between the blossom- and the fruit-time:
> Golden head, crimson head,
> Between the green tip and the root.

A landscape scene, with its soft contours, is better suited to convey an effect of indefiniteness than the townscape with its more geometrical patterns. But when the poet twice in four lines uses a 'between' as he does here, it means that he is purposely making his descriptions oblique.

In one way the indefiniteness of poetic language corresponds more closely to real thought than does a logically developed argument. As a psychic event, a real thought (a) generally moves on to several new positions (b, c, d) simultaneously, and keeps up inter-relations between them, then perhaps moving a step further to a final main conclusion (e). An argument, however, generally has to be set forth one step at a time, so that many connections are lost. A simple diagram will illustrate my meaning.

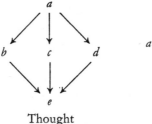

$$a \rightarrow b \rightarrow c \rightarrow d \rightarrow e$$

Rational argument

Thought

In *After Strange Gods* Eliot declares that 'in one's prose reflexions one may be legitimately occupied with ideals, whereas in the writing of verse one can only deal with actuality'. Poetry is the language of actual thought, or actual ideas. Its actuality is not merely contingent, and does not merely lie in its faithfulness to an external subject-matter: it resides far more in its faithfulness to the movements of the mind and spirit of the poet. And this is manifested in the poetic use of imagery. For actual thought also tends to move in images. 'On pense au moyen d'images,' said de Gourmont.

If we are to believe Eliot's words in *The Use of Poetry* he does not know quite why certain impressions assume a symbolical value. He has not arbitrarily chosen from his past life those memories which have been most violently dramatic and decided to turn them into symbols. The impressions have lent themselves unsolicited to symbolical interpretation, just as images may be discovered by chance to serve as 'objective correlatives'. The scene of the six ruffians in a French tavern has been put bodily into

Journey of the Magi because the poet felt that it might disclose something about reality not only to himself but objectively to others. It indicated a secret meaning of general importance. And indeed in the context of the poem the scene suggests the indifference of humanity at large to the great events which do not immediately concern them, while the dicing for pieces of silver inevitably puts us in mind of Judas, of the soldiers at the Crucifixion, and of the treachery that is already waiting for the infant Christ. Thus we are prepared for the idea of the coincidence of Birth and Death, which is part of the paradoxical and mystical import of the poem.

Dante, says Eliot, had experiences which seemed to him 'important in themselves; and therefore they seemed to him to have some philosophical and impersonal value.'[1] In the same way we may recognise the philosophical value of the personal experiences in which Eliot found a higher significance.

Eliot's symbols are sometimes ancient ones, well known to anthropology as well as to depth psychology, such as hair, sea, rain, fish and fire. Sometimes they are such as modern *Traumdeutung* has given a new or added significance to (the eye for the father-complex, drowning alternatively for the herd instinct or coition, etc.). The main symbols of *Journey of the Magi* are traditional—running water, crosses, vine-leaves, pieces of silver. They indicate a definite conception of man and a definite interpretation of history into which all men and events readily fit themselves. In contrast to these symbols the early poetry gives evidence of what Stephen Spender calls 'the crisis of symbols'[2] experienced by modern poets: the lack of a universal language of signs to express 'unreason' and anguish. But Eliot has managed to create his own private signs and to give them a general validity by resting the symbolism of his later poetry on the imagery of his earlier work. In many cases it looks as if a private memory becomes symbolical by the mere fact of being incorporated in the poetry. But it must be remembered that once a poet has used an image in a poem, it will open itself up to him in its context, and he will be able to use it again with added significance.

As one studies Eliot's images one seems to recognise a number of basic scenes which in elaborated and differentiated forms

[1] 'Dante', *SE*, p. 273.
[2] Spender, 'The Crisis of Symbols', *Penguin New Writing*, No. 19.

constitute much of his vision. There are the sea mist, the pines and thrushes of Cape Ann; things thrown up by the sea; a drowned body; an orchard and children climbing the trees in summer sunshine; an arbour, flowers and a girl in a shower of April rain; London fog and filth; and the repeated experience of lying half awake towards morning. Warfare has added little of direct imagery, but may be responsible for ideas and states of feeling, and probably for the ubiquity of death images (bones) and for the frequent images of corruption and destruction (rats, fire).

The images are used at first in a comparatively naturalistic way. As time goes on there is some shuffling and constant new assignments and differentiation. By the time he wrote the *Four Quartets*, the poet had developed almost a complete code of symbols with which one has to have some familiarity in order to understand and appreciate these poems. It makes understanding more difficult to begin with, but it enables the poet to operate very freely, exploring spiritual life by means of the evocative symbols he has evolved. It is all to the good that many of them are personal and elicit personal responses from us, for this makes them fields of force, of attraction and repulsion, which, combining both an emotional and an intellectual content, make it possible to throw an integral light forward in the direction of ultimate truths. Relevant thoughts are attracted and arranged in a pattern which the intellect alone would hardly have been able to produce. And by grouping symbols the poet achieves an effect similar to that of connecting electric batteries in series to increase the current. All this at least gives poetic satisfaction. Whether it comes anywhere near sounding the deeps of spiritual reality or whether it is just a reaching for the impossible and illimitable is a question which for the time being must be left unanswered.

When an image becomes a symbol it is simplified and reduced to bare outlines. Details and appurtenances of the particular object or event are shorn away, and usually only something that resembles a geometrical figure remains, as in heraldic beasts and plants. This again means that the formal element becomes all the more prominent. A symbol, one might say, is a point at which pure form and concentrated meaning strive to come to terms. So that the more the poet relies on symbolism, the more formal as well as meaningful does his expression become. Eliot's rose garden is nothing like the rambling area that surrounds an English cottage, but 'The single Rose / Is now the Garden'. Thus Dante's supreme vision of the blessed was of one vast white rose, whose petals they formed. The pattern is simple and very formal, but it is replete with meaning. In fact there is hardly a symbol more loaded with meaning than that of the rose. In it there is the transition from eroticism to piety, from the *Roman de la Rose* to the *Paradiso*. There is the idea of an ordered gathering around a still centre. If one cares to meditate on the symbol, its connotations and associations could be multiplied almost indefinitely. But always, the more stylised the symbol, the richer its potential meaning. The more symbolic the poetry, the more abundant its communication.

It is now relatively simple to sum up the results of this technical analysis. In texture, rhyme and rhythm, in structure and in the use of images and symbols, Eliot constantly keeps his balance between the abandonment to formal expertness and the devotion to thought for its own sake. What is more, he has found means of intensifying both form and content simultaneously, so that their fusion in his poetry approaches identification of one with the other. His later poetry employs a mystique of form which assumes that formal pattern may be used as a road to absolute knowledge. But even in his early poetry he is very careful to make his technical devices serve his vision and his moods, and to organise his ideas in appropriate patterns of sound and rhythm. Edith Sitwell thinks that 'a new reign in poetry' began with the publication of *Prufrock and Other Observations* in 1917:

> The power of English poetry had been much weakened by such poets as Matthew Arnold and Dr. Bridges, who were interested equally in matter and in manner, but who had not regarded these as an indivisible entity, treating them, instead, as railway lines, running side by side for a considerable time, but bearing a different set of trains bound for different junctions . . .
> With Mr. Eliot, we were restored to a living world in poetry.[1]

Now it might be said that the integration of form and matter is in a sense a denial of both, for they both claim complete sovereignty for themselves. Their integration is a compromise, and one which changes their very nature. Matter in the ordinary course of things is essentially loyal to what we call truth and reality, and

[1] E. Sitwell, *Aspects of Modern Poetry* (1934), pp. 99–100.

now it cannot remain so. And form is defined by its loyalty to its parents space and time, and now that loyalty is questioned. It is a common experience, however, that the more one attends to questions of style, the more frequently and easily does one produce a happy union between formal and conceptual elements. Ideally one may imagine a type of speech in which *what* one wishes to say can always be said in the *way* one wishes to say it, which generally means with the maximum of power and beauty. The English language is so rich in possibilities of expression that somewhere in its recesses one may always expect to find *the* word, *the* phrase, *the* sentence which exactly renders the meaning one wishes to communicate and at the same time gives the greatest aesthetic satisfaction. It only has to be searched for perseveringly enough. And integration is obtainable by talent and hard work. There is no 'open Sesame', and there are no special intrinsic facilities for the poet. The integration of form and matter is not regulated by a general principle, but has to be found in each detail of speech. Poets, it must be supposed, are exceptionally sensitive both to what they wish to say and to the nuances of language, and so have a special advantage in their search for *le mot juste*. But to them as to others, by accident or after protracted toil, the happy expression must come as a discovery. And if they persevere, it will set its stamp on their entire production.

As the ideal measure of what the poet can achieve in the way of integrating sense and form stands the perfect symbol, the meeting-ground, as we saw, of the fullest meaning with the most formalised expression. But of course the poet may wish to particularise his meaning more than the symbol allows him to do; in which case he will find the hardest, driest, narrowest word that suits his purpose; and that also will be a happy discovery.

Symbolism may be said to be the link between Eliot's art and his life, or rather the channel by which his beliefs flowed into his poetry and his poetry into his beliefs. 'The true claim of Baudelaire as an artist,' he says, 'is not that he found a superficial form, but that he was searching for a form of life.'[1] Eliot, too, has been searching for a form of life, and for a form of poetry, and it has all been one effort. He is an integral poet.

In calling him an integral poet, I do not mean that he has performed miracles in fusing sense and sound. But I mean that he

---

[1] 'Baudelaire', *SE*, p. 386.

has balanced the various elements of his poetry better than most writers do. To a great extent he is content with compensating for particularly formal, 'poetical' words, lines and sections of his poems by means of alternating 'prosy' parts. Deliberate parody would scarcely provide a clearer example than the stanzas of the second section of *East Coker*. But he celebrates his greatest triumphs in the memorable expressions which in themselves fuse the perfection both of matter and manner. They are everywhere in his poetry, and they also occur in his prose. He naturally believes in hard work, for such things cannot be achieved merely by talent.

It is one thing to find the best expression for what one has to say. It is quite a different thing to pretend that what one has said is what one originally meant. When an idea has been put into poetry, it appeals to the belief of the poet as well as to that of the reader. Obviously Eliot, as he says himself, has written many lines simply because they sounded well. But I cannot see that any of the important ideas in his poetry owe anything to this kind of composition.

Because what he says has meaning to him, he means what he says. But it is tempting to a reader to exaggerate the importance of ideas and attitudes; the most purely formal elements (texture, rhyme, rhythm) are so unobtrusive and the satire or the devotion seems so obvious. Besides, the formal qualities which caused surprise when the poems were first published have become more customary now, and are often taken for granted. Poets may 'find it expedient to occupy their conscious mind with the craftsman's problems, leaving the deeper meaning to emerge, if there, from a lower level'. But the ideas which emerge from a lower level, and with which the poet need not consciously concern himself, may seem all the more important to the reader *qua* ideas because they come to him clothed in poetic form. What the poet gives unconsciously the reader must receive consciously. That is why the poet may appear to be an 'irresponsible propagandist', to use Montgomery Belgion's term. But a little training in the appreciation of poetic form will help most readers to strike a right balance. It may also help one to estimate the importance of Eliot's formal work if one remembers that in the beginning his task was largely negative, consisting in a reaction against conventional manners which did not leave him his full opportunities to develop his style.

All this may not seem very sensational, but it is important to establish Eliot's intimate fusion of matter and manner, both in order to appreciate the power of poetic belief which his poems command and to approach the philosophical implications of the poems with a better understanding of why certain ideas are preferred to others and with due recognition of the importance of the poet's beliefs in the total communication provided by the poetry.

VI

APPEARANCE

'ALL art originates in an act of intuition, or vision,' says Sir Herbert Read; and as a general statement this is probably right. I shall here take 'vision' to comprise both the ways in which things impinge upon the poet's senses and the way in which he subsequently arranges the impressions in his mind. I shall also take it to include the emotive colouring in which he comes to see the phenomena involved in his experience; in other words his moods.

In Eliot's poetry, vision begins definitely with sense perception but seems to expand at once into mental images. The best word for it is probably 'awareness' or the adjective 'aware', both of which are used quite prominently in his poems: 'I am aware of the damp souls of housemaids', 'I was aware of becoming involved in her laughter', 'the awareness / Of things ill done', etc. We also find the words used significantly in Eliot's prose: 'the conscious present is an awareness of the past', 'in our awareness of the image we must be aware that the meaning is there too', etc. To Eliot awareness is a mode of perception, related to intuition, and distinct from sharp consciousness or plain knowledge. Awareness begins with a strong impression, usually of the senses, and it translates itself immediately into a state of consciousness which absorbs all the activities of the mind in the moment's concentration on an object. From the awareness of individual phenomena he fashions images and ideas, so that imagination is never far from experience. Especially in his early poetry there is a strong element of impressionism which is well served by this kind of awareness. One feels that Eliot sees objects as they appear to the naked mind, and this feeling is emphasised by the fact that many of his poems, or parts of them, are mental soliloquies.

Naturally both perception and mood have some connection with the poet's general view of life and his philosophical leanings. Eliot speaks of the transmutation of feeling into thought or vice versa, and he seems to have once regarded philosophy as being a transcendent phase of perception. 'Our philosophy should spring from our point of view,' says his Eeldrop persona.[1] To us it may be more natural to see his vision as guided by his philosophy. But in any case we cannot ignore the close connection between 'awareness' and thought.

PERCEPTION—THE 'LUNAR SYNTHESIS'

'The natural wakeful life of our Ego is a perceiving.' This line from Husserl quoted by the poet in 'Triumphal March' may serve to indicate the importance which, at the outset of his career, Eliot attached to the sense perceptions. Like Webster and Donne of his *Whispers of Immortality*, he found 'no substitute for sense, / To seize and clutch and penetrate.' He was supported in his view by all the philosophers who, as opposed to Platonists and others, have stressed the reliability of our direct impressions of the outer world. Thus Lucretius believed that the senses cannot be deceived, whereas the inferences that we draw from sensation are often wrong. But above all Aristotle would tend to turn the interest of his disciples to the sense perceptions.

According to Aristotle, the powers which characterise the human soul are those of self-nutrition, sensation, thinking and motivity. Sensation in turn comprises sight, hearing, smell, taste and touch, and it is only by means of those five senses, says Aristotle, that the outer world, including other persons, can be apprehended by us at all. If we bear this in mind, an added force will be given to these lines from *Gerontion*:

> I have lost my sight, smell, hearing, taste and touch:
> How should I use them for your closer contact?

This is an emphatic way of saying that Gerontion has lost all possibility of communication with anything or anybody outside his own mind.

[1] 'Eeldrop and Appleplex', *Little Review*, May 1917.

Perception—the 'lunar synthesis'

To Aristotle, as to Lucretius, the perception of the objects of sense is free from error, while thinking may be erroneous. He finds nothing in existence that is not inherent in sensible spatial magnitudes, and asserts that the objects of thought are in the sensible forms. By a 'sense' he means 'what has the power of receiving into itself the sensible forms of things without the matter'; in other words, the actuality of things exists in sensation, so that the senses receive not only a pale reflection of reality but reality itself. And conversely, mind, in so far as it is knowledge, only becomes actual in sensation, for knowledge is identical with its object.[1]

The mind in Aristotle's philosophy is the power of thinking, and only man is endowed with it. Thus there is a distinction between soul and mind as between the more and the less comprehensive (a distinction which may possibly be alluded to in Eliot's use of the terms soul and mind in *La Figlia Che Piange*). The mind, unlike the senses, can be in error. And unlike the soul it is conceivable apart from the body which it inhabits. So Eliot strives in his poetry not only to feed thought (mind) from the senses but also to experience reality with the fullness of the soul.

If we disregard the distinction between mind and soul, it may be said that both are activity, being nothing in themselves. They are the turning of potentiality into actuality (cp. 'Between the potency / And the existence' in *The Hollow Men*). For Aristotle, Eliot wrote in 1916,

> Soul is to body as cutting is to the axe: realizing itself in its actions, and not completely real when abstracted from what it does . . . reality is here and now; and the true nature of mind is found in the activity which it exercises. Attempt to analyze the mind, as a thing, and it is nothing. It is an operation . . . It is only then that we perceive what mind is, and in retrospect find that it was present in the simplest sensation.[2]

A poet trained in Aristotle's philosophy might confidently announce, as Eliot did, that poetry is legitimately concerned with actuality and criticism with principles. Such a poet might also try to find a revelation of the essential, that is of reality, in the particular and fortuitous. Thus the two observers of life in 'Eeldrop and Appleplex' watch from their window for the exceptional here

[1] Cf. esp. *De Anima*, III, 3, 5, 8; II, 12.
[2] 'The Development of Leibniz's Monadism', *Monist*, Oct. 1916, p. 554.

and now when life actually sallies into their silent street, and when people reveal themselves as individuals. Remembering an 'oppressively gross and vulgar' Spaniard observed in a restaurant, a man who seemed to belong to a common enough type, but who suddenly leaned forward with an unexpected remark, Eeldrop feels there was a moment of revelation:

> we were able to detach him from his classification and regard him for a moment as an unique being, a soul, however insignificant, with a history of its own, once for all. It is these moments which we prize, and which alone are revealing. For any vital truth is incapable of being applied to another case: the essential is unique. Perhaps that is why it is so neglected: because it is useless.[1]

There is not a little of Bergson as well as of Aristotle in this attitude to reality. Eliot may have repudiated and even ridiculed Bergson after his first phase of enthusiasm had passed, but the fact remains that Bergson's philosophy is reflected in his work, even in his later poetry, to a much greater extent than one might suppose. In the first part of 'Eeldrop and Appleplex' the two interlocutors end up by discussing what philosophical labels they ought to wear. Appleplex mentions Bergson and is cut short by Eeldrop, who says that 'a philosophy about intuition is somewhat less likely to be intuitive than any other'. Eeldrop refuses to adopt such labels as 'individualists' and 'anti-intellectualists' and is content to be known by his occupation 'in private life' as a bank-clerk, and by his possession of a wife, three children and a suburban vegetable garden. Eeldrop obviously disclaims Bergson because Bergson is the philosopher who most naturally comes to mind. The surest indication of his Bergsonism in spite of his disclaimer is his wish to be known by his most concrete and individual attributes: his job, his family, his Sunday gardening. For to Bergson abstractions and generalisations are suspect and only what is individual and heterogeneous is real. Bergson insists on the uniqueness of all experiences and of all living beings and asserts that nothing ever repeats itself. Laws and classifications are mechanical—useful up to a point, but having no life in them and never entirely reliable:

> Or, notre conception de la durée ne tend à rien moins qu'à affirmer l'hétérogénéité radicale des faits psychologiques profonds,

---

[1] *The Little Review*, May 1917, pp. 8-9.

et l'impossibilité pour deux d'entre eux de se ressembler tout à fait, puisqu'ils constituent deux moments différents d'une histoire.[1]

Comme la connaissance usuelle, la science ne retient des choses que l'aspect *répétition*. . . . Ce qu'il y a d'irréductible et d'irréversible dans les moments successifs d'une histoire lui échappe.[2]

It is in the spirit of such ideas that Eeldrop and Appleplex conduct their observations. And it is largely in the spirit of such ideas that Eliot wrote his early descriptive poems and portraits, both the serious and the more facetious ones. It was not the general truth that he was after, but the vital truth. And perhaps that is why he studied individual persons and particular phenomena, the exceptional in the setting of the ordinary, a Prufrock, a Sweeney 'among the nightingales'—as if his spotlight on them would bring out their secret springs of life. He may have looked for the typical, as we shall see. He may even have approached the mythical and he certainly attempted the symbolic. But he never quite relinquished the idea, basically that of Imagism too, that the fleeting instant, the particular detail, the precise expression were the things that mattered. The bitten macaroon by which the poet remembers 'Professor and Mrs. Cheetah' is in this respect as Bergsonian as the lonely cabhorse steaming in the rain at the corner of the street.

A further support for Eliot's belief in uniqueness may have presented itself in T. E. Hulme's 'theory of discontinuity'.[3] But more important, no doubt, was the teaching of Santayana, who in turn owed a great deal to William James. In James, Santayana admired a peculiar 'sense of the immediate', of 'the unadulterated, unexplained, instant fact of experience'. The following passage from Santayana might almost have been a commentary on the poems of Eliot's younger days:

Actual experience, for William James, however varied or rich its assault might be, was always and altogether of the nature of a sensation: it possessed a vital, leaping, globular unity which made the only fact, the flying fact, of our being. Whatever continuities of quality might be traced in it, its existence was always momentary and self-warranted. A man's life or soul borrowed its reality and

---

[1] Bergson, *Essai sur les données immédiates de la conscience*, Geneva, Éditions Albert Skira, 1945, p. 155.

[2] Bergson, *L'Évolution créatrice*, 1907, pp. 31-2.

[3] Cf. 'The *Pensées* of Pascal', *EAM*, p. 158.

imputed wholeness from the intrinsic actuality of its successive parts; existence was a perpetual re-birth, a travelling light to which the past was lost and the future uncertain. The element of indetermination which James felt so strongly in this flood of existence was precisely the pulse of fresh unpredictable sensation, summoning attention hither and thither to unexpected facts. Apprehension in him being impressionistic—that was the age of impressionism in painting too—and marvellously free from intellectual assumptions or presumptions, he felt intensely the fact of contingency, or the contingency of fact. This seemed to me not merely a peculiarity of temperament in him, but a profound insight into existence, in its inmost irrational essence. Existence, I learned to see, is intrinsically dispersed, seated in its distributed moments, and arbitrary not only as a whole, but in the character and place of each of its parts.[1]

The lack of belief in an absolute spiritual reality also links the first phase of Eliot's poetry very closely with the first phase of knowledge as described in F. H. Bradley's main philosophical work, *Appearance and Reality*. In the poems the experience of life is fragmentary and inconsistent, and imperfection is painfully apparent. Evil and error, on comparison with any ideal, immediately jump into prominence. All this means that actuality, the sensuous universe, has in Eliot's view precisely those properties which Bradley attributes to the unreal. The universe is just appearance.

The self is no more integrated than anything else. What is commonly regarded as a criterion of the self, the memory, dissolves on a close scrutiny. In Bradley's words: 'Memory is plainly a construction from the ground of the present. It is throughout inferential, and is certainly fallible.'[2] In Eliot's words:

> Dissolve the floors of memory
> And all its clear relations,
> Its divisions and precisions,
>
> .　　.　　.　　.
>
> And through the spaces of the dark
> Midnight shakes the memory
> As a madman shakes a dead geranium.[3]

The petals of the dead geranium are scattered far and wide, and the bunched images of the memory cling no closer. It is of little

---

[1] 'A Brief History of My Opinions', *The Philosophy of Santayana*, pp. 14-15.
[2] *Appearance and Reality*, p. 257.　　　　[3] *Rhapsody on a Windy Night*.

avail for the young man in *Portrait of a Lady* to assure himself that
he is self-possessed. His mind is not his own. He recalls 'things
that other people have desired'. And he is trapped by the question
as to whether his ideas are right or wrong.

'What is this essence of the self which never is altered?' asks
Bradley. 'Infancy and old age, disease and madness, bring new
features, while others are borne away.'[1] Change—in time, space or
circumstances—alters the identity and proves the unreality of
whatever is subject to it, whether ideas, persons or objects.[2] A
similar thought persists in Eliot's poetry. To quote from a late
poem, *The Dry Salvages*:

> 'Fare forward, you who think that you are voyaging;
> You are not those who saw the harbour
> Receding, or those who will disembark.'

Bradley was led to deny the reality of the soul, and Eliot
followed him until his conversion to Christian belief. He depicts
us as automatic creatures. 'I could see nothing behind that child's
eye,' says the speaker of *Rhapsody on a Windy Night*. And 'Gerontion' has a vision of

> . . . De Bailhache, Fresca, Mrs Cammel, whirled
> Beyond the circuit of the shuddering Bear
> In fractured atoms.

The fourth *Prelude* suggests a diffuse collective consciousness
rather than a soul:

> His soul stretched tight across the skies
> That fade behind a city block,
> Or trampled by insistent feet
> At four and five and six o'clock;

And the part played by Tiresias in *The Waste Land* might suggest
a kind of over-soul. But no individual has a soul to call his
own.

In 'Tradition and the Individual Talent' Eliot explicitly mini-
mises the importance of the individual personality. 'The point of
view which I am struggling to attack,' he says, 'is perhaps related
to the metaphysical theory of the substantial unity of the soul: for

---

[1] *Appearance and Reality*, p. 80.
[2] Cf. *Appearance and Reality*, p. 45, and *The Principles of Logic* (2nd edn.
1922), p. 143.

my meaning is, that the poet has, not a "personality" to express, but a particular medium, which is only a medium and not a personality, in which impressions and experiences combine in peculiar and unexpected ways.' The epigraph which he chose for this essay is a quotation from Aristotle, meaning 'mind is, no doubt, something more divine and impassible', *scilicet* than the personality. Eliot, however, was thinking of 'the mind of Europe'. The personal and individual mind was of little consequence.

Eliot's metaphysical scepticism in this phase of his life led him to reject philosophical theories that were too abstract. In the second of his essays for the *Monist* in 1916 he denied even Bradley's idealism, especially his theory of 'finite centres'. 'Just as Leibniz's pluralism is ultimately based upon faith,' he declared,

> so Bradley's universe, actual only in finite centers, is only by an act of faith unified. Upon inspection, it falls away into the isolated finite experiences out of which it is put together. Like monads they aim at being one; each expanded to completion, to the full reality latent within it, would be identical with the whole universe. But in so doing it would lose the actuality, the here and now, which is essential to the small reality which it actually achieves. The Absolute responds only to an imaginary demand of thought, and satisfies only an imaginary demand of feeling. Pretending to be something which makes finite centers cohere, it turns out to be merely the assertion that they do. And this assertion is only true so far as we here and now find it to be so.[1]

'Here and now' seem to be key words. We shall find them again in quite different contexts, as we shall find Bradley again in a different interpretation. But for the present it is important to recognise that there is a considered and coherent attitude behind Eliot's scepticism as behind his imagism. He believed that reality was only in the here and now and that only the unique was essential.

One feels that his vision of unrelatedness must have something to do with a general view of life which has refused to submit to Absolute Idealism or any other integrating philosophy. One is reminded of 'the weeping philosopher' Heraclitus, whose belief in flux and change evidently found a strong echo in Eliot's mind. Very likely, too, the Epicurean atomism of Lucretius lent support

[1] *Monist*, Oct. 1916, p. 571.

to Eliot's perception of an un-unified universe. He constantly re-verts to *De Rerum Natura* in his criticism. In the philosophy of Epicurus and Lucretius, the particles of matter which compose the universe are combined only by accident and disintegrate again readily to form new bodies. Even the soul is merely made up of solid atoms and void, in which transient images and notions are formed by repeated impressions. This is not very different from Eliot's view of the soul in his third *Prelude*, where he speaks of 'The thousand sordid images / Of which your soul was consti-tuted'; or the very Lucretian fourth *Prelude*, in which the worlds are described as revolving 'like ancient women / Gathering fuel in vacant lots'. The same conception of the soul and rendering of mental processes recurs in nearly all the non-Christian poems.

A certain solipsism would naturally accompany an atomistic philosophy. If the soul consists of combinations of material par-ticles, it can have no real communication with other souls, and if its particles are combined in accidental groups, souls cannot be essentially but only superficially alike in organisation. Thus the mind which experiences is to itself the only actual universe. And this perhaps helps to explain why, from *The Love Song* to *Ash-Wednesday*, the people and objects that we meet are really sub-jective, 'Tenants of the house, / Thoughts of a dry brain in a dry season'. Most of Eliot's poems are in the first person and spoken as monologues. And the speakers feel turned-in upon themselves.

> We think of the key, each in his prison
> Thinking of the key, each confirms a prison

These lines from *The Waste Land* are also related, in Eliot's own note, to Bradley's philosophy. The poet quotes from *Appearance and Reality*:

> My external sensations are no less private to myself than are my thoughts or my feelings. In either case my experience falls within my own circle, a circle closed on the outside; and, with all its ele-ments alike, every sphere is opaque to the others which surround it. . . . In brief, regarded as an existence which appears in a soul, the whole world for each is peculiar and private to that soul.

An atomistic philosophy would be a very good starting-point for a revolutionary young poet intent on breaking up the com-placencies and conventions and all too coherent views of life of his predecessors; and a useful platform for a poet experimenting with his technique and desirous of using his subject-matter freely. A view of life which decomposed that subject-matter into immediate facts of experience would enable him to bring objects and ideas together at the dictate of his formal needs and not according to the relatedness of the objects and ideas among themselves.

The trouble was that though a sceptical and atomistic philosophy might be interesting for a time, it could not in the long run satisfy the constructive poet, and hardly the man, unless he were content to make of scepticism itself a belief. 'The natural wakeful life of our Ego is a perceiving'—but what is the use of perceiving if what we perceive is invariably superficial, the perception of a crowd waiting with its stools and sausages, aware of '5,800,000 rifles and carbines, 102,000 machine guns' but quite unaware of what is 'hidden under the dove's wing'?

The weakness of a philosophy which is interested only in the unique event is that the reality which it tries to establish may not amount to very much. In the passage on William James quoted from Santayana, a certain uneasiness is betrayed in the final sentence, where existence is considered as 'arbitrary not only as a whole, but in the character and place of each of its parts'. Eliot, too, must have had a sense of arbitrariness as long as he clung to his isolated facts. And possibly there was something lacking in his conviction that only the unique was real or that the individual was the only valuable unit. Even Aristotle had not made up his mind completely on this latter point as it seemed to Eliot.[1] In Eliot's poetry the spotlight singled out the individual and the X-rays 'threw the nerves in patterns on a screen', but they obstinately refused to reveal more than hollow men. So to a great extent his perception was merely of the individual and unrelated and fragmentary fact; which enabled him to become an admirable imagist, and admirably to follow Hulme's precept 'to prove that beauty may be in small, dry things', as well as Poe's recommendation to write short, static poems; but which held his vision within relatively narrow confines.

In his early poetry he writes of the 'smell of steaks in passageways', of 'broken blinds and chimney-pots' and so on, and no effort to force these things to join together can deprive us of the impression that we have to do with odds and ends in a vast

[1] Cf. *Monist*, Oct. 1916, p. 544.

jumble of particularities. They do make up a 'picture', and this picture of reality may be coherent, but the reality is itself incoherent. And frequently the picture too, or the scene, is given only in flashes and glimpses. *The Love Song*, though narrative in a way, proceeds fitfully, with numerous digressions from the 'story' if not from the main nebula of vision. In *Rhapsody on a Windy Night* the glimpses of a concrete night scene are almost submerged in the roaming thoughts and memories of the protagonist. Here, if anywhere, immediate perception may be said to be ideal as well as sensory, but it is none the less fragmentary. The senses are all at work, bringing in impressions of sight and hearing, of taste, smell and touch. But though the poet may be aware of several kinds of sensation at once, there is no principle other than his awareness to unite them; and they can be readily analysed into their component parts.

Eliot thinks that 'perhaps one reason why Donne has appealed so powerfully to the recent time is that there is in his poetry hardly any attempt at organization; rather a puzzled and humorous shuffling of the pieces; and we are inclined to read our own more conscious awareness of the apparent irrelevance and unrelatedness of things into the mind of Donne'.[1] The sense of the irrelevance and unrelatedness of things is not undisputed in Eliot's early poetry, but it is certainly very powerful up to, and including, *Coriolan*.

'These fragments I have shored against my ruins,' says the 'I' of *The Waste Land*. In some of his moments of intense awareness Eliot must have seen life as the broken fragments of what might have been originally a harmonious whole, but which it was impossible now to piece together. And only fragments of various philosophies jostled each other in his mind, as, at the end of *The Waste Land*, do the Catholic philosophy of Dante, the eroticism of *Pervigilium Veneris*, the hopelessness of Gerard de Nerval's *El Desdichado*, the mysticism of the Vedanta.

The French Symbolists believed in the inter-relatedness of things. And it is quite apparent in Eliot's poetry that, in spite of his atomistic view of life, he searched for connectedness as well, for that fusion of disparate elements which would really make them one. His perception of immediate facts co-existed with a reaction against their fragmentariness, which made him join

[1] 'Donne in Our Time', *A Garland for John Donne*, p. 8.

impressions as it were by force, perhaps in an effort to find a hidden significance in them.

It is characteristic that metaphors, in which disparate elements are seen as identical, are much more common in Eliot's poetry than similes. He excels in metaphors of a daring and delightfully surprising kind, such as: 'all the works and days of hands / That lift and drop a question on your plate', 'His laughter tinkled among the teacups', 'the last fingers of leaf / Clutch and sink'. A 'smile falls heavily among the bric-à-brac', housemaids have 'damp souls'. The images are often extremely successful. And they do give a meaning—but a limited meaning which describes one fragment in terms of another.

Another device by which an effect of identity is often attempted is that of juxtaposition. There is a good example in 'The Fire Sermon', where the typist's gramophone, by the mediation of Ariel's music in *The Tempest*, turns into the fishmen's pleasant mandoline. In *Rhapsody on a Windy Night* the moon, without a transition, becomes a bedraggled prostitute.

Sometimes there seems to be an attempt at interpretation by interpenetration, when the poet renders external objects as subjective impressions and subjective impressions as objective. Thus in *Morning at the Window* there is a 'smile that hovers in the air'. It is the smile of a passer-by, but really it is only the observer's lingering impression of that smile that seems to hover in the air as he moves his glance upwards. As no separate and integral perceiving organ is recognised in Eliot's early belief, the self, or the soul is able to mingle with its environment. In *Hysteria* the man is 'aware of becoming involved in' the woman's laughter 'and being part of it'. And the fourth *Prelude* begins characteristically:

> His soul stretched tight across the skies
> That fade behind a city block,

What happens in these cases is a dissolution of individualities rather than an integration of anything. It may suggest, but it is really different from, the merging of one's self in a monistic Absolute. The boundaries between subjective and objective have been broken down, and there is an illusion of some secret revealed, but no more. The synthesis is a 'lunar synthesis', a trick of the light and of the poet's mood. An image in *Morning at the Window* comes near to finding a real significance. The street is seen as a sea where people are drowned. This is interpretation of life. But on the whole the effort to find a hidden meaning in or behind the freakish phenomena of life results in little more than a pretence that the meaning is there. When, for instance, in the third *Prelude*, the experiences of a city dawn are gathered in the lines 'You had such a vision of the street / As the street hardly understands', this remains no more than an assertion to the reader, though the word 'vision' may stand for a remembered moment of exaltation or illumination to the poet himself.

Now the facts of existence, as observed by the phenomenologists, have no ulterior significance. And unique, vital truth as it appears to an individualist or an empiricist is gratuitous and essentially useless: Eliot says so himself in 'Eeldrop and Appleplex'. On the other hand, a phenomenologist like Alexius Meinong particularly emphasises the fact that we do perceive things in their relations, and not only as isolated objects—'dass mit zwei Vorstellungen auch deren Relationen zu einander gegeben sind'[1]— and Eliot argued this point in his doctoral dissertation on Meinong and Bradley.

Eliot was not content with Aristotle's relatively primitive conception of reality. In his dissertation he recognises that knowledge and its objects are one in immediate experience, but not that immediate experience is simply the unqualified sense perceptions. What we experience immediately is not just objects, but relations, and the wholeness of a sentient experience is not just a sum of various sensations. Much that we generally call ideal has immediate reality.[2] And so perception and knowledge mean a complicated awareness of both particularity and relationships, in sensations, emotions and thoughts. I think perhaps we may find these ideas reflected in Eliot's poetry in the constant attempt to find an organisation in complex experiences.

Where no other meaning is apparent, the relations found in sense perceptions can be taken to indicate at least a principle of order. There are the beginnings of integration in them. So Eliot extracted as much poetry as he could from 'pure observation' but

[1] Meinong, *Abhandlungen zur Erkenntnistheorie u. Gegenstandstheorie* (1913), I, p. 46. Cf. also II, p. 388. Bradley has a similar view, but speaks of wholeness instead of relations, 'relations' to Bradley being mere appearance; they disintegrate experience.

[2] See R. W. Church, 'Eliot on Bradley's Metaphysic', *Harvard Advocate*, Dec. 1938.

he also went on and tried to exploit the relationships that he found or forged between objects and experiences.

There is another way in which Eliot tries to integrate his sensations in his early poetry: by means of the typical.

The feature of Greek philosophy which has had the most telling and enduring influence on Eliot's thought is possibly its concern with the typically human rather than with individual differences.[1] The mind to Aristotle was a type-mind, not a personality. Even Heraclitus emphasised the common reason and frowned on peculiar insights.[2] And the importance of the type was re-affirmed by Bradley. 'From the very first beginnings of intelligence it is the type that operates and not the image,' says Bradley. 'The lower we descend in the growth of our own functions, or in the scale of animate nature, the more typical, the less individual, the less distinct, the more vaguely universal and widely symbolic is the deposit of experience.'[3]

Amid the confusion of fragments and particularities Eliot generally selects for us those experiences which point to something typical, something that we all recognise. And in presenting the particular as the type of a great number of phenomena of the same kind he not only achieves the aim of the satirist, but he also begins to create symbols.

A general vision of urban life is rendered by means of concrete scenes recognised as typical. The conventional drawing-room of polite society, with its interminable tea-drinking—'you have the scene arrange itself'—is glimpsed in *The Love Song, Portrait of a Lady* and *Mr. Apollinax*. The women wandering to and fro 'talking of Michelangelo', make a fitting background to Prufrock, with his desperately conventional appearance:

> For I have known them all already, known them all—
> Have known the evenings, mornings, afternoons,
> I have measured out my life with coffee spoons;
> I know the voices dying with a dying fall
> Beneath the music from a farther room.
> So how should I presume?
>
> And I have known the eyes already, known them all—

---

[1] Cf. *Monist*, Oct. 1916, p. 544.
[2] Cf. the epigraph to *Four Quartets*.
[3] F. H. Bradley, *The Principles of Logic*, p. 37.

And so, amid 'the cups, the marmalade, the tea', Prufrock's individuality founders miserably. Even when a death occurs in another poem (*Aunt Helen*) the undertaker 'was aware that this sort of thing had occurred before'.

Somewhat lower down the social scale life is typified by the 'smell of steaks in passageways', by 'dingy shades / In a thousand furnished rooms', and by the rattling of breakfast plates in basement kitchens. The smells and noises penetrate to the street, of which we are intermittently reminded in *The Love Song* and *Portrait of a Lady*, and which is the actual scene of some of the other poems.

The poet's vision of the street takes in not only its sordidness, but its sameness and unimaginativeness. The streets 'follow like a tedious argument'. There are 'the sunsets and the dooryards and the sprinkled streets', where a street piano 'reiterates some worn-out common song'. The *Preludes*, *Morning at the Window* and *Rhapsody* must be read in their entirety to fill out the picture of the typical street in its various aspects, 'at four and five and six o'clock', morning, afternoon, evening and night. For the better-off citizens outdoor existence is perhaps slightly less grimy, but hardly less trivial:

> —Let us take the air, in a tobacco trance,
> Admire the monuments,
> Discuss the late events,
> Correct our watches by the public clocks.
> Then sit for half an hour and drink our bocks.
> *(Portrait of a Lady)*

These glimpses of urban life chiefly typify a certain phase of civilisation. They outline a view of modern existence whilst retaining their character of direct impressions. They do not, however, reveal a meaningful organisation or oneness in the people, objects and scenes described. Sameness is not unity, and adherence to type does not necessarily imply communication or communion. Eliot's early world, therefore, is none the less a heap of discrete phenomena for displaying the qualities of typicality. Whatever belongs together in this world belongs merely by habitual association.

To record and present his vision Eliot apparently exploited modern mechanistic theories in psychology. I cannot determine to what extent he was influenced by Freud, but certainly without Freud's influence it may be reasonably doubted whether any modern poetry would have been what it is, in technique or in ideas. No doubt the facts which Freud studied existed long before his time. Poets employed dreams and symbols before they were systematically examined, and in recent times the Symbolist school of poetry may even have provided Freud with useful suggestions. The work of William James, especially his theory of associations, probably meant a great deal to Eliot and others before Freud became well-known. But even in Eliot and his contemporaries the method of associations in poetry, the recognition of the subconscious and of the importance of dreams, all derive to some extent from psychoanalysis. Not till the reports of clinical studies of the mind were available did literature receive a real impetus to draw directly upon the subconscious.

It seems obvious that psychoanalysis gave Eliot the material for much of his character-drawing, such as it is. It helped him to 'look into the cerebral cortex, the nervous system, and the digestive tracts'.[1] We need only think of the inhibited Prufrock, the neurotics of *Gerontion*, *The Waste Land* and *Sweeney Agonistes*, and above all, perhaps, of the figures of *The Family Reunion*. Harry complains that 'Of the past you can only see what is past, / Not what is always present. That is what matters.' 'What is always present' is in one of its aspects the subconscious impressions of past events. Mr C. L. Barber sees the Eumenides as 'the *voyeurs* in the typical nightmare of nakedness', and finds the same exhibitionistic motive in the beginning of *Burnt Norton*.[2] Harry at any rate suffers from a guilt-complex[3] which we can trace from one of Eliot's earliest poems in the *Harvard Advocate*, *Nocturne*, in which the hero smiles to see the effect of his mistress's blood on the moonlit ground. The story of the play is a complicated mixture of psychoanalytical patterns, including incest-urge, with, of course, many things besides that cannot be covered by such formulae. In the early poetry, the death-wish, or the disguised wish to return to the womb, is clearly apparent. In the later poetry it is sublimated as religious self-annihilation.

What often constitutes a difficulty to the readers of Eliot's

[1] 'The Metaphysical Poets', *SE*, p. 290.
[2] See Unger's *Selected Critique*, pp. 418, 440.
[3] Compare Rosmer in Ibsen's *Rosmersholm*.

poetry is the fact that the associations are not just those of the fictitious characters of the poems. If Eliot had simply invented a stream of consciousness for Prufrock or Gerontion he might have made all of it psychologically quite plain. But the associations are obviously his own, and sometimes too private to be completely intelligible to the reader. They do, however, admirably support the impression of irrelevance in the things observed; in fact they emphasise it to a degree perhaps not intended by the poet, for all his philosophical scepticism.

It may be remarked in passing that Eliot has denied having any first-hand knowledge of the psychology of Carl Jung. I quote from the 'Statement of the Committee of Fellows of the Library of Congress in American Letters' made on the occasion of the dispute about the award of the Bollingen Prize to Ezra Pound in 1948:

> ... we have Mr Eliot's word that so far from being a disciple of Jung, he has, he believes, never read a word of this writer, and knows his work only by rumor and report. The notion may have arisen through the fact that Miss Elizabeth Drew, in *T. S. Eliot, the Design of His Poetry*, makes use of Jungian concepts and treatments of symbols in her interpretation of Mr Eliot's poems. ... But this can scarcely make Mr Eliot himself a Jungian.[1]

I need only add that Miss Drew's book, apart from the debt to Jung which it may wrongly suggest, is well worth reading for its intrinsically interesting approach to Eliot's symbolism.

MODALITY—DISGUST AND LONELINESS

In Eliot's poetry up to *Sweeney Agonistes* we rarely find conventionally beautiful subject-matter. And only exceptionally is the atmosphere tragic or solemn, at least on the surface. The subjects of the poems are trivial, trite, ugly, ludicrous. And the mood, accordingly, is predominantly one of irony or disgust, more rarely one of serious concern.

In the *Prufrock* collection the irony is often levelled at the 'I' of the poems. But the poet also directs it against his age and the sort of life which surrounds him. In some of the poems, and in most of the 1920 collection, irony turns into a feeling of nausea and

[1] *The Case Against the Saturday Review of Literature*, published by *Poetry*, Chicago, 1949, pp. 5–6.

disgust both with the age and with life in general. The bitter satire of *The Hollow Men* makes this poem one of the gloomiest that Eliot has ever written, while the satire of *Sweeney Agonistes* is facetious, yet with an undertone of solemnity. Despair and bewilderment, even fear, are apparent in many poems, and in some, like *Gerontion*, there is a pronounced note of sadness, disillusionment and nostalgia.

The origins of these dark moods were probably very complex. In part they may have been constitutional, and they were possibly strengthened by experiences of a private character. In poem after poem we find indications of the personal suffering which Eliot thought must be the true subject-matter of poetry. Mr Edmund Wilson hints at the 'dark rankling of passions inhibited'. But Eliot's pessimism was to a large extent assumed deliberately in protest against the facile 'cheerfulness, optimism, and hopefulness'[1] of the nineteenth century which he so much disliked. In contrast to the vapidity of English Romantics and Victorians, he found many of the French writers strangely bracing. Baudelaire's prostitutes and corpses, the spleen of Verlaine and Laforgue, Flaubert's corrosive view of the small bourgeoisie appealed strongly to him, and undoubtedly much of his dismal outlook was caused directly by literary influences.

Plainly Eliot's despondency had very real causes in the outer world as well. It seems certain, at any rate, that his love of tradition and culture was at the root of his despairing view of modern civilisation, just as his avowed affection for London was at the bottom of his gloomy picture of the city in *The Waste Land* and elsewhere. Tradition and culture as Eliot ideally imagined them, as he may have dreamt of them from across the Atlantic, were beauty and order and purposeful living: the 'inexplicable splendour of Ionian white and gold', 'the Rialto', 'the eagles and the trumpets', the 'fishmen' in the heart of the City. Not the beauty of the countryside, the order of the natural universe, the purposeful life of simple rustics. These things meant little to Eliot except as parts of his childhood memories. He wished to find his ideals manifested in human society and in man-made civilisation. But what did he actually see? The Paris of *Bubu de Montparnasse*. A drab London of swarming, aimless existences and joyless activities.

Modern civilisation was a civilisation of dingy streets and sooty

---

[1] *SE*, p. 262.

houses, all alike, enlivened only by a street piano, 'mechanical and tired' (Laforgue's piano, reduced to this); of genteel teas, of 'faint stale smells of beer', of 'restless nights in one-night cheap hotels'. The images of this paltry civilisation are legion. Life is trivial, monotonous and pointless. 'In a thousand furnished rooms' people do exactly the same mechanical things. They walk about in a fog of unknowing, damp of soul, and their smiles vanish aimlessly above the roof-tops.

In the 1920 *Poems* Eliot stresses the ugliness and corruption of our age compared with previous ages. The keynote in these poems is the decay that has occurred. The degenerate race of to-day, the race of modern cities, is represented by such individuals as Bleistein and the phthisic Princess Volupine, Sweeney and his hysterical lady, and *le garçon délabré*. Behind them stand the shadows of Shylock, Nausicaa and Polypheme, *Phlébas le Phénicien*, Hercules, Ariadne, Agamemnon and Napoleon—an altogether more impressive assembly. The heroes of Homer were worth writing poetry about. Eliot feels that he can only ridicule the representatives of modern man, and in fact the poems of the 1920 collection are more grotesque than anything he wrote either before or since. He does not compare his own age merely to the historical past, however. He knows well enough what corruption was seen in Carthage and in the England of Elizabeth. Therefore it is an ideal rather than a real past and ideal heroes rather than real heroes which provide material for his comparisons.

Into this pitiful world came the turmoil of the Great War to increase its likeness to an Inferno. It was not for nothing that the *Prufrock* poems were inscribed to a victim of the War. There are not many references to actual fighting in Eliot's poems—*Gerontion* has some, and *The Waste Land* a few indirect ones—and it does not look as if war itself was regarded as the greatest evil. In fact, in *Gerontion*, the fighting at 'the hot gates' and 'in the warm rain' is felt as a salutary activity contrasted with the decay by which the 'old man' is surrounded. But the decay is associated with the fighting, as were the estaminets of the enemy-occupied towns of Antwerp and Brussels. The civilisation which remained after the Great War was hollowed-out from within, and it was inevitable that the note of disillusion should be strong, especially among town-dwellers. Only speculating industrialists and contractors, smart tradesmen, militarists and amusement-caterers could really like it. On the other hand, as Eliot has pointed out,[1] the post-war period was just as much a period of illusions as of disillusion. Its effete, effeminate, romanticising society was castigated in Benda's *Belphégor*, which Eliot much admired.

Eliot does not see post-war people in quite the same way as for instance Fitzgerald, Hemingway, Huxley and Waugh. There is less individual substance in Eliot's types than in the characters of the novelists. Eliot's characters are phantom-like in their disembodied neuroses, as in the miniature portrait gallery of *Gerontion*. Sometimes we meet the fast, disillusioned members of the lost generation in his poems—Sweeney among the prostitutes or the Lithuanian lady of *The Waste Land*. But there is a dreariness and paltriness about them of which the poet is perfectly aware. Not their private lives only are tainted by it, but the whole of the civilisation to which they belong. The age is one of superstition and deep-seated uneasiness.

There is no need to expatiate on the many excellent reasons for a sensitive person to feel discouraged in this period. In outer facts and concrete events the reasons were plentiful. Eliot's poetry, however, shows not only moods of discouragement, but there is also such a consistent attitude of despondency that we are forced to look for more than contingent reasons. I have already suggested his temperamental make-up and his literary bias. There is also a strong connection between the moods of his poetry and his philosophical ideas. Just as his perceptions were in part directed by his ideas, so his moods were partly governed by them.

In 1933 Eliot wrote in one of his Commentaries: 'It is the use of irony to give the appearance of a philosophy of life, as something final and not instrumental, that leaves us now indifferent.'[2] I see here an acknowledgment of the fact that his ironical mood was once felt to belong to a general philosophy of life.

Apparently Eliot's whole philosophical bent was at one time negative and inverted, as if he despaired of metaphysics and clung to his very despair. If the interests evidenced in his writings are to be trusted, he more or less gave up metaphysics for art about 1917. In 1916 he wrote that no philosophy could make anything either more or less valuable to us than we actually find it to be.[3] He had

[1] *CR*, April 1933, p. 469.
[2] Ibid., April 1933.
[3] *International Journal of Ethics*, 1916, p. 287.

apparently searched the realms of philosophy without finding a permanent foothold, and so he decided that a poet must give himself up to art entirely and cut himself off from everything else. But his liberation was not complete, and he admits as much in *Whispers of Immortality*, which I take to be something more than a literary pastiche. Doubt and uncertainty were at the origin of Eliot's aestheticism. But 'doubt and uncertainty', he tells us, with especial reference to these attitudes in *The Waste Land*, 'are merely a variety of belief'.[1]

He has Christian belief in mind in this context, and it may be that his despair of metaphysics was more particularly a despair of Christianity (though he also seems to have suffered a revulsion from Bradley's idealism). The fourth *Prelude* contains a clear indication of this:

> I am moved by fancies that are curled
> Around these images, and cling:
> The notion of some infinitely gentle
> Infinitely suffering thing.

The 'infinitely gentle / Infinitely suffering thing' suggests both Jesus and the Virgin Mary. It is the objective correlative of an emotion, which is again transmuted from the idea of Christianity. But the whole complex of emotion, idea and symbol is rejected in the three final lines of the poem.

No doubt Eliot's Unitarian scepticism made it hard for him to accept Christianity. His philosophical training would also make it difficult to give adherence to any definite belief. Perhaps such scepticism as that of Heraclitus meant something to him, and perhaps he was struck by the anti-religious fervour of Lucretius.[2] Yet there can be no question, even without his own statement about doubt being a variety of belief, but that he was much occupied with the Christian view of life. His *alter ego*, the bank-clerk Eeldrop in 'Eeldrop and Appleplex' takes an interest in theology, like himself. It may have been primarily an intellectual interest with Eliot. But Christianity is not mainly a philosophical system, and no degree of assent to it or repudiation of it can be exclusively

---

[1] 'A Note on Poetry and Belief.'
[2] There are several echoes of Lucretius' 'nil posse creari de nilo' in his poetry, e.g. 'I can connect / Nothing with nothing' (*The Waste Land*, III).

intellectual. Eliot was uncommonly capable of sensing the emotional value-implications of philosophical and theological theories (a fact which goes far to explain his double role as philosopher and poet). Long before he believed in Christian orthodoxy, he let Eeldrop deplore 'the decline of orthodox theology and its admirable theory of the soul', because owing to this decline 'the unique importance of events has vanished'.

Eliot thinks that 'the intellectual soul' must necessarily experience moments of despair and disillusion in its development. His recognition of Pascal's despair contains a clear confession: this despair is more terrible than Swift's, he says, 'because our heart tells us that it corresponds exactly to the facts and cannot be dismissed as mental disease'.[1]

The despair caused in the early phase by the loss or lack of a philosophy, particularly a Christian philosophy, is manifested in intricate ways in the poems. Much of it is projected into the portrayal of the various characters encountered there. Thus what is felt to be wrong with Sweeney, Bleistein, Mr Eugenides, the 'small house agent's clerk' and their numerous company, is not so much their immorality, or sexual perversion, as the fact that they have no sense of immorality or perversion, lacking knowledge of Good and Evil. This is an idea dear to Eliot, and it has also been exploited by other writers. Eliot finds in Baudelaire a perception of the fact

> that what distinguishes the relations of man and woman from the copulation of beasts is the knowledge of Good and Evil (of *moral* Good and Evil which are not natural Good and Bad or Puritan Right and Wrong). Having an imperfect, vague romantic conception of Good, he was at least able to understand that the sexual act as evil is more dignified, less boring, than as the natural, 'life-giving', cheery automatism of the modern world. For Baudelaire, sexual operation is at least something not analogous to Kruschen Salts.[2]

Eliot's characters lack Baudelaire's awareness, and it is hardly far-fetched to assume that, in a sense, they are an objectification of his irreligious self.

In *Gerontion* disbelief in the Christian faith is a central theme. History, says 'Gerontion',

[1] *EAM*, p. 152.   [2] 'Baudelaire', *SE*, pp. 390–1.

> . . . gives when our attention is distracted
> And what she gives, gives with such supple confusions
> That the giving famishes the craving. Gives too late
> What's not believed in, or if still believed,
> In memory only, reconsidered passion. Gives too soon
> Into weak hands, what's thought can be dispensed with
> Till the refusal propagates a fear . . .

Knowledge and understanding of religion is often given too late —when belief has passed, and it becomes lifeless theological learning. Mr Wolf Mankowitz, commenting on this poem, says that 'The whole of Gerontion's complex inquisition really would seem to constitute an apology for his failure to passionally believe, or having intellectually conceded the required belief, his constitutional inability to accept its corollary in faith.'[1]

'After such knowledge, what forgiveness?' There would seem to be none. Instead, there is punishment, there are 'Rocks, moss, stonecrop, iron, merds'. Here, for the first time, we clearly find the idea of the corruption of civilisation being due to the decay of religion, an idea which is more fully developed in *The Waste Land*.

It is tempting to mention the name of Oswald Spengler in connection with Eliot's early poetry. Eliot's criticism, however, is noticeably silent about Spengler, and it may be doubted whether he had read *Der Untergang des Abendlandes* before its author won international renown by its republication in 1923. This does not prevent the similarities between Eliot's views and those of Spengler from being frequently quite striking. Thus the cultural decline of the West was in Spengler's view associated with the exhaustion of the vital energy of all culture, which is religion. And one of the phenomena of decay was the rootless, barren life of the modern metropolis. The civilisation that Eliot describes might well be the same as 'civilisation' according to Spengler's terminology: a culture that has passed its peak and is doomed to extinction.

One of the deepest needs of human nature is for society and communion, and Eliot, reticent of disposition, must have felt it keenly. But in life such as he found it human intercourse was as inconsequent and confused as almost everything else. Complete communication between mind and mind and complete union

[1] B. Rajan (ed.), *T. S. Eliot*, p. 134.

between heart and heart were impossible. And so the soul's incurable loneliness became one of the main themes of his poetry.

We may imagine, as the lady in the *Portrait* does, that we have friends, and that friendship is real. 'Without these friendships—life, what *cauchemar*'; the further development of the poem is a sufficient commentary on this remark. The woman's effusions are resumed in the second section:

> 'I am always sure that you understand
> My feelings, always sure that you feel,
> Sure that across the gulf you reach your hand.'

But she is sadly mistaken. Whatever others may say, think, or do, and whatever may happen to other people,

> I keep my countenance,
> I remain self-possessed

says the man. And the word 'self-possessed' has an extra weight of meaning: 'I remain shut-off and impregnable', is what it conveys.

Friendship is 'faithless as a smile and shake of the hand',[1] a phrase which has added a great load of bitterness to Laforgue's 'sans foi comme un bonjour'. And at any rate friendship is destroyed by age and death and bloodshed, as so many friendships were brutally destroyed during the Great War. 'I that was near your heart was removed therefrom,' says 'Gerontion'—'I have lost my sight, smell, hearing, taste and touch: / How should I use them for your closer contact?' In *The Love Song* lonely men in shirtsleeves lean symbolically out of the windows of their isolation, smoking meditatively. In *The Waste Land* men herd in crowds, but a crowd is no company: 'each man fixed his eyes before his feet.' The lady of 'A Game of Chess' hysterically demands

> 'What are you thinking of? What thinking? What?
> 'I never know what you are thinking. Think.'

There is no communication, though all are equally miserable:

> In this last of meeting places
> We grope together
> And avoid speech
> Gathered on this beach of the tumid river [2]

---

[1] *La Figlia Che Piange.*   [2] *The Hollow Men*, IV.

Even in *The Family Reunion*, Harry is haunted by a 'sense of separation, / Of isolation unredeemable, irrevocable.' Only Agatha, and those who have learnt what she has learnt, know by what means one may 'try to penetrate the other private worlds / Of make-believe and fear.' In Eliot's early vision it is impossible for human beings to share their deepest feelings with one another. 'Formulated phrases', yes, and talk about Michelangelo, but Prufrock wonders

> . . . how should I begin
> To spit out all the butt-ends of my days and ways?
> And how should I presume?

The need and longing to communicate, to establish contact, is there, but it is frustrated, and therefore can only cause suffering, and the wish to escape still further from the company of men:

> I should have been a pair of ragged claws
> Scuttling across the floors of silent seas.

It is only natural that the relation between man and woman, in which the closest union between human beings is generally thought to be possible, should be used by Eliot to illustrate the theme of loneliness. At one end he depicts the prostitution of sex: Sweeney and his paramours in a number of poems, Grishkin, the typist and other figures of *The Waste Land*. In the latter poem, rape, artificial abortion, homosexuality, impotence, and frigidity are indicated. At the other end there are the inane dialogue and the lack of understanding and sympathy of such poems as *Portrait of a Lady* and *Conversation Galante*. Between them we see such sterile love as that of *Lune de Miel*.

Even true love is doomed to futility. The episodes of *La Figlia*, of the 'hyacinth girl', of *Dans le Restaurant* (where the situation is directly connected with the boyhood love of Dante for Beatrice[1]) are really variants of one episode, which has also lent features to most of the true love relationships in the other poems and the plays. Even the purest affection cannot lead to the consummation of a complete union between two human beings.

Not only are human beings isolated from their fellows, but nature also appears unfeeling and unsympathetic. The evening sky in *The Love Song* is described as 'a patient etherised upon a table'.

[1] Cf. 'Dante', *SE*, p. 273.

And in *Rhapsody on a Windy Night*, 'la lune ne garde aucune rancune', for

> The moon has lost her memory.
> A washed-out smallpox cracks her face,
> Her hand twists a paper rose,
> That smells of dust and eau de Cologne,
> She is alone
> With all the old nocturnal smells
> That cross and cross across her brain.

'She is alone'—the same key-note again. It would be dangerous to stress this point too much in its application to nature, because natural objects are used in these poems mostly to provide supporting imagery, and rarely for their own sake. But what we can safely say is that the poet finds no comfort in nature. There is no impulse from a vernal wood nor any society where none intrudes.

The poet's isolation is still more complete than it often appears to be. For he learned from Laforgue, as we have seen, the trick of a *'dédoublement* of the personality', which enabled him to commune with himself. And some of his poems are dramatic monologues or dialogues in which what sound like answering voices are often mere echoes of the solitary ruminator's spoken thoughts.

The *'dédoublement* of the personality' may be enjoyable. Mr Roy Basler even thinks that *The Love Song* is a love song to the poet's self and that the main emotion of the poem is pleasurable—an enjoyment of the undisturbed possession of self.[1] If the same conception be applied to Eliot's other poems, we get a quite different picture from the customary one. However, though there is no doubt an *element* of self-enjoyment, this by no means exhausts, or even dominates, the emotions of the poems. There is no narcissism. Rather, to the introspective mind, 'every moment is a new and shocking / Valuation of all we have been'. The division of the personality can only cover up, it cannot cure, the soul's incurable loneliness. The mind perceives, but it feels cut off from what it perceives, and one must go far for a remedy.

A certain comfort and invulnerability may be found, perhaps, in a misanthropic pose, and Eliot's misanthropy may be largely a pose of this kind. It appears as a view of life and not merely as a passing mood in his poems. But the bitterness with which it is

[1] R. P. Basler, 'Psychological Pattern in "The Love Song of J. Alfred Prufrock"', in W. S. Knickerbocker (ed.), *Twentieth Century English* (1946).

invested perhaps indicates that the original and obscurely persistent emotion of the poet was the love of his fellows, a love that was sadly disappointed in its contacts with the world.

Wanting a positive belief, the poet seems to have been haunted not only by misanthropy, but by a feeling of determinism, and even fatalism:

> Every street lamp that I pass
> Beats like a fatalistic drum,

Our actions are mere reflexes, like those of animals:

> So the hand of the child, automatic,
> Slipped out and pocketed a toy that was running along the quay.[1]

The deterministic view is terrifying, but it is also comforting because it relieves one of responsibility. 'History to blame', is Stephen's comfort in Joyce's *Ulysses*. And in a way it is Gerontion's comfort too—as well as his nightmare. History deceives us and 'guides us by vanities'. And

> Neither fear nor courage saves us. Unnatural vices
> Are fathered by our heroism. Virtues
> Are forced upon us by our impudent crimes.

There seems to be a fatal development which we cannot resist. The symbol of the wheel is often used in Hindu and Buddhist scriptures to denote the endless round of unredeemed life and death. And Eliot uses it—notably in *The Family Reunion*—to describe a sense of hopeless frustration. Harry and Agatha feel it very strongly until they are released by the illumination of faith:

> To and fro, dragging my feet
> Among inner shadows in the smoky wilderness,
> Trying to avoid the clasping branches
> And the giant lizard. To and fro.
> Until the chain breaks.
> > The chain breaks,
> The wheel stops, and the noise of machinery,
> And the desert is cleared, under the judicial sun
> Of the final eye . . .

The whirlpool of 'Death by Water' and the 'water-mill beating the darkness' of *Journey of the Magi* are among the Protean forms of the same wheel.

[1] *Rhapsody on a Windy Night.*

Thus the poet's despondency, from being a disappointment with human intercourse and modern civilisation, broadens into an all-embracing pessimism, which certainly owes something to Indian, especially Buddhist, philosophy. His interest in the Buddha was of long standing. As a boy he came across a poem for which he has preserved a warm affection, *The Light of Asia* by Edwin Arnold, a long epic on the life of Gautama Buddha. 'I must have had a latent sympathy for the subject-matter, for I read it through with gusto, and more than once,' he tells us.[1] The Buddha's 'Fire Sermon' he has directly drawn upon in *The Waste Land*. All things, says the Buddha, are on fire, visible things are on fire, the ear and the tongue and what they perceive, the body and the mind, everything is on fire 'with the fire of passion, say I, with the fire of hatred, with the fire of infatuation; with birth, old age, death, sorrow, lamentation, misery, grief, and despair are they on fire'.[2] And in another famous passage the Buddha declares:

> This, monks, is the noble truth of suffering: birth is suffering; decay is suffering; death is suffering; presence of objects we hate is suffering; separation from objects we love is suffering; not to obtain what we desire is suffering.
>
> In brief, the five aggregates which spring from grasping, they are painful.
>
> This, monks, is the noble truth concerning the origin of suffering: verily it originates in that craving which causes the renewal of becomings, is accompanied by sensual delight, and seeks satisfaction now here, now there; that is to say, craving for pleasures, craving for becoming, craving for not becoming.[3]

We are reminded of Eliot's constant insistence, both in his prose and his poetry, on pain and suffering. Awareness is painful, creation is painful, sincerity is painful, doubt is painful, belief is painful. In *Journey of the Magi*, we are told of the hardships of the journey, the pain of conviction, the discomfort of belief. Life is death, as in *The Hollow Men*, and both terrible to those who have not passed over the river to 'death's other Kingdom'.

[1] 'What is Minor Poetry?', *Welsh Review*, Dec. 1944.
[2] From the *Maha-Vagga*. H. C. Warren, *Buddhism in Translations* (1896), p. 352.
[3] Quoted from Ballou's *World Bible*. (Viking Press, 1944).

The human mind is perpetually driven between two desires, between two dreams each of which may be either a vision or a nightmare: the vision and nightmare of the material world, and the vision and nightmare of the immaterial. Each may be in turn, or for different minds, a refuge to which to fly, or a horror from which to escape. We desire and fear both sleep and waking; the day brings relief from the night, and the night brings relief from the day; we go to sleep as to death, and we wake as to damnation.[1]

Eliot knows that insensibility, obtuseness, stupidity would bring relief, as they bring relief to a Sweeney 'letting his arms hang down to laugh'—before he has become the philosopher of *Sweeney Agonistes*—or to the chattering uncles and aunts of *The Family Reunion*. He knows that Grishkin's 'friendly bust / Gives promise of pneumatic bliss'. But he has heard 'whispers of immortality', he is above the mob, he disdains the vulgar pleasures which cost us all our human dignity. Nirvana attracts him. Simeon says: 'I am tired with my own life and the lives of those after me', and asks only for the peace of obliteration. The protagonist of *Ash-Wednesday* also wishes to be freed from the eternal cycle and to find peace in oblivion:

> Because I do not hope to turn again
> Because I dc not hope
> Because I do not hope to turn
> Desiring this man's gift and that man's scope
> I no longer strive to strive towards such things

There is even the death-wish pure and simple. Eliot may have exploited theories of mass psychology, but we can safely assume that the death-wish in his poetry, especially in *The Waste Land* and *The Hollow Men*, has been personally experienced. It is not, however, identical with the morbid fascination of destruction. As befits a post-war period, and in accordance with the poet's temperament, it is rather a feeling of fatigue, like the tiredness of Simeon, or like the infinite weariness of the Sibyl whose ἀποθανεῖν θέλω ('I wish to die') occurs in the epigraph of *The Waste Land*. There is a certain similarity to the disdainful refusal of life of many of the French Symbolists and decadents, for instance de l'Isle-Adam (whose *Axël* seems to have lent a number of images to *The Waste*

---

[1] *Revelation*, I, p. 31.

Land) and Huysmans.[1] It is likely enough that these writers in their way, and Webster, Tourneur and other Elizabethans in theirs, helped to induce a mood of morbidity in Eliot. But the mood is none the less personal. This is borne out by Eliot's pronouncements on Cyril Tourneur. *The Revenger's Tragedy*, he says in his essay on that playwright, 'is a document on humanity chiefly because it is a document on one human being, Tourneur; its motive is truly the death motive, for it is the loathing and horror of life itself. To have realized this motive so well is a triumph; for the hatred of life is an important phase—even, if you like, a mystical experience—in life itself.'[2]

However, both the poetic belief in Nirvana and the death-wish are challenged by other beliefs, particularly by Christian ideas of a hereafter. The peace of winter cannot last: 'In the juvescence of the year / Came Christ the tiger.'[3] The contemplation of Nirvana is disturbed, and peace of mind must be found elsewhere. In any case, the poet recognises that oblivion, too, is a mode of flight and unworthy of a philosopher. It resembles too closely the death-in-life of the 'hollow men' or of the crowds flowing over London Bridge. Better to follow the example of the Stoics and recognise life for what it is without being discouraged. Better still, perhaps, to embrace suffering as being itself a virtue, in the spirit of the Christian mystics, until we learn that 'la sua voluntate è nostra pace'.

The outcome of it all, to begin with, was that the poet gave himself up, with a certain heroism, to a pessimistic view which, in the opinion of at least one critic, is the most absolute and despairing since Swift.[4] And this in spite of F. H. Bradley, who thought that pain was ultimately unreal, that it was transcended by a higher experience, and that there is a preponderance of pleasure in the universe.[5]

Before closing this chapter it may be useful to attempt a general interpretation of the main work of the poet's early phase, in the light of what we have here discussed.

---

[1] Wilson's treatment of these writers in *Axel's Castle* is very illuminating in this connection.

[2] *SE*, p. 190.

[3] *Gerontion*.

[4] H. W. Häusermann, *L'Oeuvre poétique de T. S. Eliot* (1939), p. 2.

[5] See *Appearance and Reality*, p. 199.

THE WASTE LAND

Eliot himself has pronounced on two interpretations of *The Waste Land* both of which he declares to be incomprehensible to him. The first is that of I. A. Richards, who said that Eliot 'had effected a complete severance between his poetry and all beliefs'; and the second is the common interpretation of the poem as the expression of the 'disillusionment of a generation'.

In Richards's opinion, Eliot felt a sense of desolation because it had now become impossible to hold the beliefs of bygone days; and his readers derived the same sense of desolation from his poetry. Richards later explained that when he spoke of 'a complete severance between his poetry and all beliefs' he was 'referring not to the poet's own history, but to the technical detachment of the poetry'.[1] But we have Eliot's own statement that 'a "sense of desolation," etc. (if it is there) is not a separation from belief; it is nothing so pleasant. In fact, doubt, uncertainty, futility, etc., would seem to me to prove anything except this agreeable partition; for doubt and uncertainty are merely a variety of belief.'[2] We need discuss this no further. The question has already been dealt with in the present chapter and in that on 'Poetic Belief'; and the general considerations there are fully applicable to *The Waste Land*.

Since the view was first popularised by 'the more approving critics', it has become almost axiomatically accepted that *The Waste Land* is the most significant expression of a certain feeling of disillusion and neurotic boredom in the period after the First World War; particularly of the disenchantment felt by the so-called 'lost generation'. This notion Eliot simply calls nonsensical. What he objects to is the term 'generation'.[3] A poet expresses his own ideas and emotions, not those of a generation, if it may be said to have any. A great poet may be writing his time, but he does so in writing himself, and anyhow the outlook of a 'time', or an age, is not identical with the outlook of a 'generation', which suggests a mere clique of self-conscious and self-important contemporaries. As a matter of fact he seems to have thought that disillusionment was precisely what the inhabitants of modern

---

[1] Richards, *Science and Poetry*, p. 70, note.
[2] 'A Note on Poetry and Belief.'
[3] *Thoughts after Lambeth* (1931).

Europe did not suffer from—what, indeed, they might have been all the better for achieving. Human beings may lose one set of illusions, but they quickly acquire others. And Eliot was disinclined to commiserate with a generation which was perhaps smugly satisfied with its sense of disillusionment if the truth were known. What he depicted through his personal dilemma was a predicament of modern humanity more general than that of a generation, a predicament which he had begun to see quite clearly years before the Great War broke out.

Those who repeat the standard view usually disregard the fact that most of the essential moods and features of *The Waste Land* were present in the poems that Eliot wrote before the Great War. Their point of view tends to make *The Waste Land* seem rather superficial, as it does seem to Dr H. V. Routh, who has written an otherwise excellent appreciation. 'The poem,' he says, 'despite its erudition, is essentially superficial. Eliot not only overlooks the undercurrent of inventiveness and humanity, which is struggling against the curse of Adam, but he trifles with the symptoms of our alleged demoralization . . .; blemishes which always have and always will disgrace society even at its best. . . .'[1] This objection might have been justified if Eliot had been concerned with merely presenting 'social aimlessness', as Dr Routh puts it. But it is this explanation of the poem that is superficial. Eliot was concerned with something more or something else than social aimlessness. And at any rate he thought, with Croce, that it is 'the intensity of the artistic process', not the 'greatness' or originality of the emotions and ideas, that counts most.

One of the critics who has best understood Eliot is Mr E. M. Forster. Concerning *The Waste Land* he wrote in 1929:

> . . . if I have its hang, it has nothing to do with the English tradition in literature, or law or order, nor, except incidentally, has the rest of his work anything to do with them either. It is just a personal comment on the universe, as individual and as isolated as Shelley's *Prometheus*.
>
> In respect to the horror that they find in life, men can be divided into three classes . . . those who have not suffered often or acutely; . . . those who have escaped through horror into a further vision;

---

[1] H. V. Routh, *English Literature and Ideas in the Twentieth Century* (2nd edn. 1948), p. 164.

... those who continue to suffer. Most of us belong to the first class, and to the elect outside it our comments must sound shallow. ... Mr. Eliot ... belongs to the third.[1]

Mr Forster's awareness of suffering enables him, if nothing else does, to understand something fundamental in Eliot's outlook.

The Waste Land certainly expresses disgust with modern civilisation and with post-war society. What else could one expect of an American who wrote as early as 1909 of 'the failure of American life' and of the many Americans whose 'hearts were always in Europe': he could hardly fail to be disappointed on a closer acquaintance with European civilisation. We must also take into account the feelings expressed in the quotation from Hesse's *Blick ins Chaos* in the Notes to *The Waste Land*. But it is much nearer the mark to call the poem 'a personal comment on the universe'. The 'waste land', in one of its aspects, is the wilderness of thought into which Eliot's studies and speculations had led him, a wilderness unenlivened by a vital faith. He is himself the Fisher King, who has only fragments of ideas to shore against his ruins. And at the same time the Fisher King, who is conspicuously absent from most of the poem, is the God whom he cannot find. The poet is unable to surrender to belief. This inability was already hinted at in *The Love Song*. It is notable that throughout Eliot's poetry the themes of human union and divine union are accompanied by feelings both of ecstasy and of *fear*. The despair of *The Waste Land* is a despair of metaphysics,[2] and the horror of life has its source in this despair. The scorn of humanity is really a loathing of anything that reminds the poet of the meaninglessness of existence. *The Waste Land* is determined by its religious attitude. It is a criticism of life from a Christian and Hindu and Buddhist point of view, but without the faith of any of these religions, or rather with the faith of them all but with a still more powerful scepticism.

There is plain personal suffering too, caused in part by the feeling of isolation which neo-Kantian philosophy helped to make vividly conscious. There is no doubt much purely personal matter that the reader cannot trace. But it is all made to contribute to the *pessimisme absolu* which is caused by the absence of the Absolute.

[1] E. M. Forster, 'T. S. Eliot and his Difficulties' in *Life and Letters*, 1929.
[2] Cp. Eliot's opinion of *In Memoriam*: '*In Memoriam* is a poem of despair, but of despair of a religious kind.' (*EAM*, p. 187.)

The personal emotions of the poet, however, have been objectified in accordance with his theory and usual practice. The poet's tiredness of life has become the death-gravitation of a society. The objective images of a sterile civilisation have been seized upon to express the poet's sense of sterility in his soul. In comparison, *Gerontion*, with its 'thoughts of a dry brain in a dry season', presents itself much more directly as a personal confession. The objectification of *The Waste Land* is clearly justified, because the poet felt strongly about the aspects of modern life that he used for his objective correlatives as well as about the states of his own soul. And he successfully transposed the poem, as he had often done before, from being lyrical in its genetic impulse to being descriptive, narrative and dramatic. In so doing he availed himself of his technical skill, and he was carried along, no doubt, by his technical interest, which in turn helped to shape his thought in many places. Ezra Pound's poems and other modern poetry were also there to exercise their suggestive influence. The result was a broken sequence in which the order and unity were not merely of technique, as Dr Richards contends, but of mood, of negative belief, of doubt. The fragments of the poem are not just aspects of modern civilisation, but images of the desires, pains, thoughts and misgivings of the poet, who had stocked his mind with metaphysical ideas which held no comfort, and in his 'natural wakeful life' incessantly 'perceived' objects and events which had no meaning.

This being the case, and given the unaccustomed technique of the poem, it was perhaps inevitable that readers should be content if they found the disillusionment of a generation to be its subject. Otherwise they might have found nothing. This meaning is the poet's 'bit of nice meat' for the house-dog of the premises he is breaking into. What is more, it has made the poem useful to the generation it is assumed to satirise by making it conscious of its plight. *The Waste Land* may well be regarded as 'a cry from the wilderness, a call to repentance'.[1] When a poem arouses suitable emotions in the reader, it is already justified as poetry. We must remind ourselves again of Eliot's view that a sensitive reader is as well qualified to determine the meaning of a poem as is the poet himself.

We are at liberty to interpret *The Waste Land* as the expression

[1] H. R. Williamson, *The Poetry of T. S. Eliot* (1932), p. 87.

of the feelings of a particular generation if we like. But it must be because we personally find this significance, not because we have been told to find it. We may recognise the social satire of *The Waste Land*, and the generation which has survived the Second World War will find it as urgently topical as their parents—and perhaps as salutary. But much of the poem cannot find its true perspective or become properly intelligible unless we regard it as the experiences of a mind looking into itself. And if the poem continues to captivate our great-grandchildren, it will not be because it describes a particular historical situation but because it describes a human soul tormented by eternal problems which the historical situation only served to actualise.

VII

REALITY (Part One)

As early as in the *Prufrock* poems Eliot reaches out, as we have seen, for an experience of totality. He often seems to be making deliberate efforts to fuse disparate impressions, the noise of the typewriter and the smell of cooking, and force them to reveal their occult relationships. Distinctions between objects are suppressed, and impressions are made to represent wholes of feeling:

> The winter evening settles down
> With smell of steaks in passageways.

The poet often imparts to us a sense of completeness which almost convinces us that he must have discovered it in the outside world. But there is a feeling of unfulfilment besides. For the wholeness is not really discovered in outer things and recorded as a perception. There is no essential unity between a suburban evening and the smell of steaks in passageways, but only one of habitual togetherness. The unity which we feel is one of mood, which the perceptions only serve to express. There are unifying moods but no unifying ideas to support them. In the *Quartets* it is different. The smell of wild thyme and the sight of winter lightning have no spatial or temporal connection, but an ideal unity nevertheless. And in the beginning of *East Coker* the objects mentioned have no unity of mood, but an essential oneness of substance and significance:

> Old stone to new building, old timber to new fires,
> Old fires to ashes, and ashes to the earth
> Which is already flesh, fur, faeces,
> Bone of man and beast, cornstalk and leaf.

The 'deep lane' does not exist in its own right, but 'insists on the direction / Into the village', and 'the sultry light / Is absorbed, not refracted, by grey stone', making itself one with it.

Eliot declared in 'Eeldrop and Appleplex' that the general and universal was superficial and without interest; it was the particular that counted. But he obviously found it difficult to content himself with the particular or even to remain assured of its prime reality. There were strong influences, Plato's perhaps most pervasive among them, urging that reality was not in the particular, as Bergson and other modern philosophers asserted, but in the universal. His own longing for metaphysical certitude, we may assume, made it impossible for him to ignore these voices. And his interest in Symbolism made him all the more attentive to them. This interest was no doubt mainly concerned with the formal aspects of Symbolism at first. But it drew him on to try to express the ineffable. It pointed to final causes, to hidden meanings, to correspondences between phenomena, in fact to just those things which he wished to find and communicate, but long failed to discover. His view of this life as unreal and of a transcendent existence as real owes a great deal to the Symbolists as well as to more purely philosophical sources. For Symbolism, though to a large extent a matter of form and technique, was essentially a search for the mystic reality behind physical manifestations. So it was understood by Symons, who hardly interested himself in the technical aspects of French Symbolism at all. In his Introduction to *The Symbolist Movement*, Symons wrote that 'the literature of which I write in this volume [is] a literature in which the visible world is no longer a reality, and the unseen world no longer a dream'. And it was this literature that he held up as the only hopeful model to his times. Symons's conception of Symbolism was no doubt passed on to Eliot, whose dependence on Symons right up to recent years appears clearly enough in his work.

There is something in what Middleton Murry says, that it is the highest function of imagery 'to define indefinable spiritual qualities. All metaphor and simile can be described as the analogy by which the human mind explores the universe of quality and charts the non-measurable world.' In these things, he says, 'however much we struggle, we cannot avoid transcendentalism'.[1] In fact,

[1] J. Middleton Murry, *Countries of the Mind*, Second Series (1931), pp. 9, 15.

imagery is a means of approaching religious understanding, and it is used deliberately in this way in Eliot's later poetry. In the words of Cecil Day Lewis: 'The image cannot, of course, reproduce the soul of things: what it can do is to persuade us, by the force of its own vitality, and our own answering sense of revelation, that soul there must be—or, if you dislike the word "soul", to persuade us that there is beneath the appearance of things a life whose quality may not be apprehended in our everyday intercourse nor be gauged by the instruments of science.' 'The poetic image,' he says, 'is the human mind claiming kinship with everything that lives or has lived, and making good its claim.'[1] We have here a representative modern poet and critic speaking with the voice of the Symbolists.

It is interesting to study the development of Eliot's imagery and to see how it reflects the development of his thought. For whatever images and symbols he uses—personal and traditional—his use of them is marked at all stages by his individual needs and adaptations.

The sexual urge can be traced through many stages of sublimation—'the transition from Beatrice living to Beatrice dead, rising to the Cult of the Virgin'.[2] 'The moment in the arbour where the rain beat', which is remembered in *Burnt Norton*, is transformed into a symbol of religious illumination. The little girl of *Dans le Restaurant* rings the changes through 'la figlia che piange', Marie and the hyacinth girl of *The Waste Land*, and Marina, to the Lady of *Ash-Wednesday* and *Four Quartets*. Eliot is aware of this development and of its Freudian significance. In the same way the murder theme with its accompanying sense of guilt travels through many stages (e.g. the philanthropically stabbed Juliet in the early *Nocturne*, the 'pained surprise' of la figlia, the Philomela myth in *The Waste Land*, the actual murder reported in *Sweeney Agonistes*, the contemplated murders in *The Family Reunion* and the vicarious murder in *The Cocktail Party*) to acquire a deep spiritual significance. To grasp the essential of this significance it is not necessary to 'dissect / The recurrent image into pre-conscious terrors', for the image is not private but general in its poetic contexts.

The wind throughout Eliot's poetry is a symbol of emptiness and nothingness. At the end of *Gerontion* a gull fights vainly

[1] C. Day Lewis, *The Poetic Image* (1947), pp. 107, 35.
[2] *SE*, p. 275.

against the wind, to disappear completely—'White feathers in the snow'. The dialogue of 'A Game of Chess', which partly echoes a poem by Thomas Hardy, uses the wind symbol very significantly:

> 'What is that noise?'
>   The wind under the door.
> 'What is that noise now? What is the wind doing?'
>   Nothing again nothing.
>   'Do
> 'You know nothing? Do you see nothing? Do you remember
> 'Nothing?'

In *Marina*, the various categories of the vain and wicked 'are become unsubstantial, reduced by a wind'. And the wind retains the same significance in *Burnt Norton*, where it sweeps the gloomy hills of a London which knows only

> Tumid apathy with no concentration
> Men and bits of paper, whirled by the cold wind
> That blows before and after time,

In *Burnt Norton*, however, the wind is not the only effective power in human lives.

The image of the sea is somewhat ambiguous in the *Prufrock* and 1920 poems. But mainly it suggests all the phenomena and events of life, which, like Hamlet's 'sea of troubles', impinge upon the individual without his being able to order or relate them in his mind, or utilise them in any way. He is choked, and the sensation is one of drowning. His individuality is dissolved, his bones are picked, as in the case of 'Phlébas, le Phénicien' or his counterpart, 'le garçon délabré', who is unable to cope with his reality. A precarious existence can be led among all the uncoordinated phenomena by means of dreams, and thus the sea itself can come to represent dreaming and unreality, as in *The Love Song* ('should have been a pair of ragged claws / Scuttling across the floors of silent seas'; 'We have lingered in the chambers of the sea / By sea-girls wreathed with seaweed red and brown / Till human voices wake us, and we drown').

Because the phenomena of life have their existence within our consciousness, the sea, too, is within us. And the idea of the sea as a confusion of unrelated matter contained in the mind is seen clearly in *Rhapsody on a Windy Night*:

> The memory throws up high and dry
> A crowd of twisted things;
> A twisted branch upon the beach
> Eaten smooth, and polished
> As if the world gave up
> The secret of its skeleton,
> Stiff and white.

Connected with the sea and drowning are the symbols of fog and smoke. *Morning at the Window* joins the two sets of symbols in 'the brown waves of fog'. More directly than the sea, the fog suggests ignorance and bewilderment, the sense of being lost and of not knowing where to go.

In *The Waste Land*, the sea is '*Oed' und leer*'. We again meet Phlebas the Phoenician. 'The king my brother's wreck'—death at the bottom of the sea—means no more than death in the earth: 'White bodies naked on the low damp ground / And bones cast in a little low dry garret.' And yet it is not for nothing that Madame Sosostris warns against death by water, for there is the chance of a sea-change ('Those are pearls that were his eyes. Look!'), of a resurrection, just as the body buried in the earth may be dug up again by 'the Dog . . . that's friend to men,'—or it may begin to sprout! Thus the sea becomes the symbol of a mysterious transformation 'into something rich and strange': bewilderment and confusion may turn into knowledge.

Music also, like the sea in one of its aspects, seems to represent illusion and delusion, especially the delusion provided by art. It betrays itself by its false notes, by the instruments being broken and cracked and out of tune. The titles of some of the poems suggest music: *The Love Song, Preludes, Rhapsody*, but the poems—except in their formal aspects—do not give us the harmony of music; in fact they parody what we usually understand by harmony. In *The Love Song*, the 'music from a farther room' is part of the conventional and meaningless atmosphere. In *Portrait of a Lady*, Chopin's Preludes echo at first 'among velleities and carefully caught regrets / Through attenuated tones of violins / Mingled with remote cornets'. And soon

> Among the windings of the violins
> And the ariettes
> Of cracked cornets

Reality (Part One)

Inside my brain a dull tom-tom begins
Absurdly hammering a prelude of its own,
Capricious monotone
That is at least one definite 'false note'.

In *Conversation Galante* the man remarks:

> . . . 'Someone frames upon the keys
> That exquisite nocturne, with which we explain
> The night and moonshine; music which we seize
> To body forth our own vacuity.'

'To body forth our own vacuity'—illusion and hypocrisy—is what music stands for in these poems.

The music symbol has acquired a different significance in *The Waste Land*. Music and singing now stand for purity and meaningfulness ('this music crept by me upon the waters'). The nightingale's song is something in the nature of a revelation of the spirit: it fills 'all the desert with inviolable voice'. There are the 'voix d'enfants, chantant dans la coupole'. And finally, there is the 'pleasant whining of a mandoline' among the fishmen. But music, too, is vitiated and turns into gramophone records, the cries of crickets and bats, and the singing of the dry grass. In 'What the Thunder Said', a woman fiddles 'whisper music' on her hair—ghostly, unreal music—a symbol of unreality joined to a symbol of life (the hair).

By the time we come to the *Four Quartets*, the transformation is complete. The sea has not become a symbol of timeless eternity; rather, in *The Dry Salvages*, it represents limitless time. But at least it is no longer within us, 'the sea is all about us'. It still tosses up curious things on its beaches, but they no longer confuse, they are merely hints of something beyond our comprehension. And music is used as a symbol of absolute Reality. It is no longer mechanical and out of tune, but something 'heard so deeply / That it is not heard at all.' The development of these images marks a development in the poet's mind from a feeling of helplessness in a world of appearances and illusions to a sense of a transcendent reality which human beings may not be able to grasp but of which they can receive intuitive glimpses.

The world of Prufrock and Sweeney is, on the whole, the familiar, material world of every day. And yet it is bewildering enough, because, as we saw in the previous chapter, there appears

to be no necessary relation between its phenomena, and no ultimate meaning. There is the obtrusive and disturbing fact of death,
the thought of which may bring 'whispers of immortality' to
some; but the young man in *Portrait of a Lady* is entirely baffled
by it. 'What if she should die some afternoon,' he asks—

> Should die and leave me sitting pen in hand
> With the smoke coming down above the housetops;
> Doubtful, for a while
> Not knowing what to feel or if I understand

More and more the poet becomes aware that there are two
worlds, two planes of existence. They are both at first unreal, both
'death's kingdoms', as in *The Hollow Men*. But this life, the 'life' of
the crowds flowing into the City, is 'death's dream kingdom', is
more definitely unreal than 'death's other kingdom' which we do
not know, and which only flashes on our awareness like 'sunlight
on a broken column'. Then through *Marina* and *Ash-Wednesday*
the certainty of an immaterial, transcendent world beyond this
deepens towards the mystic conviction of the *Four Quartets*, in
which the two planes of existence are seen to be really connected:

> We move above the moving tree
> In light upon the figured leaf
> And hear upon the sodden floor
> Below, the boarhound and the boar
> Pursue their pattern as before
> But reconciled among the stars.

THE INFLUENCE OF BRADLEY

I suggested that the mystic conception of reality which we find
in Eliot's later poetry owes a great deal to Plato. But the philosophy which seems to have exercised the most direct influence on
Eliot's poetry from first to last is that of Francis Herbert Bradley,
particularly his theory of knowledge. This is not surprising seeing
that it was to Bradley's philosophy that Eliot mainly applied himself in the last years of his purely academic career.

Eliot's quest for knowledge is reflected in his poetry throughout. And in this quest the nature of Reality is a main objective.
The phrase 'Unreal City' in *The Waste Land* has far-echoing
philosophical implications to a person familiar with Bradley's

Appearance and Reality. And in *The Hollow Men* 'the Shadow' falls, accompanied by similar echoes, 'Between the idea / And the reality'. The child of *Animula* is offended and perplexed 'With the imperatives of "is and seems"'. *The Family Reunion* is much concerned with the problem of real existence. But it is mainly in the *Four Quartets* that the nature of reality becomes a subject of sustained meditation. The recurrent phrase 'human kind cannot bear very much reality', a repetition of Becket's words in *Murder in the Cathedral*, indicates the trend of the poet's thought.

In Bradley's theory of knowledge, as in Aristotle's, the senses play an important part. 'To be real,' says Bradley, 'is to be indissolubly one thing with sentience.' But the particular and individual is eliminated in the kind of sentience that Bradley describes in *Appearance and Reality*:

> . . . if, seeking for reality, we go to experience, what we certainly do *not* find is a subject or an object, or indeed any other thing whatever, standing separate and on its own bottom. What we discover rather is a whole in which distinctions can be made, but in which divisions do not exist . . . to be real is to be . . . something which, except as an integral element of such sentience, has no meaning at all.[1]

Actually sentience, according to Bradley, is not enough to constitute reality, although there is no reality without it. Reality includes the sense perceptions while transmuting them. It also includes and transcends the perceiver. Bradley regards human beings as isolated from each other as finite persons. But the self is not isolated from the objects it perceives, nor from the 'Absolute' of which it is a part. In this Absolute everything finite is completed. And by a kind of intuition, which is more than both thought and feeling, or perhaps a Hegelian synthesis of thought and feeling, the finite mind is able to gain a faint realisation of totality.[2]

Every part of Bradley's Absolute contains within itself the whole, and to grasp a part means to grasp the whole. He thinks that 'we should get a way of thinking in which the whole of reality was a system of its differences immanent in each difference. In this whole the analysis of any one element would, by nothing but the self-development of that element, produce the totality.'[3]

---

[1] Op. cit., p. 146. [2] Cf. ibid., p. 172; also pp. 159–60.
[3] *The Principles of Logic*, p. 489.

Generally, however, we grasp nothing completely, which is why some things seem bad to us. For not only truth and goodness are contained in the Absolute, but error and evil as well. Bradley, like Meinong, recognises falsehood and fiction as equally real with 'fact'. The important thing is that they exist in experience, an experience which is not purely rational. But such things as error, evil and pain are altered in quality when they are made to fit into the pattern of the whole; and Bradley is convinced that there will ultimately be a balance of goodness, beauty and pleasure. It matters little in the present connection that his main reason for believing these things seems to be an urgent desire that they should be so.

In religion Bradley is a complete sceptic. 'Like morality,' he says, 'religion is not ultimate. It is a mere appearance, and is therefore inconsistent with itself.' 'Religion,' he goes on, 'naturally implies a relation between Man and God. Now a relation always . . . is self-contradictory.' Man, on the one hand, is a finite subject, yet, on the other hand, apart from God, he is merely an abstraction. God again is a finite object. But sundered from relations God is emptiness.[1]

Eliot criticised Bradley's conception of the Absolute in one of his early philosophical essays. Yet he followed Bradley imaginatively beyond the phenomenal stage, even while he himself was still in his first phase of scepticism. We have seen that his poetry shows an awareness of connectedness and wholeness co-existing with the prevalent awareness of dissolution. The fact that the objects described in Eliot's poetry are often broken in itself points to an ideal, complete existence in which they are whole, or, in Bradley's terms, to a transmutation of the parts in the individuality of the total experience. (The very word 'transmute', in Eliot's use of it, has a distinct Bradleyan flavour.[2]) Thus in *The Hollow Men* sunlight falls on a broken column as if to continue it in a world beyond. Things only *appear* to be incomplete and imperfect because we have usually no awareness of totality.

This awareness seems to be what Eliot aims at in a number of his later works. And in so far as he consciously strives to arrive at an understanding of the Absolute he may be said to be modelling his efforts on those of Bradley. The word 'pattern' which recurs so

[1] *Appearance and Reality*, pp. 444–5.
[2] See, for instance, *SE*, pp. 18, 137, 290.

frequently in his later poetry is again reminiscent of Bradley, who thought that the broken pattern of the life which we perceive is completed in the Reality which contains it.

Murder in the Cathedral several times reaffirms the importance of the 'here and now' which we found so significant in Eliot's early work. But the 'here and now' has finally become part of a larger pattern from which it derives its meaning:

> The critical moment
> That is always now, and here, Even now, in sordid particulars
> The eternal design may appear.

The dramatic relevance of this idea is shown immediately and vividly in Becket's first encounter with the Knights, when he accepts their attack 'Now and here!'

Eliot's larger pattern is Bradley's Absolute interpreted in the spirit of Christian teleology. After the first exchange with the Knights, Thomas promises comfort to his people:

> This is one moment
> But know that another
> Shall pierce you with a sudden painful joy
> When the figure of God's purpose is made complete.

Bradley's idea of completion is again reflected in *The Family Reunion*, where Harry, in his climactic conversation with Agatha, discovers that

> . . . in the end
> That is the completion which at the beginning
> Would have seemed the ruin.

Similarly the fulfilment envisaged from time to time in the *Four Quartets* is thought of as a completion of the incompleteness which is now, as a filling of the concrete pool 'with water out of sunlight', as a reconciliation among the stars. This implies an eschatology based on the belief that this world is to be transfigured, not destroyed or superseded, that the earthly paradise is to be rediscovered. There will be:

> both a new world
> And the old made explicit, understood
> In the completion of its partial ecstasy,
> The resolution of its partial horror.
>   (*Burnt Norton*, II)

See, now they vanish,
The faces and places, with the self which, as it could, loved them,
To become renewed, transfigured, in another pattern.

(Little Gidding, III)

If Bradley's ideas were not altogether acceptable to Eliot when he became a Christian poet, there was always Royce's variety of idealism to fall back upon, so that the belief in God and in the individual soul might be supported. It should be pointed out, perhaps, that his recognition of the behoveliness of sin and evil owes still more to Royce (who regarded these things as being willed by God in order that greater good might ensue) than to Bradley. But even so there is a good deal of Bradley's optimism in Eliot's assurance that 'Sin is Behovely' and that

> . . . all shall be well and
> All manner of thing shall be well
> When the tongues of flame are in-folded
> Into the crowned knot of fire
> And the fire and the rose are one.

(Little Gidding, V)

Even in *Marina*, when the speaker of the poem rejoices that those who sinned in various ways have become 'By this grace dissolved in place', one is tempted to think of Bradley's dissolution of the elements of evil to be regrouped in a wider synthesis and thus turned into good.

On a more technical level, and on the level of critical theory, Eliot remains in close touch with Bradley. His impersonal theory of poetry seems to owe something to *Appearance and Reality*, as when he speaks of Shakespeare's struggle '—which alone constitutes life for a poet—to transmute his personal and private agonies into something rich and strange, something universal and impersonal'.[1] Another favourite idea is that of the possibility, in poetry and ordinary experience, of 'a direct sensuous apprehension of thought'.[2] This idea, too, finds complete support in Bradley, who writes as follows:

. . . feeling belongs to perfect thought, or it does not. If it does not, there is at once a side of existence beyond thought. But if it does belong, then thought is different from thought discursive and rela-

---

[1] *SE*, p. 137.   [2] Ibid., p. 286.

tional. To make it include immediate experience, its character must be transformed . . .

. . . feeling and will must also be transmuted in this whole, into which thought has entered. Such a whole state would possess in a superior form that immediacy which we find (more or less) in feeling; and in this whole all divisions would be healed up. It would be experience entire, containing all elements in harmony. Thought would be present as a higher intuition. . . .[1]

Bradley becomes quite rhapsodical as he further develops this view and has visions of the harmony of a 'higher bliss'. Eliot may well have caught some of his enthusiasm for the fusion of thought and feeling which would bring about 'experience entire'.

The fact that Bradley's philosophy has been so important to Eliot means that his poetry is indirectly, but profoundly, influenced by Hegel's philosophy as well. One might almost say that Eliot uses Bradley (and Hegel) in the same way that he thinks Lucretius used Epicurus or Dante used St Thomas: as a groundwork on which to construct the edifices of his poems. It is remarkable that the main line of development of Eliot's poetry follows the main trend of Bradley's philosophy: whereas the early poems roughly correspond to the demonstration of everything as appearance, the later poems correspond to the phase, or aspect, of reality.

It would be foolish to suggest that Eliot simply tries to expound and illustrate Bradley's philosophy. Nor is this philosophy the only groundwork of his poetry; it is not even the main influence in his later work. There are many other things besides. The correspondence to the two phases of appearance and reality, for instance, has a parallel in the correspondence to Dante's *Inferno* and *Paradiso*. Christianity and Oriental mysticism have powerfully contributed to the meaning of the poems. Kant is nowhere far to seek in them. And one is often reminded of Spinoza's 'amor intellectualis Dei'. But for many of these influences it is likely that Bradley paved the way.

ARISTOTLE

Bradley's idealism is similar to Plato's in positing a state of perfection beyond our common experience. But Bradley's transmuta-

---

[1] *Appearance and Reality*, pp. 171–2.

tion is not Plato's transcendence. Where Plato is a dualist, Bradley is a monist and believes in a basic reality inherent in all appearances. Eliot's platonism should not be underestimated, but he seems on the whole to adopt Bradley's view of appearance and reality. Perhaps this means that his aristotelian belief in the concrete and particular has been transmuted, by a typical compromise, into an idealist philosophy.

Certain aspects of Aristotle's philosophy have always remained strongly evident in Eliot's work. Thus the idea of everything striving towards perfection ('Everything tends towards reconciliation'[1]) and that of everything being essentially good or necessary, are Aristotelian as well as Bradleyan. There is even a tentative monism in the suggestion in *De Anima*, III, 8 that 'the soul is in a way all existing things', though Aristotle leaves this suggestion undeveloped.

Aristotle's philosophy of form is particularly interesting in the present connection. The form of an object is its actuality, or entelechy. And as form is the principle of individuation, of realisation and of fulfilment, so pattern is the principle of fulfilment in Eliot's poetic usage. 'Only by the form, the pattern, / Can words or music reach / The stillness.'[2] Eliot speaks constantly of pattern, not only the pattern of words, or pattern in art, but pattern in history, pattern in the life of individuals, etc. We shall have to consider this idea more closely, but it seems clear that what Eliot partly means by pattern is potentiality and vocation: a latent purpose in the lives of communities and individuals, as well as in the existence of objects, which demands to be realised. In fact, something akin to Aristotle's form.

The form of an animate object is what Aristotle calls its soul. As such the soul is an ordering principle of the matter of which the body is constituted. The soul of a human being is manifested in its activities, which in turn can give form to inanimate matter, stamping it with an idea. Eliot takes a similar view in the ninth Chorus of *The Rock*:

Out of the formless stone, when the artist united himself with stone,
Spring always new forms of life, from the soul of man that is joined to
    the soul of stone;

---

[1] *The Family Reunion*, p. 104.   [2] *Burnt Norton*, V.

Aristotle's first mover is a divine mind, or νοῦς, which ceaselessly thinks itself, and which causes all activity by the love which it inspires:[1]

> Love is itself unmoving,
> Only the cause and end of movement.[2]

This is straight from Aristotle, and similar passages occur elsewhere in Eliot, for instance:

> Here the past and future
> Are conquered, and reconciled,
> Where action were otherwise movement
> Of that which is only moved
> And has in it no source of movement—
> Driven by dæmonic, chthonic
> Powers.[3]

Eliot thinks we must 'find meaning in *final causes* rather than in origins. . . . The final cause is the attraction towards God.'[4] He applies this particularly to our notions of sex, and it is obvious that much of the sexual imagery of his poetry is meant to convey the idea of 'the attraction towards God' as the mover of all things, the end of all activity.

Since reality, to Aristotle, is in activity, reality, Eliot infers,[5] must be in the 'here and now'. This is an interpretation, however, which looks suspiciously modern, and which brings us naturally to a closer consideration of Henri Bergson's philosophy.

BERGSON, AND THE PROBLEM OF TIME

According to Bergson's *Essai sur les données immédiates de la conscience*, the human intellect concerns itself with quantitative factors contained in a homogeneous environment, that of space, while our more intuitive consciousness experiences everything as absolute quality and gathers every moment of such experience into an organic pattern, that of *durée*. This *durée* is a moving present which accumulates all the past and holds preparedness for the future. Bergson compares the experience of *durée* to listening to a piece of

---

[1] *Metaphysica*, XII, 7, 9.   [2] *Burnt Norton*, V.   [3] *The Dry Salvages*, V.
[4] 'Dante', *SE*, p. 274.   [5] *Monist*, Oct. 1916, p. 554.

music, where each note is separate, yet dependent for its effect on all the others.

Thus there are two levels or kinds of consciousness: intuition and intellect. And only the former gives experience of reality. From a slightly different approach, in *Matière et mémoire*, Bergson sees consciousness as the meeting-ground of perception and memory, of which the former is the mechanical impression of matter, whereas the memory is mainly subconscious and represents the free and integrated life of the spirit, the *durée* of every individual. The memory has no 'before' and 'after' in time. It allows no experience to lapse into oblivion but, whether we are consciously aware of it or not, arranges all our past moments in a simultaneous order which is always in the making. The same view is stated in *L'Évolution créatrice* and anticipated in the *Essai*:

> En réalité le passé se conserve de lui-même, automatiquement. Tout entier, sans doute, il nous suit à tout instant: ce que nous avons senti, pensé, voulu depuis notre première enfance est là, penché sur le présent qui va s'y joindre . . .[1]

> La durée toute pure est la forme que prend la succession de nos états de conscience quand notre moi se laisse vivre, quand il s'abstient d'établir une séparation entre l'état présent et les états antérieurs . . . il suffit qu'en se rappelant ces états il ne les juxtapose pas à l'état actuel comme un point à un autre point, mais les organise avec lui, comme il arrive quand nous nous rappelons, fondues pour ainsi dire ensemble, les notes d'une mélodie.[2]

> la vérité est que chaque surcroît d'excitation s'organise avec les excitations précédentes, et que l'ensemble nous fait l'effet d'une phrase musicale qui serait toujours sur le point de finir et sans cesse se modifierait dans sa totalité par l'addition de quelque note nouvelle.[3]

Eliot's vision of concrete phenomena, especially in his early poetry, is related to Bergson's perception of distinct qualities in a heterogeneous world. And his attempts to bring disparate perceptions into an organic unity is related to Bergson's ideas of *durée* and intuition.

Eliot, too, believes in different levels of consciousness, and his levels are much more Bergsonian than Freudian. Examples can be

[1] *L'Évolution créatrice*, p. 5.
[2] *Essai sur les données immédiates*, pp. 84–5.
[3] Ibid., pp. 88–9.

found plentifully in *The Family Reunion*, where Harry says (rather unkindly) of his brother John:

> A brief vacation from the kind of consciousness
> That John enjoys, can't make very much difference

Most people, he thinks,

> ... don't understand what it is to be awake,
> To be living on several planes at once

Harry is 'the consciousness of [his] unhappy family'. He has awareness. And Eliot's awareness corresponds to Bergson's intuition, the means by which reality is known, ordinary perception being confused, fragmentary and meaningless.

Eliot, like Bergson, thinks our entire being, past and present, is continually being modified by our new experiences, or, as he says in *East Coker*,

> ... the pattern is new in every moment
> And every moment is a new and shocking
> Valuation of all we have been.

There is a further striking correspondence between Bergson's conception of personal memory and Eliot's idea of historical tradition. The historical sense, according to Eliot, 'involves a perception, not only of the pastness of the past, but of its presence' and 'a feeling that the whole of the literature of Europe ... has a simultaneous existence and composes a simultaneous order'. Eliot makes tradition practically synonymous with the mind of a country or continent. He declares that this is 'a mind which changes, and that this change is a development which abandons nothing *en route*'. He could not have got closer to *L'Évolution créatrice*. Whenever a new work of art arrives, he says, 'the *whole* existing order must be, if ever so slightly, altered'. For Eliot finds it natural 'that the past should be altered by the present as much as the present is directed by the past'.

This leads us into the heart of the problem of time, which we must now consider, both as a general preoccupation of Eliot's poetry and in its more specific connection with Bergson's philosophy.

Even in his young days Eliot was constantly preoccupied with the passing of years, the withering of flowers, the coming of old age. Looking back into the past, there was the interminable sequence of history, looking into the future there was a measureless void. But for many years the time problem seems to have engaged mainly his feelings. In his early poetry he had a tendency to describe time in concrete metaphors ('the smoky candle-end of time', 'devoured the afternoon', 'fragments of the afternoon', 'time's ruins', etc.). No doubt this kind of imagery constituted a poetic aim in itself, and there may have been no further significance in the metaphors than in such common phrases as 'a wet afternoon' or 'a sunny day'. But they do in a playful way suggest that the reality of time is a matter of subjective impressions, that time depends on our feelings of time.

From a very youthful age Eliot also appears to have been intrigued by philosophical speculations about time. One recognises in his poetry a number of the modern ideas concerning the nature of time which most people are familiar with at least in a popularised form. In a poem which originally appeared as *A Lyric* in the *Smith Academy Record* for April 1905 (Eliot was then sixteen and a half), and which was reprinted with slight alterations as *Song* in the *Harvard Advocate* two years later, the young poet takes issue with the sages:

> If space and time, as sages say,
> Are things that cannot be,
> The fly that lives a single day
> Has lived as long as we.
> But let us live while yet we may,
> While love and life are free,
> For time is time and runs away,
> Though sages disagree.

At the other end of a long career, we find the following lines in *Little Gidding*:

> The moment of the rose and the moment of the yew-tree
> Are of equal duration. A people without history
> Is not redeemed from time, for history is a pattern
> Of timeless moments.

It seems that the sages prevailed.

In the early poems there is a frequent contrast of past glories with present grossness and triviality, as in *Lune de Miel*. But it is not till *The Waste Land* that the attempt to distinguish between different conceptions of time begins to be important. More or less clearly indicated in *The Waste Land* there are the germs of at least three different conceptions: (i) time as succession, flow, history or development; running endlessly from the future into the past, it brings age but no conclusion, and is aptly symbolised by the figure of Tiresias, the deathless old prophet of Thebes, or by the crowd flowing over London Bridge to the sound of Saint Mary Woolnoth keeping the hours; (ii) time as a 'perpetual revolution' and repetition; the cycles of the seasons, as in 'The Burial of the Dead' and the cycles of civilisation mechanically reproducing the same events and the same problems; the migrant Lithuanian woman who goes south every winter is probably the best symbol for this view of time, or perhaps Phlebas the Phoenician, caught in the backward whirlpool; (iii) time as eternal extension without any direction or order, blowing, like the wind, where it listeth, and symbolised by the lady of 'A Game of Chess' with her hysterical 'What shall we do tomorrow? / What shall we ever do?'

I take it to be mainly an illustration of the third conception that the past and the future are continually merged in the most disconcerting ways. Thus 'April is the cruellest month . . . mixing / Memory and desire.' The 'reminiscent bells' of Part V, tolling upside down, toll for the future as well as for the past. Golgotha and the Thunder of the *Upanishads*, belonging to the past, are brought into the present, and we already hear the rain which may fall in the future, and which therefore falls and does not fall. History becomes a Heraclitean flux.

The speaker of *Ash-Wednesday* has tired of worrying over the problems of time and place and sought refuge in renouncing ultimate understanding:

> Because I know that time is always time
> And place is always and only place

But in *The Rock* and *The Family Reunion* the distinctions suggested in *The Waste Land* are worked out more clearly. *The Rock*, being a historical pageant play, is necessarily based in part on the idea of development in time. But it also very emphatically illustrates the idea of repetitive cycles:

> O perpetual revolution of configured stars,
> O perpetual recurrence of determined seasons,
> O world of spring and autumn, birth and dying! (Chorus I)

Reality (Part One)

The Family Reunion, particularly in the words of Amy, gives a very vivid sense of the loss of direction in a frightening wilderness of time, or even of being suspended in a void, not of timelessness in any exalted sense, but of no time, when the clock stops in the dark of night.

Coming between *Murder in the Cathedral* and *The Family Reunion*, *Burnt Norton* seems to have developed time speculations originally perhaps intended for the former play. And as far as I can see it introduces yet another conception of time not exactly similar to any of those we have just considered:

> Time present and time past
> Are both perhaps present in time future,
> And time future contained in time past.
> If all time is eternally present
> All time is unredeemable.
> What might have been is an abstraction
> Remaining a perpetual possibility
> Only in a world of speculation.

The idea recorded in these lines is not the ancient idea of eternity as a present moment in the mind of God, what Carlyle calls the 'Everlasting Now', otherwise why should time be called unredeemable? It is rather connected with Bergson's *durée*. According to Bergson, time has no extension, in fact no similarity at all to spatial things. The only reality is the present, which contains the past and may be said to contain the future in germ. To Bergson 'what might have been' is an intellectual abstraction which has nothing to do with reality: all that was or might have been points ineluctably to the present.

The *Four Quartets* confirm the realisation of the poet of *Ash-Wednesday* that 'time is always time' in the usual conditions of earthly life, and the first lines of *Burnt Norton* may to this extent be said to be an acceptance of Bergson's theory of time: 'all time is eternally present'. Indeed, Bergson's whole theory of creative evolution seems to have helped to inspire the thought processes of the *Four Quartets*. Thus the idea of all life being characterised by movement, as opposed to rigidity and quiescence, is of basic importance. Eliot, it is true, continually speaks of a final 'stillness', but it is a stillness which is also a dance, and he reminds us that 'We must be still and still moving'. And it is entirely in the spirit of Bergson that Eliot, in *The Dry Salvages*, mocks at 'superficial notions of evolution', which, by our feeling of superiority to our remote ancestors, become 'a means of disowning the past'. The past cannot be disowned, for we carry it with us in our present.

Including Bergson's *durée*, there are at least four conceptions of time in Eliot's poetry. The analysis of the time concept, however, is no end in itself. The poet's main purpose is apparently to find a solution to the problem of living. What constitutes the identity in time of a human being or a civilisation? Has life any aim or purpose in time or outside of it? Can past omissions and failures be atoned for and obliterated? All these questions add up to one: 'Is time redeemable?', which in a sense is the major question of all of Eliot's poetry. 'Redeemable' in this context I take to apply both to the past, which one would wish to buy back and change, and to time as such, which needs to be redeemed from being merely a quasi-spatial, deterministic succession of moments.

The analysis of the time concept does seem to indicate certain solutions. Thus according to the cyclic theory there ought to be a possibility of returning to former states and, with greater insight derived from experience, of acting differently and more wisely than at first. Agatha, in the opening scene of *The Family Reunion*, must be hinting at some such idea:

When the loop in time comes—and it does not come for everybody—
The hidden is revealed, and the spectres show themselves.

The 'loop in time', however, is not enough. It cannot of itself provide release from temporal conditions and freedom of action. Time, whether considered as a sequence, a cycle, a vague vastness, an eternal present, or, for that matter, a fourth dimension, remains just as obstinately unredeemable. *Durée* is not enough for salvation, for it is 'simply not final'. There must be something beyond it from which time starts, towards which it moves or in relation to which it has meaning. In his search for the means of redeeming time the poet therefore finally repudiated Bergson and denied at least the completeness of his theories.

Even so, Bergson not only forced him to search but also helped him to find a solution. As a matter of fact, Eliot had always known of a solution, provided he could only believe in it. Plato, Augustine, Kant and many other thinkers pointed to a transcendent reality in which time, as we know it, is non-existent. Who will hold the heart of man, asks Augustine,

> and so fix it, that it may stand a while, and a little catch at a beam of light from that everfixed eternity, to compare it with the times which are never fixed, that he may thereby perceive how there is no comparison between them . . . and that all both past and to come, is made up, and flows out of that which is always present?[1]

To Bradley as to the Vedantists time is an illusion and reality is timeless.[2] Even Bergson's *durée* is very similar to timelessness, since at least it is not quantitative or measurable. The scientific theories of Einstein perhaps, as filtered through the explanations of Whitehead, could also be used to support belief in an ultimate timeless reality, in which the infinite number of possible time systems were mere transient fabrics of thought.

Eliot seems to have been particularly attracted by the changeless eternity of the ancients and the timelessness reported in the experience of mystics of various religions. The possibility of a fullness of life divorced from time altogether has always been either a mirage or a faith in his work. In *The Love Song of J. Alfred Prufrock* the idea of Lazarus returning from the dead or the image of lingering 'in the chambers of the sea / By sea-girls wreathed with seaweed . . .' is related to the idea of timelessness. In *The Waste Land*, the seasons follow each other 'year to year'. But now and again there is a moment of pause:

> At the violet hour, when the eyes and back
> Turn upward from the desk, when the human engine waits
> Like a taxi throbbing waiting,

And under a rock, red with the vertical noonday sun, there is timeless shadow where you may be shown

> . . . something different from either
> Your shadow at morning striding behind you [the past]
> Or your shadow at evening rising to meet you [the future]

Time and the timeless are represented by Madame Sosostris and the 'hyacinth girl' respectively. One looks into the past and future,

---

[1] Augustine, *Confessions*, Bk. XI, ch. xi.

[2] In his essay on Leibniz and Bradley of 1916 Eliot says that Bradley's 'finite center' (i.e. our perceiving self) 'is not in time, though we are more or less forced to think of it under temporal conditions'.

the other provides a vision into 'the heart of light, the silence'. In *The Hollow Men* there is a juxtaposition of 'death's dream kingdom' and 'death's other kingdom' implying a similar contrast. And the concern with timelessness becomes more and more apparent in the poetry as one approaches the *Four Quartets* and the later plays. 'To be conscious,' says the poet of *Burnt Norton*, 'is not to be in time.'

The timeless condition, however, is a matter of experience, not of speculation. It can only be arrived at in enchanted moments, the moments frequently symbolised in Eliot's work by a scene in a rose garden or apple orchard. And such moments of absolute insight are as rare as the moments of intuition of which Bergson says: 'Bien rares sont les moments où nous nous ressaisissons nous-mêmes à ce point: ils ne font qu'un avec nos actions vraiment libres.'[1]

Eliot seems to have had various experiences of sudden illumination, and it will no doubt be useful to enquire what significance he attaches to them. They seem to be of somewhat different kinds in different contexts but can roughly be considered under four heads:

(i) Poetic fulfilment. This is the kind of event referred to in the 'fusion' image in 'Tradition and the Individual Talent' and described in *The Use of Poetry*, in terms that remind one a little of *Tintern Abbey*,[2] as 'the sudden lifting of the burden of anxiety and fear' resulting in 'an outburst of words which we hardly recognise as our own'. The event is analogous to mystical experience, he says, but is really 'a very different thing'. Poetic fulfilment takes place after 'a long incubation' and it is often precipitated by ill-health.[3] A similar account is given in Eliot's essay on 'The *Pensées* of Pascal', which also compares literary composition to religious illumination.[4]

(ii) Pure observation. The moments prized by the two observers of 'Eeldrop and Appleplex' are moments of a heightened aesthetic awareness in which a person or situation is experienced in its

---

[1] *L'Évolution créatrice*, p. 218.
[2]   . . . that blessed mood,
       In which the burthen of the mystery,
       In which the heavy and the weary weight
       Of all this unintelligible world
       Is lighten'd:
[3] *UPC*, pp. 144-5.   [4] *EAM*, p. 142.

uniqueness. This aesthetic attitude has a certain importance, as we have seen, in a great many of the poet's visions. It is manifest in *La Figlia Che Piange*, and it is not entirely absent from 'the intense moment / Isolated, with no before and after' of the *Four Quartets*. It is probable that a memory of Pater occasionally lingered in the poet's mind when he was describing such moments. There is even something that might be a faint echo of Pater in the winter scene described at the beginning of *Little Gidding*:

> When the short day is brightest, with frost and fire,
> The brief sun flames the ice, on pond and ditches,

Here are Pater's words from the Conclusion of *The Renaissance*:

> While all melts under our feet, we may well catch at any exquisite passion, or any contribution to knowledge that seems by a lifted horizon to set the spirit free for a moment. . . . Not to discriminate every moment some passionate attitude in those about us, and in the brilliancy of their gifts some tragic dividing of forces on their ways, is, on this short day of frost and sun, to sleep before evening.

(iii) The rapture of love. This is suggested as a possibility in *The Love Song*, aestheticised in *La Figlia*, mockingly vulgarised in *Dans le Restaurant* ('J'éprouvais un instant de puissance et de délire') and described as a reality in *The Waste Land* ('I could not / Speak, and my eyes failed'), *Burnt Norton*, *The Family Reunion* and *The Elder Statesman*.

(iv) Transfiguration. This is really what the *Four Quartets* are about, and what Harry experiences in *The Family Reunion*. The intensest moments in Eliot's spiritual experience seem to have been those he referred to in a broadcast talk on 'The Significance of Charles Williams' given in 1946, where he said that 'there are pages in [Williams's] novels which describe, with extraordinary precision, the kind of unexplainable experience which many of us have had, once or twice in our lives, and been unable to put into words.'[1] In one of my conversations with Mr Eliot I asked him if he was seeking a spiritual revelation in the *Four Quartets*. He replied that he was not seeking a revelation when writing them, but that he was 'seeking the verbal equivalents for small experiences he had had, and for knowledge derived from reading'. Such 'small

---

[1] *Listener*, Dec. 19, 1946.

experiences' may not be comparable to the ecstasies of the saints, but they are what, for most of us, come closest to the beatific vision.

> For most of us, there is only the unattended
> Moment, the moment in and out of time,
> The distraction fit, lost in a shaft of sunlight,
> *(The Dry Salvages, V)*

To describe the illumination which comes in these unattended moments, Eliot is fond of using the word 'pattern', and it is time to find out what exactly he means by this word. I think our best clue will be found in a few lines from his essay on John Marston, which, to my knowledge, have never received the attention they deserve. After giving a number of quotations from Marston's *Sophonisba*, Eliot continues:

> The quotations are intended to exhibit the exceptional consistency of texture of this play. . . . In spite of the tumultuousness of the action, and the ferocity and horror of certain parts of the play, there is an underlying serenity; and as we familiarize ourselves with the play we perceive a pattern behind the pattern into which the characters deliberately involve themselves; the kind of pattern which we perceive in our own lives only at rare moments of inattention and detachment, drowsing in sunlight. It is the pattern drawn by what the ancient world called Fate; subtilized by Christianity into mazes of delicate theology; and reduced again by the modern world into crudities of psychological or economic necessity.[1]

The 'shaft of sunlight' has become an almost permanent symbol of such moments of illumination. It is found again in *Murder in the Cathedral*, where the Chorus, still waiting for the unknown to happen, feels that

> Destiny waits in the hand of God, shaping the still unshapen:
> I have seen these things in a shaft of sunlight.

The shaft of sunlight suggests both drowsiness and suddenness. Illumination comes in an unattended moment, a 'distraction fit'. Similarly Henri Bergson believes that certain states of 'détache-ment' are favourable to intuitive insight:

> Mais si notre passé nous demeure presque tout entier caché parce qu'il est inhibé par les nécessités de l'action présente, il retrouvera

---

[1] *SE*, p. 232.

la force de franchir le seuil de la conscience dans tous les cas où nous nous désintéresserons de l'action efficace pour nous replacer, en quelque sorte, dans la vie du rêve. Le sommeil, naturel ou artificiel, provoque justement un détachement de ce genre.[1]

Bergson thinks that the past can be revived in dreams or in moments of disinterestedness and relaxed meditation.[2] And this is not very different from what Eliot says in the essay on Marston. What the poet has experienced in the enchanted moments which have taken him by surprise is comparable, he thinks, to finding an 'exceptional consistency of texture' in a play 'in spite of the tumultuousness of the action'. His own life, in other words, may have seemed untidy and disordered, but he suddenly discovers a pattern in a new vision of the past as if a playwright had all the time been shaping it according to a master-plan.

> See, now they vanish,
> The faces and places, with the self which, as it could, loved them,
> To become renewed, transfigured, in another pattern
> (*Little Gidding*, III)

The pattern which he glimpses may be called Fate or Destiny. The important thing is that there is a meaningful arrangement of a transcendent order, and that in moments which seem to be out of time this pattern is experienced as real, in fact as the only reality. His whole past fits into the pattern. Nothing needs to be changed but everything needs to be transmuted and illuminated.

'This,' then, 'is the use of memory: / For liberation.'[3] Ordinary memory is not sufficient. It either presents just a 'few meagre arbitrarily chosen sets of snapshots',[4] or it simply makes the past intolerably present and unredeemable:

> The memory throws up high and dry
> A crowd of twisted things;
> (*Rhapsody on a Windy Night*)

---

[1] *Matière et mémoire*, 1906, pp. 167-8.
[2] Compare: 'But to what purpose / Disturbing the dust on a bowl of rose-leaves / I do not know.' (*Burnt Norton*, I.)
[3] *Little Gidding*, III.
[4] *UPC*, p. 148.

Bergson, and the Problem of Time

There is no use in

> Lying awake, calculating the future,
> Trying to unweave, unwind, unravel
> And piece together the past and the future,
> Between midnight and dawn, when the past is all deception,
>
> (*The Dry Salvages*, I)

Only that memory is useful which can reveal the hidden symphony of the past and enable us to recognise the present in the entire composition. 'Ideally,' says Eliot in his Introduction to Valéry's *Art of Poetry*, 'I should like to be able to hold the whole of a great symphony in my mind at once.' This is the idea poetically expressed in the last movement of *Burnt Norton*:

> Not the stillness of the violin, while the note lasts,
> Not that only, but the co-existence,
> Or say that the end precedes the beginning,
> And the end and the beginning were always there
> Before the beginning and after the end.
> And all is always now.

This realisation, that 'all is always now' at the end of *Burnt Norton* is different from the feeling at the beginning of the poem that 'all time is eternally present'. A vision lies between the two statements. The present has become an all-inclusive and meaningful pattern. And so time is redeemed.

In case Eliot's idea of pattern is still not clear, he has himself provided us with an illustration in concrete, dramatic terms, namely *The Family Reunion*. Harry, Lord Monchensey, is obsessed by the past and by feelings of guilt which haunt him in the shape of the Furies. He cannot satisfactorily account for these feelings, and he cannot even distinguish between what he actually did in the past and what he merely wanted to do. On his return to Wishwood he meets his superficial past again: Amy has tried to keep everything unchanged till his return. But the mere reawakening of his memories makes things worse rather than better:

> Here I have been finding
> A misery long forgotten, and a new torture,
> The shadow of something behind our meagre childhood,
> Some origin of wretchedness.

It is only when Agatha reveals the secret of her love for Harry's father that he understands his own memories and is able to complete them (and again this is an awakening of the past which is Bergsonian rather than Freudian). Harry now sees his own guilt as part of something more universal and is able to explain the shadow behind his 'meagre childhood'. The fact that, like his father, he has wished to kill his wife indicates an inherited guilt, or, in theological terms, original sin. But there is grace in the simultaneous discovery that, though his mother in the flesh is the possessive Amy, on a more important level he belongs to Agatha. This spiritual kinship is the hidden pattern of his life which explains his bewildered feelings and actions and liberates him both from what was and what might have been: As Agatha says:

> relief from what happened
> Is also relief from that unfulfilled craving

In a rather more mechanical way, which smacks of Oscar Wilde, the pattern of Colby's past and his true identity are revealed to him in *The Confidential Clerk*. In *The Elder Statesman* it is the act of confession that forces Lord Claverton's life into focus and pattern.

Thus the poet shows how, by going back to face the past in a spirit of acceptance, or rather by discovering the whole past in a deeper understanding of the present, the imprisoning cycle of time may be broken. We are required to become conscious of ourselves, of our own minds and the influences which have worked upon them to make them what they are. We cannot fully succeed in this life, for 'to be conscious is not to be in time', but we can achieve a measure of success. And if we thus manage to heighten our awareness, we can contrive to live, like Harry in *The Family Reunion*, on several planes at once.

Ultimately, of course, Eliot's pattern derives its meaningfulness from being not merely a structure of the mind or the product of an obscurely operating 'Fate', but from being definitely supernatural. We cannot construct a vision out of our own past and present alone. We must somehow get in touch with an Absolute Reality which can provide a teleological basis for our lives. 'The decision will be made by powers beyond us / Which now and then emerge', says Agatha. And in *Murder in the Cathedral* Thomas makes the Christian implication perfectly clear:

> This is one moment
> But know that another
> Shall pierce you with a sudden painful joy
> When the figure of God's purpose is made complete.

Whatever the theories of time as such, then, the answer to the time problem as it affects the moral and spiritual being of man lies outside the province of physicists and systematic philosophers, in the province of experience and belief. Eliot may not strictly speaking be a mystic, nor are all those who have had experiences similar to his, but there is an essential similarity between his glimpses of a higher pattern in his personal history and the ecstatic union with the divine which the great mystics have attempted to describe.

More and more in Eliot's later work the idea of timelessness is connected with the Christian revelation. Dr Staffan Bergsten, in his recent dissertation on *Time and Eternity* in Eliot's *Four Quartets*, reminds us that Eliot's conception of the state of bliss as timeless may be unbiblical, since the basic idea of the Bible would seem to be that of a termination of terrestrial history in time and a continuation of time in eternity. Eliot may have superimposed favourite philosophical ideas of his own on the Christian teaching. But in doing so he undoubtedly has the support of Christian as well as Hindu and Buddhist mystics. And on the basis of his own 'small experiences' and on 'knowledge derived from reading' he has interpreted the central Christian doctrine of the Incarnation in a completely poetical, a completely modern and a profoundly reverent way as 'the intersection of the timeless with time'.[1] Thus the Incarnation just as much as the Passion means Atonement and Salvation. It is the redemption of all history:

> Then came, at a predetermined moment, a moment in time and of time,
> A moment not out of time, but in time, in what we call history:
> transecting, bisecting the world of time, a moment in time but not like a moment of time,
> A moment in time but time was made through that moment: for without the meaning there is no time, and that moment of time gave the meaning.
>
> (*The Rock*, Chorus VII)

---

[1] Cp. Bergson: 'Il y a une durée réelle . . . dont chaque moment peut être rapproché d'un état du monde extérieur qui en est contemporain . . . le trait d'union entre ces deux termes, espace et durée, est la simultanéité, qu'on pourrait définir l'intersection du temps avec l'espace.' *Essai*, p. 91.

It is interesting to note that this view of the Incarnation is fore-shadowed in *Gerontion*, in its bringing together of Christ the tiger and History: 'The tiger springs in the new year . . .'

Before leaving the subject of time I think a few words should be said of a rather special theory which has had a certain influence on the work of some modern writers. I refer to J. W. Dunne's theory of time as developed in *An Experiment with Time* and *The Serial Universe*. The former book was first published in 1927 and was reissued in a revised form as a paperback by Faber and Faber in 1958.

Dunne believes in different levels of awareness at which events appear with greater or less dependence on the ordinary time sequence. Our 'observer 1', the everyday waking consciousness, perceives only a chronological flow in which memories are in the past and the future is blocked from view. But 'observer 2', who is able to function in dreams when the more limited consciousness is asleep, commands a view of a wider 'field of presentation', a four-dimensional one in which future as well as past events can be perceived. Theoretically an 'observer 3' would see a still wider field, and so on in a series *ad infinitum*, i.e. till final reality is known.

Dunne's theory is not altogether speculative. It is based first on the experience of chance moments of illumination or clairvoyance, secondly on experiments in which he and others recorded their dreams and watched for elements of these dreams to 'happen' afterwards. Of the strange experiences of premonitions and dreams 'coming true' that most of us may occasionally have had, Dunne offers a surprisingly plausible explanation. And whatever we think of his theory as such, it cannot be denied that in its assurance of the reality and immortality of the soul it has a strong emotional appeal. Dunne's prose, too, is often of a poetic order:

> We must live before we can attain to either intelligence or control at all. We must sleep if we are not to find ourselves, at death, help-lessly strange to the new conditions. And we must die before we can hope to advance to a broader understanding.

To a Christian and a poet Dunne's ideas and formulations might well recommend themselves quite strongly, and I would not be surprised to find that his time theory had suggested certain inci-dents and trains of thought in Eliot's works. The meditations on the nature of time in the *Four Quartets*, particularly in *Burnt Norton*, may have absorbed something from Dunne's general ideas, as when the poet reflects that

> Time past and time future
> Allow but a little consciousness.
> To be conscious is not to be in time

And in *The Cocktail Party* Reilly's premonition of Celia's violent death is not just the development of a platonic idea suggested by Shelley. It may quite possibly owe something to Dunne's belief in our knowledge of the future. Certainly Reilly has some of the same expository manner as Dunne:

> When I first met Miss Coplestone, in this room,
> I saw the image, standing behind her chair,
> Of a Celia Coplestone whose face showed the astonishment
> Of the first five minutes after a violent death.
> If this strains your credulity, Mrs. Chamberlayne,
> I ask you only to entertain the suggestion
> That a sudden intuition, in certain minds,
> May tend to express itself at once in a picture.
> That happens to me, sometimes.

One should not attach too much importance to the possible influence of Dunne or to that of other somewhat eccentric philosophers like P. D. Ouspensky, the author of *A New Model of the Universe*; but these writers at least help to show that Eliot's interest in time is typical of a widespread movement of modern thought.

VIII

REALITY (Part Two)

ORIENTAL MYSTICISM

J UST as Eliot's interest in Western philosophy can be clearly traced in his poetry, so his study of Oriental philosophy has left indelible marks. It is not always easy to distinguish these marks from those left by Christian mysticism, and one risks attaching too much importance to concrete references, such as the quotation from the *Bhagavad-Gita* in *The Dry Salvages*. There are obvious points of contact between Eastern and Western thought. The two currents meet in the New Testament, while in the Old Testament, which has become part of the basis of Western culture, we really meet a tributary of the Oriental tradition. Thus *Ecclesiastes*, which has been much used by Eliot, presents a view of life related to that of Buddhism. If, however, the distinctions between Eastern and Western mysticism are not always easy to draw, Eliot's allusions show at least that he has often had the Oriental mystics in mind; and occasionally he introduces the peculiarities of Oriental thought into his poetry.

The more obvious references to Oriental religions and mysticism are to be found in *The Waste Land*, the *Quartets* and *The Cocktail Party*. In *The Waste Land*, the Buddha, a representative of Eastern asceticism, is 'collocated' with St Augustine, a representative of Western asceticism. And in the final section of the poem the ethical mystic teachings of the *Upanishads* are drawn upon. *Burnt Norton* introduces the Oriental image, which is superficially incongruous in its context, of a lotos floating on the water of the empty pool; its import may be phallic, but its Buddhist associations are far more immediate.[1] *The Dry Salvages* reminds us in

---

[1] In *Burnt Norton* it appears to be a symbol of the complete reality of which sensible things (the concrete pool) are only a part. This, of course, would attach it to Hinduism rather than to Buddhism.

section II of Vishnu and Siva of the Hindu trinity by the notion that 'Time the destroyer is time the preserver', and in section III quotes from Krishna's admonitions to Arjuna in the *Bhagavad-Gita*. In *The Cocktail Party*, the admonition of the psychiatrist to his patients, 'work out your salvation with diligence', are the words of the dying Buddha.

These allusions call our attention to a far profounder saturation of Eliot's poetry with Hindu and Buddhist thought than they immediately indicate.[1]

In the *Bhagavad-Gita* Krishna discourses thus:

> They do not know my nature
> That is one with Brahman, changeless, superhuman.
>
> Veiled in my Maya, I am not shown to many.
> How shall this world, bewildered by delusion,
> Recognize me, who am not born and change not?

I know all beings, Arjuna: past, present and to come. But no one knows me.

All living creatures are led astray as soon as they are born, by the delusion that this relative world is real. This delusion arises from their own desire and hatred. But the doers of good deeds, whose bad karma is exhausted, are freed from this delusion about the relative world. They hold firmly to their vows, and worship me.

Men take refuge in me, to escape from their fear of old age and death. Thus they come to know Brahman, and the entire nature of the Atman, and the creative energy which is in Brahman. Knowing me, they understand the nature of the relative world and the individual man, and of God who presides over all action. Even at the hour of death, they continue to know me thus. In that hour, their whole consciousness is made one with mine.[2]

Eliot calls the *Bhagavad-Gita* 'the next greatest philosophical poem to the *Divine Comedy* within my experience'.[3] This passage from the *Gita* not only expounds one of the most fundamental ideas in Eliot's philosophy, that of one absolute Reality, but might also have been his own expression of many more incidental attitudes, for instance the fear of old age and death. There is no

---

[1] See also H. E. McCarthy, 'T. S. Eliot and Buddhism', *Philosophy East and West*, II, 1 (April 1952).

[2] *Bhagavad-Gita*, trans. by Prabhavananda and C. Isherwood, London, 1947, p. 93.

[3] 'Dante', *SE*, p. 258.

need to repeat what I have said before concerning Absolute Idealism in the poet's work. It is enough if we see that it has been inspired by ancient Indian philosophy as well as by Western thinkers of more recent times. The imagery by means of which Eliot conveys his ideas and intimations is mostly modern, it is true, but this is no indication of the age or origin of the ideas.

The ancient Indian philosophers, especially Śaṁkara, are very close to the Absolute Idealists in their interpretation of reality. Reality, they thought, was one and spiritual, Brahman. And the world of sense perception was relative and deceptive, māyā, though there were various degrees of unreality.

The Brahman is 'the unmoved and the moving'.[1] One of his aspects is ubiquitous presence, the Atman.

> Not subject to change
> Is the infinite Atman,
> Without beginning,
> Beyond the gunas:[2]

Brahman is timeless; therefore whoever seeks illumination must become oblivious to the passing of time, just as those who seek Nirvana must detach themselves from temporal relations. Such detachment cannot depend on a 'distraction fit' or accidental illuminations, but must be practised deliberately and wholemindedly. Our karma follows us always, but it can be controlled by a disciplined observance of the yogas. If this is to be successful humility is required. The insistence on this virtue in Hinduism and still more in Buddhism reminds us that Eliot does not see it exclusively as a Christian virtue.

The end of Yoga is liberation—

> The inner freedom from the practical desire,
> The release from action and suffering, release from the inner
> And the outer compulsion,

> (*Burnt Norton*, II)

And liberation means divine union and the annihilation of the individual (the word yoga is derived from the Sanskrit yuj = join). The divine union may be best described by the word 'shantih', which concludes *The Waste Land* and which Eliot makes equivalent to our phrase, 'the Peace which passeth understanding'.

---

[1] *Bhagavad-Gita*, p. 125.   [2] Ibid., p. 138.

Only in the divine union is there true existence:

> The awful daring of a moment's surrender
> Which an age of prudence can never retract
> By this, and this only, we have existed
> ('What the Thunder Said')

To achieve union with Brahman, however, only intuitional knowledge is of any avail, for Brahman is 'the negative of everything
that is positively known',[1] and knowledge as we commonly understand it must therefore be eliminated.

One of the basic features of Oriental religions is the belief in
metempsychosis. This belief never appears very clearly on the surface in Eliot's poetry, but there are obvious traces of it. Thus, in
the *Four Quartets*, the 'travellers' who start on a journey are not
the same when they arrive at their destination. They are asked to
meditate during their journey upon Krishna's words to Arjuna
concerning re-incarnation:

> On whatever sphere of being the mind of man may be intent at
> the time of death, to that he goes . . . having been used to ponder
> on it.[2]

Their change will be a part of their spiritual progress. And the
final goal of all changes is freedom from the self.

Another doctrine, closely connected with metempsychosis, is
used far more overtly by Eliot: that of the universal cycle. The
Gita uses the old symbol of the wheel, 'the terrible wheel of re-
birth and death'.[3] This terrible wheel may be an illusion, but it
nevertheless holds us prisoners:

> Maya makes all things: what moves, what is unmoving.
> O son of Kunti, that is why the world spins,
> Turning its wheel through birth
> And through destruction.[4]

The wheel, as we have seen, is a frequent symbol in Eliot's work.
And generally it has a significance more or less as in the *Bhagavad-
Gita*. I assume that in the Tarot pack of cards alluded to in *The
Waste Land*, the Wheel originally symbolised the cycle of life and

---

[1] *Encyclopaedia Britannica*, art. on Indian Philosophy.
[2] Quoted from R. Preston, '*Four Quartets*' *Rehearsed* (1946), p. 44. Cf.
Prabhavananda and Isherwood, *Bhagavad-Gita*, p. 95.
[3] *Bhagavad-Gita*, p. 44.   [4] Ibid., p. 102.

the seasons. It appears significantly in 'Death by Water', where Phlebas the Phoenician enters 'the whirlpool'. And in an earlier section, Madame Sosostris sees 'crowds of people, walking round in a ring'. In *Murder in the Cathedral* the wheel is again a major symbol. Only the fool, says Becket on one occasion, 'may think / He can turn the wheel on which he turns'. And Harry in *The Family Reunion* speaks of 'the burning wheel' and 'the human wheel'.[1]

By successful re-incarnations, the wheel of Hinduism and Buddhism can be turned into an ascending spiral. This idea also enters into Eliot's poetry, especially in the image of the winding stairs in *Ash-Wednesday*.

As long as we are climbing the stairs, however, or turning on the wheel, we are bound to suffer. Eliot's conception of life as suffering found its most consistent philosophical support in Oriental mysticism. The Buddha's Fire Sermon, alluded to in *The Waste Land*, is an account of the sterile and painful burning of the senses, of desires and thoughts, and of all their objects. We found that the poet's pessimism had nourished itself on these ideas. Without their background it is hard to explain what I can only call the thoughtfulness of Eliot's *Weltschmerz*, or to account adequately for the death-wish expressed in such poems as *The Waste Land*, *Ash-Wednesday* and *A Song for Simeon*.

Only by the practice of disaffection, by spiritual discipline and askesis, can release from the circle of suffering be attained. Krishna explains the 'Karma Yoga' to Arjuna, and declares that 'even a little practice of this yoga will save you from the terrible wheel of rebirth and death'.[2]

Eliot's study of Patanjali left him, he says, in a 'state of enlightened mystification'. But his knowledge of Yoga, even if imperfect, has nevertheless been extremely fruitful for his poetry. In the self-mortification and austerities enjoined by Patanjali he found not only the answer to a religious need, but also the matter for a poetry of contemplation which should be both intense and dramatic. In the repetitive muttering of Vedic hymns he may have found the idea for some of his own hypnotic effects.

The practice of Yoga tends to consist in renunciation and in abstention from movement, physical and mental. Bearing this in

---

[1] *The Family Reunion*, pp. 30, 101.
[2] *Bhagavad-Gita*, p. 44.

mind, we can approach such passages as the following from *Burnt Norton* with an increased sensibility to their range of suggestion:

> Descend lower, descend only
> Into the world of perpetual solitude,
> World not world, but that which is not world,
> Internal darkness, deprivation
> And destitution of all property,
> Desiccation of the world of sense,
> Evacuation of the world of fancy,
> Inoperancy of the world of spirit;

The symbol of darkness is a Hindu as well as a Christian symbol, as Philip Wheelwright has pointed out. He quotes from the *Bhagavad-Gita*:

> In that which is night to all things, therein the self-subjugated remains awake; but where all else is awake, that is the night for the knower of self.[1]

Purification by fire is also a Hindu symbol:

> The blazing fire turns wood to ashes:
> The fire of knowledge turns all karmas to ashes.
> On earth there is no purifier
> As great as this knowledge,[2]

Patanjali's 'Eightfold Path' aims at the suppression of mental activity (and similarly the Buddha's 'Aryan Eightfold Path', which otherwise differs considerably from it, consists largely in abstentions). But all Yoga is not passivity. Krishna urges Arjuna to pursue the course of right action, for 'freedom from activity is never achieved by abstaining from action'[3]:

> The wise see knowledge and action as one:
> They see truly.
> Take either path
> And tread it to the end:
> The end is the same.
> There the followers of action
> Meet the seekers after knowledge
> In equal freedom.[4]

---

[1] Rajan (ed.), *T. S. Eliot*, p. 103. Cp. the fragment from the *Isa Upanishad* quoted by J. J. Sweeney, in Unger's *Selected Critique*, p. 406.
[2] *Bhagavad-Gita*, p. 66.   [3] Ibid., p. 51.   [4] Ibid., p. 70.

This passage reminds one strikingly of a number of passages in Eliot. There is a special yoga of action which Eliot no doubt has in mind when he urges us to be 'still moving' or to 'fare forward'. And by reference to Hindu mysticism we see how Eliot's insistence on inaction can be reconciled with his insistence on activity. The action must be that which we are destined to fulfil, and there must be no thought of its fruits. 'You have the right to work, but for the work's sake only. You have no right to the fruits of work', says Krishna.[1] And further, 'You must perform every action sacramentally, and be free from all attachment to results.'[2] And similarly Eliot, 'For us, there is only the trying. The rest is not our business';[3] 'And do not think of the fruit of action.'[4] Krishna: 'Action rightly performed brings freedom.'[5] And Eliot: 'And right action is freedom / From past and future also.'[6]

There is a certain contrast between *East Coker* and *The Dry Salvages*: the former deals mainly with the dark night of the soul, while the latter has right action for its theme. But the opposite themes are combined in the poem of reconciliation, *Little Gidding*, in which all the activity of history is seen to be a pattern of timeless, motionless moments, and all our exploration to lead us back to our starting-point.

If we turn to the *Upanishads*, we find a kind of 'right action' indicated by 'what the Thunder said': 'datta, dayadhvam, damyata' —'give, sympathise, control'. The main significance of these words is that one should subdue oneself and give oneself to others, and to the Brahman, who is in all things; and this is how Eliot uses them in *The Waste Land*. If the voice of God in the thunder is obeyed, it means a breaking out of the isolation which prevents a fruitful intercourse, and the consummation of a final union.

The Yoga of Patanjali counts on an irresistible will in its addicts to see them through their spiritual discipline. And in spite of an admixture of fatalism in Hindu belief, it would seem that the idea of the perfect efficaciousness of human effort rightly applied is implicit in all Oriental asceticism. Yoga leads to union with the Brahman without divine interference. Eliot is strongly attracted

---

[1] *Bhagavad-Gita*, p. 46. (Contrast Christ's 'the labourer is worthy of his hire'.)
[2] Ibid., p. 52.
[3] *East Coker*, V.
[4] *The Dry Salvages*, III.
[5] *Bhagavad-Gita*, p. 69.
[6] *The Dry Salvages*, V.

to this idea, as we have already seen. But at the same time his Christian orthodoxy prevents him from accepting it completely. His dilemma resembles that of his own spiritual hero, Thomas Becket, who is tempted to win saintliness by deliberate martyrdom, but who realises that only divine grace can bestow it. Eliot seems to stop half-way, from either point of view, or even to contradict himself. He believes strongly in human effort, and yet he denies its efficacy. In the same breath as he tells us to 'be still, and wait without hope', he declares, not only with hope but with seeming confidence, 'So the darkness shall be the light, and the stillness the dancing'.[1] The apparent opposition between human passivity and human activity can be reconciled. But it is harder to reconcile the reliance on divine grace with the reliance on human effort. That Eliot is fully conscious of the difficulty we can tell from his essay on 'The *Pensées* of Pascal'.[2] A reconciliation is effected in Catholic theology, where the will is considered to be really free only if it acts under grace. But this part of Catholic theology has not been drawn upon to any extent in Eliot's poetry. The result is that the Oriental view of spiritual discipline has been given great prominence and is juxtaposed with the Christian view of grace. There is an unresolved conflict in these ideas, which we can only feel as a conflict in the poetry, though it does not necessarily impair the value of the poetry.

PRIMITIVE MYTH AND RITUAL

Eliot's interest in Oriental religions is part of a wider interest in the history and the essence of all religion. The work of the leading anthropologists of the early part of our century, such as Frazer, Durkheim and Lévy-Bruhl, is well known to him. And he almost retraces in his poetry the development of human beliefs from primitive myth and ritual to the higher faiths and forms of worship.

The influence of his anthropological studies makes itself felt particularly in *The Waste Land*. Stephen Spender is worth quoting for his lucid summing-up of this influence:

Instead of a basis of accepted belief, the whole structure of Eliot's poem is based on certain primitive rituals and myths, which, he

---

[1] *East Coker*, III.   [2] *EAM*, p. 153.

seems to feel, must be psychological certainties, being a part of what psychologists call our 'race memory'. He is appealing to scientific legend, where Yeats appeals to poetic legend. The authority behind *The Waste Land* is not the Catholic Church, nor romantic lore, but anthropology from the volumes of Sir James Frazer's *The Golden Bough*. Eliot has tried to indicate, beneath the very ephemeral and violent movements of our own civilization, the gradual and magical contours of man's earliest religious beliefs. The effect he sets out to achieve is illustrated by Freud's remark in *Civilization and its Discontents* that the growth of the individual mind resembles the growth of Rome, supposing that modern Rome, as it is to-day, were co-existent with the buildings of Rome at every period in her history; and that beneath the modern architecture was found the architecture of every earlier period, in a perfect state of preservation.[1]

Eliot's awareness of the whole past of religion and culture is no doubt as distinct as his consciousness of the past of words. And this awareness informs not only *The Waste Land*, but practically his entire production. In one of the *Rock* Choruses (VII) he summarises the history of religion from its cradle among early savages. And even in the *Four Quartets* the connection is recognised between religion and the 'primitive terror':

> the past experience revived in the meaning
> Is not the experience of one life only
> But of many generations—not forgetting
> Something that is probably quite ineffable:
> The backward look behind the assurance
> Of recorded history, the backward half-look
> Over the shoulder, towards the primitive terror.

Anthropological lore gives a meaning to the dance around and through the bonfire in the first section of *East Coker*. And anthropology provides the background for the poetic vision of the river as 'a strong brown god' in the beginning of *The Dry Salvages*. In *Animula* there is a correspondence between the pleasure of the child and the cult of fertility symbols in the childhood of the race; while the 'running stags around a silver tray' remind one of the magic drawings of primitive hunters. 'The wind, the sunlight and the sea' in the same poem are favourite symbols and are well known to anthropology (they are connected with the 'elements' of air, fire and water, which, with the fourth element, earth, are

[1] Spender, *The Destructive Element* (1936), pp. 145–6.

often referred to by the poet). Fire, one of the most frequent symbols in Eliot's poetry, is also one of the most ancient known to man.

Thus the whole history of religion is behind Eliot's Christianity. I think it is right to say, nevertheless, that anthropological learning only plays a subordinate part in his work, and that he uses it entirely as he thinks fit. In *The Waste Land* it certainly helped to fashion his general outlook, but in the rest of his poetry it has little influence on his ultimate views. His later poetry, in particular, is mainly determined by religious faith.

CHRISTIANITY

The basis of Eliot's poetry changed as a Christian philosophy supervened on his former agnosticism. His vision changed at the same time. Instead of a jumble of irrelevancies life began to look like a complete system in which even sin was 'behovely' and nothing at all was irrelevant. The poet found a pattern when the man found a faith. For one of the main effects of Christianity in Eliot's poetry is the provision of a unifying principle to his vision. In comparison, such a feature as the presentation of doctrine in his poems is altogether insignificant.

I would not assert that poetry must necessarily render the impression of unity that we find in the *Four Quartets*, or even that it is better poetry if it does. There is wonderful poetry which relies on a mere picturesque harmony, or in which the unity is only that of the poet's mood. But we must not mistake mood for philosophy, so as to miss the vision of disconnectedness in Eliot's early work and fail to understand the change which occurred later.

Apart from the imagery in which it is clothed, his vision has become far less concrete than it was at first. It endeavours to grapple with pure ideas, and in this endeavour it changes itself into symbols and mental images. This means that it is both more indirect, more synthetic and more reminiscent than formerly. At the same time as the philosophical pendulum may be said to have swung from Aristotle to Plato, the poet's manner has swung, on the whole, from impressionism to expressionism; and there would seem to be some natural connection between these changes. We still, no doubt, find the indistinctness of association which used to characterise his poetry in spite of the sharpness of individual perceptions, but now it is caused by a different kind or degree of metaphysical ignorance—not the sceptical exploitation but the hopeful exploration of spiritual mysteries.

It is likely that much of the imagery which is used to suggest religious experiences may have its origin in purely personal and a-religious memories and associations. Thus the shaft-of-sunlight symbol may have been originally connected with 'la figlia'— it is the sunlight playing in her hair. And the aridity symbols may derive from the sight of the 'barren New England hills'. One might say that the later poetry is merely 'emotion recollected in tranquillity'. It is not beliefs, one is tempted to think, that have made Eliot's poetry, but personal suffering. What is behind such a line as 'looking into the heart of light, the silence'? Is it merely 'J'éprouvais un instant de puissance et de délire'? Is this all the 'distraction fit' amounts to? And what is the origin of the religious fear that is often felt, the fear of reality, the 'fear in a handful of dust'? Is it only some trivial experience such as that of being scared by a dog?

It would be absurd to think the whole truth could be found in a reduction to childhood impressions and literary reminiscences. Nor does it invalidate a religious experience to find its human roots in everyday events. If religion is true, all events must have some connection with it. And the Symbolist teaching that what we perceive conceals some inner reality, that the universe is all a mass of symbols, follows as a corollary.

Christian ideas are ubiquitous in Eliot's work, but the emphasis on various dogmas and aspects of faith is very personal. We need not dwell upon the many satirical references to Christian doctrines in the 1920 *Poems*, or the apparently blasphemous comparison of Sweeney in his bath to Christ in the Jordan. But the early poems, like *The Love Song* and *Portrait of a Lady*, also show the poet frequently puzzling over the problem of immortality; and they are pervaded by a sense of guilt and sinfulness, clearly expressed in *Gerontion*.

These early poems seem to show that their author suffered by reason of his disbelief in the spiritual oneness of the individual. Prufrock feels despondent because of his age, and the idea of the ravages of time constantly crops up, echoing through all the poetry down to *Little Gidding*, in which the stranger of the blasted London streets discloses 'the gifts reserved for age'.

Eliot's obsession with old age, in so far as it is serious, can be best explained by his horror at the idea of the dissolution of the personality, so carefully hedged about by its owner. At one time he probably disbelieved both in the 'substantial unity of the soul' and in any kind of universal soul; which may well have caused a sort of metaphysical despair,[1] till he recognised that in Christianity belief in the supreme worth of the particular soul could be reconciled with belief in a supreme superhuman spirit.

Whatever the contributary causes, Eliot's early pessimism was changed from the inside. For the despondency engendered by the difficulties of embracing a positive faith was supplemented at first by the 'Catholic philosophy of disillusion', which Eliot found exemplified in Dante's *Vita Nuova*, and which may be summed up in the precepts: 'not to expect more from *life* than it can give or more from *human* beings than they can give; to look to *death* for what life cannot give.'[2] This philosophy is not necessarily bitter. It softens the bitterness of disappointed expectations in life. But it demands a high degree of resignation. In his early poems Eliot shows little of this resignation, unless it is to be found in his constant preoccupation with the theme of death. Even in such poems as *Ash-Wednesday* he finds resignation difficult. But in time the Catholic philosophy of disillusion, with its serene recognition of the world for what it is, engulfs his more rebellious and bitter disillusion. This has happened in the *Four Quartets*, where the author has taken a further step and expressed a mood or experience of beatitude only occasionally glimpsed before, and where the impression of communication has replaced the earlier impression of solitary rumination.

The Catholic philosophy of disillusion is connected, of course, with the doctrine of sin. The Eastern religions are more aware of evil as suffering than as unrighteousness, more as personal than as social, and this view seems to predominate in Eliot's poetry. But certainly in his later poems the note of gloom is often struck by the idea of sin. This idea already appears as 'the shadow' in *The Hollow Men*. In *Ash-Wednesday* the realisation of sin is fully conscious and informs the prayers of the poem: 'Pray for us sinners

---

[1] Cp. 'Eeldrop and Appleplex': 'With the decline of orthodox theology and its admirable theory of the soul, the unique importance of events has vanished.'

[2] 'Dante', *SE*, p. 275.

now and at the hour of our death.' *Marina* mentions such definite
sins as hatred, vanity, gluttony and lust. And in Chorus V of *The
Rock* the feeling of sinfulness is particularly keen: 'The heart is
deceitful . . . and desperately wicked.'

On the whole, it seems as if sin is inextricably bound up with
existence in time. It is *original sin*, the heritage of mankind. *Animula*, however, indicates another point of view: that childhood is
a period of innocence, when the soul which has issued from the
hand of God retains its purity and simplicity—whereas experience
of this life and adult age bring corruption. The poem may be
interpreted, it is true, as a general statement of what temporal
existence does to man, who was originally shaped in the image of
God. But it would be hard to deny that it shows some belief in the
essential goodness of human kind. Eliot's view in *Animula* is influenced by Aristotle by way of Dante.[1] In his younger days he
may also have inclined to the Romantic notion that man is essentially good and only corrupted by his environment. But as far
back as his poetry takes us he was obviously drawn much more
strongly to the opposite view, that man is fundamentally imperfect but can be improved and civilised.

The conviction of sin is not always conscious. The Magus and
Simeon, for instance, are not consciously aware of it. Simeon
even has a strong sense of his own righteousness:

> I have walked many years in this city,
> Kept faith and fast, provided for the poor,
> Have given and taken honour and ease.
> There went never any rejected from my door.

But the Magus feels that 'this Birth was / Hard and bitter agony
for us, like Death, our death', obviously because he realises sub-
consciously how worthless he is in comparison with the perfection
he has seen. Simeon, we must suppose, has some such realisation
too, though he does not explain it in terms of agony and death,
but in terms of tiredness. It is the old man's fear, also seen in
Gerontion, which is thus disguised.

In the early poems, the subject of sin is rarely introduced
directly. Nor is the contemplation of death (which is fairly constant) frequently connected with the idea of doom. But in *Gerontion* and occasionally in *The Waste Land* we do find such a

---

[1] Cf. 'Dante', *SE*, pp. 259-61.

connection between death and the judgment for sins. 'The tiger [i.e. Christ] springs in the new year,' says Gerontion: 'Us he devours.' And Madame Sosostris admonishes her clients to 'Fear death by water', with a similar meaning.

A number of critics, among them Dr Richards, have pointed to Eliot's preoccupation with sex. One cannot help noticing this preoccupation, and it is sometimes hard to avoid the impression that sex is regarded as in itself evil and sinful. This impression, however, is easily exaggerated if we imagine that the sinfulness of sex is a matter of Christian doctrine or philosophy. Apart from the doctrine of original sin, which perhaps has a special application to sex, there is no such teaching in the theology to which Eliot subscribes. Catholic dogma, despite the doctrine of the Immaculate Conception, does not regard sexual intercourse as in itself tainted or sinful. Anglican theology, as expounded in *Doctrine in the Church of England*, emphatically does not. And I do not think Eliot very often had sinfulness in mind when he wrote about or alluded to the abuse of sex. If a philosophy is required to explain this preoccupation, it will sooner be found in the Oriental ideas of desire as suffering and as distraction from the path of holiness. We must also remember that the sexual imagery of Eliot's poems stands for a number of other things besides physical eros, especially for his view of spiritual isolation or communion.

It is particularly noteworthy that Celia in *The Cocktail Party* comes to a sense of sin not because she feels guilty in respect of her affair with a married man, but because that very affair was a sufficiently wonderful experience to stir her into a spiritual awakening. She guesses the existence of something supremely desirable which she has failed to recognise before and failed to live up to. And she is able to guess it because the experience of love was itself a vision and an ecstasy:

> I abandoned the future before we began,
> And after that I lived in a present
> Where time was meaningless, a private world of *ours*,
> Where the word 'happiness' had a different meaning
> Or so it seemed.

This is what Celia tells Edward at their parting. Later she tells the psychiatrist that she does not feel immoral, although she may have been a fool. She took nothing from Edward's wife, Lavinia,

that Lavinia wanted. Her sense of sin, therefore, so different from
the conventional ideas of bad form or psychological maladjust-
ment which she has been brought up to believe in, leaves her both
intellectually and emotionally bewildered. She has to learn that
nobody can become aware of absolute perfection without developing a corresponding sense of human imperfection. Anti-Puritan
critics, stubbornly reading their own interpretation of Christian
morality into the action of Eliot's play, have censured the cynical
cruelty of Reilly in inflicting a painful death on Celia as a punishment for her sexual transgression. They have not seen, or understood, that she herself wishes to atone for a universal sin, which in
Eliot's view has no more and no less to do with sex than it has to
do with many other aspects of life.

In this connection it may be remarked that Mr Edmund Wilson
is stating only one half of a general truth when he observes in
Axel's Castle that 'the drying up of the springs of sexual emotion'
may cause a 'straining after a religious emotion which may be
made to take its place'.[1] It might be maintained with equal justice
that the drying up of the springs of religious emotion causes a
straining after sexual emotion which may be made to take its
place. Very little is gained by either explanation. And at any rate
an interest in metaphysics, and in religious emotions, positive or
negative, are as original in Eliot's poetry as his interest in sexual
emotions. We may admit, and Eliot admits, a connection as in an
ascending scale between sexual love and divine love, but this does
not make either a substitute for the other.

To sum up this minor discussion, it may be confidently affirmed
that sex in Eliot's poetry is often corrupted by sin, and may even
be peculiarly susceptible to corruption, but it is not essentially
sinful except in being an important part of life in general and
sharing the general burden of original sin.

In *The Waste Land* it is continually implied that sin and guilt are
shared by everybody. And this is stated directly in *Sweeney
Agonistes*:

> I knew a man once did a girl in
> Any man might do a girl in
> Any man has to, needs to, wants to
> Once in a lifetime, do a girl in.

---

[1] Op. cit., p. 105.

In *Ash-Wednesday* we hear of those who 'affirm before the world and deny between the rocks', 'spitting from the mouth the withered apple-seed'—which reminds us of the Fall of man in the Garden of Eden, the perpetuation of the Fall symbolised by the withered seed. The events of *The Family Reunion* are described by Agatha as a story 'of sin and expiation' and Harry feels that there must be 'some origin of wretchedness'. *East Coker* has a highly 'metaphysical' image of the Church as a 'dying nurse'

> Whose constant care is not to please
> But to remind of our, and Adam's curse,
> And that, to be restored, our sickness must grow worse.

And the Fall is again alluded to in *The Dry Salvages*—'The bitter apple and the bite in the apple'.

The doctrine of original sin was at first welcomed, perhaps, chiefly because it lent a semi-mythical support to Eliot's opposition to the romantic-humanistic view of life. But this opposition was inspired in turn by a deep realisation of human failure, the causes of which we have discussed. We remember that Eliot was so depressed by the spectacle of modern civilisation that he regarded the possibility of damnation as in itself a relief. And in one way, if evil was regarded as the common human lot, it was easier to bear. We do not, in Eliot's poetry, find the reflection that 'I am the chief of sinners'. The conviction of sin is objectified, and generally experienced in a sort of communion of either wretchedness or hope. We are at least companions in misfortune, even though we have no real contact with one another.

The question of the freedom of the will has always been entangled with that of sin, for how can we be held responsible if we are not free to choose our own acts and modes of action? Eliot's debt to the ancient Greeks for the outlines of some of his plays occasionally brings him close to an idea of Fate in which human beings are considered as the instruments or the victims of the gods: 'Destiny waits in the hand of God, shaping the still unshapen,' says the Chorus of *Murder in the Cathedral*. In *The Family Reunion* Agatha at one point declares:

> The decision will be made by powers beyond us
> Which now and then emerge.

Reality (Part Two)

And in *The Elder Statesman*, Lord Claverton, thinking of his death, remarks:

> The place and time of liberation
> Are, I think, determined.

The poet's concept of 'pattern' sometimes reminds one, in addition, of the doctrine of predestination.

Neither Fate nor predestination, however, seems to belong to Eliot's basic beliefs. His main position seems to be rather that there is an ideal pattern or design, a divine plan for every human life, but that we are free to conform to it or reject it at our own risk. Thus in *Murder in the Cathedral* it sounds like a version of predestination when Becket states that both the agent and the patient 'are fixed / In an eternal action, an eternal patience'. But he immediately continues:

> To which all must consent that it may be willed
> And which all must suffer that they may will it,
> That the pattern may subsist . . .

His words are repeated mockingly later on by the Fourth Tempter, but he nevertheless finds his peace in submitting to the eternal design. We may remember Eliot's comment on Dante's words 'la sua voluntate è nostra pace' that 'the statement of Dante seems to me *literally true*. And I confess that it has more beauty for me now [1929], when my own experience has deepened its meaning, than it did when I first read it.'[1]

It may be remarked before leaving this question of free will that Eliot's attitude is again strongly supported by Bergson. I am not referring to Bergson's belief in the essential indeterminism of the vital impulse, but to his constantly reiterated faith that our consciousness and our actions are only truly free when we take cognisance of the deep pattern of our being, its *durée*. There is only one reason, he thinks, why this fact is not generally recognised: 'C'est que, si nous sommes libres toutes les fois que nous voulons rentrer en nous-mêmes, il nous arrive rarement de le vouloir.'[2]

If the will is free it should follow that our actions are efficacious. It was natural that the poet, in his pre-Christian phase, should stress the efficacy of human effort in the working-out of salvation, that is, if he envisaged the possibility of salvation at all. More and

---

[1] 'Dante', *SE*, pp. 270–1.
[2] *Essai sur les données immédiates de la conscience*, p. 183.

198

more, however, the striving for perfection came to be seen as an effort of expiation on the one hand and an attempt at mystical penetration on the other.

The Waste Land, after leading us through all the rigour and nausea of a modern wilderness, shows us in the last section that it has all been part of a journey to a definite goal, the Chapel Perilous, where the Holy Grail is to be found. In other words, by braving dangers, looking evil in the face and toiling onwards, a regeneration may perhaps be attained. Life must be an ascetic discipline, akin to the mystic disciplines of the East. There is no question yet of grace. The 'awful daring of a moment's surrender' might be a surrender to a deity without attributes. But in *Journey of the Magi* and *A Song for Simeon* we hear of the cost of seeking Christ: 'A cold coming we had of it'—'They shall praise thee and suffer in every generation.' And the little poem *Usk* directs us to 'the hermit's chapel, the pilgrim's prayer'.

In the third section of *Ash-Wednesday*, the protagonist labours up the stairs of spiritual life, 'Struggling with the devil of the stairs who wears / The deceitful face of hope and of despair'. Ugliness, darkness and terror are there to deter him. He is also tempted by a view of life as an enchanting pastoral scene. But he goes on climbing. And in *The Family Reunion* a way to salvation is pointed out 'across a whole Thibet of broken stones / That lie, fang up, a lifetime's march'.[1]

The effort and the action may consist in suffering. Many Christian mystics, especially perhaps Meister Eckhart, have found a virtue in suffering. And the Church has always tried to find a place for suffering in the scheme of things, regarding it as meritorious if accepted in the right spirit. In Eliot's mind this idea finds a strong response because he was predisposed, as an artist, to regard suffering as a source of value. Becket declares several times that 'action is suffering / And suffering is action'. In his case it is a question of martyrdom, and martyrdom, we are made to understand, is as necessary to the Church in our age as in the twelfth century. *The Rock* actually contains a call to martyrdom. And Celia Coplestone is a modern martyr. But all cannot be martyrs. Obviously, then, suffering must be significant in lesser degrees or in other ways besides, though we are not told precisely how.

'Right action' is an internal as well as an external affair, in fact

[1] Op. cit., p. 103.

it is chiefly a matter of making 'perfect the will'. It demands renunciation. Becket has to resist the temptations of youth, popularity, temporal and spiritual power. In *Ash-Wednesday*, too, there
is much to forego:

> the lost heart stiffens and rejoices
> In the lost lilac and the lost sea voices
> And the weak spirit quickens to rebel
> For the bent golden-rod and the lost sea smell

Life may be an exile, but the consciousness of having to lose
cherished, familiar things increases the doubt and incertitude. We
stand 'Wavering between the profit and the loss / In this brief
transit where the dreams cross'. But, says St John of the Cross,
'the soul cannot be possessed of the divine union, until it has di-
vested itself of the love of created beings'. Eliot used these words
as an epigraph to *Sweeney Agonistes*.

If renunciation is to be complete each individual self must be
annihilated. This is the eternal paradox of nature: *si le grain ne
meurt—*. And it is the paradox at the heart of Christianity. Lord
Claverton discovers it in the end: 'in becoming no one,' he says,
'I begin to live.' He has renounced his former self by what
amounts to a sacramental act of penance, which includes con-
trition and confession.

Renunciation and askesis have always played an important part
in Christianity, and they have obviously appealed strongly to Eliot,
who is very much in earnest about these things because he has
seen the great need of the modern world for spiritual discipline.
In an essay on 'Religion without Humanism' he wrote (in 1930):

> I found no discipline in humanism; only a little intellectual disci-
> pline from a little study of philosophy. But the difficult discipline is
> the discipline and training of emotion; this the modern world has
> great need of; so great need that it hardly understands what the word
> means; and this I have found is only attainable through dogmatic
> religion. . . . There is much chatter about mysticism: for the modern
> world the word means some spattering indulgence of emotion,
> instead of the most terrible concentration and askesis. But it takes
> perhaps a lifetime merely to realise that men like the forest sages,
> and the desert sages, and finally the Victorines and John of the Cross
> and (in his fashion) Ignatius really *mean what they say*. Only those
> have the right to talk of discipline who have looked into the Abyss.[1]

---

[1] N. Foerster (ed.), *Humanism and America* (1930), p. 110.

The austerity of this passage reminds one of *Ash-Wednesday*. But the note of renunciation is heard in practically all of Eliot's poems from *The Love Song* onwards. The more definite note of askesis is struck in *Whispers of Immortality* and continues down to *Little Gidding*. Eliot has always been attracted to what is difficult, and the corruption of mankind has made him see the need of discipline; but he has also found askesis to be the best way of integrating the personality. These motives are clearly exemplified in his dramas and in his later poems. In his earlier poetry there is another motive as well that draws him to an annihilation of the personality: the fear of judgment, the fear of reality, the very fear of losing his individuality. Prufrock is prompted by such a fear. But it is best illustrated in a poem in which it has already been overcome: *Ash-Wednesday*. In the magnificent vision of the scattered bones, 'Forgetting themselves and each other, united / In the quiet of the desert', we have a perfect image of the human desire for escape and oblivion.

The alternative to escape is the way which Harry discovers: to 'turn again' and face the ministers of vengeance, to accept renunciation and suffering as a penance. In the purpose of penance both action and suffering find their chief importance. This is the 'lifetime's death in love' of *The Dry Salvages*. Its symbol is usually that of voluntary isolation in a desert, which because of its association with the story of Christ in the wilderness, includes the idea of a gain in spiritual power as the result of the victory over temptations. Eliot was also inspired by the lives of saintly men and women. Thus he was greatly struck by Bazin's biography of Charles de Foucauld, and wrote that 'there is no higher glory of a Christian empire than that which was here brought into being by a death in the desert'.[1] Like Charles de Foucauld, Harry chooses to go 'to the worship in the desert, the thirst and deprivation'. His way is the way of solitude described in *Burnt Norton*:

> Internal darkness, deprivation
> And destitution of all property,
> Desiccation of the world of sense,
> Evacuation of the world of fancy,
> Inoperancy of the world of spirit.

---

[1] 'Towards a Christian Britain', *The Church Looks Ahead* (1941), p. 117.

Harry chooses something that very much resembles a Purgatory on earth. We have noticed the frequency of the Purgatory theme in Eliot's works. So constantly does he revert to it and so much significance does he attach to it that it may safely be called a central motif of his poetry. He sees man as hovering in a twilight between salvation and damnation. It is impossible for most people, because of their weakness, their nothingness, to cross 'With direct eyes, to death's other Kingdom'. So our only hope, if we are to avoid damnation, and if we realise that it is useless to dissemble, is in the purgation of sin:

> The only hope, or else despair
> Lies in the choice of pyre or pyre—
> To be redeemed from fire by fire.
>
> (*Little Gidding*, IV)

It is mainly Dante's visions of Purgatory that have appealed to Eliot. There is one episode that he seems to have found particularly striking: that in which Arnaut Daniel asks that his pain may be remembered, and then dives back into the purifying fire:

> 'Ara vos prec, per aquella valor
> que vos guida al som de l'escalina,
> sovegna vos a temps de ma dolor.'
> POI S'ASCOSE NEL FOCO CHE GLI AFFINA.[1]

These few lines have provided the title for one of Eliot's collections of poems (the 1920 *Poems* were first called *Ara Vos Prec*), and for one of the sections of *Ash-Wednesday* as first published ('Som de l'escalina'); they have provided a quotation at the end of *The Waste Land* ('Poi s'ascose nel foco che gli affina'); a quotation in *Ash-Wednesday*, IV ('Sovegna vos'); an allusion in *Little Gidding* ('that refining fire') and other references besides. What Eliot chiefly found striking in the episode, conceptually, was no doubt the voluntary acceptance of the 'refining fire' by the spirits who were bent on attaining salvation.

The images and ideas of Purgatory are fairly constant throughout, mixed in the beginning with images of Hell and later with those of Paradise. The epigraph of *The Love Song* has the hopelessness of the *Inferno*, and *The Waste Land* alludes to all those in Hell (or Limbo) whom Death has undone. The poems of the *Ash-Wednesday* phase are more exclusively associated with Purgatory.

[1] Cf. *SE*, p. 256.

Purgatory is definitely suggested by the allusion to the three steps leading to Dante's Purgatorio, or the three stages of ascent through the Purgatorio. In the recent poems there are such allusions to the *Paradiso* as the 'heart of light' (in *Burnt Norton*) and the Rose of *Little Gidding*. But there is no clear progression in Eliot's work from one stage to another. The 'heart of light' occurs in *The Waste Land*, and the images of Purgatory are as dominant in *The Family Reunion* and the *Quartets* as are those of Heaven. The vision of earth as an immense hospital, which occurs in both the latter works, is akin to that of Purgatory. And Harry is regarded as the consciousness of his unhappy family, 'Its bird sent flying through the purgatorial flame'.

We are put in mind of a Purgatory after this life by the frequent allusions to Dante. But on the whole the poet tends to see Purgatory as a state of life on this earth, as in the image of the hospital. It is a self-imposed discipline in 'death's dream kingdom'. The explanation lies partly in the fact that the distinction between physical life and physical death means very little to Eliot—much less than the distinction between the different planes of life which may be visualised as Hell, Purgatory and Heaven. Life and death fight for the upper hand both in 'this life' and 'the next', in 'death's dream kingdom' and in 'death's other Kingdom'. And partly the state of Purgatory is identified with the life of askesis inaugurated by the saint or the penitent here on earth. Besides, it gives significance to much of the suffering which often seems unprovoked and meaningless. If this suffering is accepted as purgatorial it may work towards our spiritual health.

We saw that Eliot believes with the Catholic Church that human beings may work effectively for their salvation by their own actions. But this belief is countered and complemented by another, which is almost Molinistic. For the poet also thinks that action is useless and that we must submit passively to the will of God, or rather make his will our will and our peace. Even the action that is required of Becket and of Harry is very much like inaction. And in the *Quartets* the poet now tells us to 'fare forward', and now to 'be still, and wait without hope'. In one of his striking phrases, he joins the two ideas indissolubly: 'We must be still and still moving.'[1] We are reminded of the two ways of liberation indicated by Agatha in *The Family Reunion*: the 'present moment

[1] *East Coker*, V.

of pointed light' and the 'lifetime's march' 'across a whole Thibet of broken stones'. And here we come nearer to a full understanding of the purpose of askesis and purgation. Their ultimate purpose is to consummate a union of the spirit with God. It is to achieve this end that St John of the Cross preaches a divesting oneself of the love of created beings and destitution of property. And it is for this that he exhorts us to descend into the 'dark night of the soul'.

Eliot's debt to St John and other Christian mystics is well known. Mr Raymond Preston brings it out clearly in his commentary on the *Four Quartets*. In St John of the Cross Eliot chiefly found support for the idea (derived first, perhaps, from Indian philosophy) of a way of contemplation by voiding the mind of everything save faith:

I said to my soul, be still, and wait without hope
For hope would be hope for the wrong thing; wait without love
For love would be love of the wrong thing; there is yet faith
But the faith and the love and the hope are all in the waiting.
Wait without thought, for you are not ready for thought:
So the darkness shall be the light, and the stillness the dancing.

(East Coker, III)

St John provided Eliot with much of the imagery of darkness with which he symbolises both the evacuation of the mind and the ignorance of God and his ways; with paradoxical statements such as 'the way up is the way down', also borrowed from Heraclitus, to denote the humility that is necessary if the soul is to be exalted; and with the image of the stairs by which the soul ascends to God, and which are glimpsed in *Ash-Wednesday* (joined with reminiscences from Dante), in *A Song for Simeon* and in the *Four Quartets*. A metaphor very similar to that of the 'dark night' is 'the cloud of unknowing', the title of a work by an anonymous English mystic of the fourteenth century, alluded to both in *The Family Reunion* and *Little Gidding*. There is further Dame Julian of Norwich, who 'was much troubled by the thought of the origin of sin in a world created by infinite Goodness' but heard a voice saying, 'Sin is behovable, but all shall be well, and all shall be well, and all manner of things shall be well.' Eliot has used these words and this thought to excellent purpose in *Little Gidding*.

Christianity

According to Christian doctrine, a divine revelation is an act of grace. Eliot recognises this—most of the time. The climbing of the stairs in *Ash-Wednesday* would not have brought the protagonist *'al som de l'escalina'* if he had not been invested with 'strength beyond hope and despair'. Grace, symbolised by the colour blue, is one of the leading themes of section IV of *Ash-Wednesday*. And in *The Dry Salvages* the poet sees our only hope in the 'Prayer of the one Annunciation', the message of grace to humanity. It is because divine grace is necessary in the last resort that the soul must wait even without hope—so that no thought of our ability to earn salvation shall supervene.

Grace is made manifest in the Incarnation of Christ. Mr H. R. Williamson approves of the Catholic emphasis on the doctrine of the Incarnation and thinks that Protestants stress the Atonement to a dangerous extent.[1] As far as Eliot is concerned there is, of course, no exclusion of the Atonement, either from his beliefs or from his poetry. It is significant, for instance, in the Good Friday poem *East Coker*. But it is true that the Incarnation seems to mean much more to him. This is partly, we may suppose, because the doctrine of the Incarnation attaches a greater value to human nature and human life than does that of the Atonement. But it is also because the former doctrine lends itself much more easily than the latter to Eliot's speculations about the nature of reality and of time. His revelations are associated with The Revelation; and his moments of illumination seem to give him, however remotely and vaguely, an integral experience of God.

Eliot has frequent visions of a garden bathed in sunlight. His garden obviously stands for a vision of ultimate reality. But it only stands for the vision: it is not the vision itself. And the fact that it occurs so frequently is due to its representing something else besides, namely the poet's nostalgia for Paradise and happiness. As a symbol of reality it falls into line with the many tentative metaphors which are rejected as inadequate almost as soon as they are conceived:

> The wild thyme unseen, or the winter lightning
> Or the waterfall, or music heard so deeply
> That it is not heard at all, but you are the music
> While the music lasts. These are only hints and guesses,
> (*The Dry Salvages*, V)

---

[1] *The Poetry of T. S. Eliot*, p. 161.

The poet does not see God in his historical Incarnation. Eliot's supreme visions are different from those of Dante and from those of a number of medieval mystics to whom it seemed that Christ or the Virgin appeared in a visible shape. St Francis, it is said, had a vision of a six-winged seraph carrying a crucifix. In comparison with such experiences, Eliot's are indeterminate. This is not because Francis of Assisi was a saint and Eliot probably is not. Dante was no saint but a poet, yet his visions were definite enough. And there must have been many poets in the Middle Ages and later who were far from saintly and still described heavenly sights with the utmost confidence. The reason why Eliot experiences the Absolute as a timeless inexpressible something, while Dante saw a host of the blessed gathered as the petals of a bright rose, is rather a matter of cultural and religious environment. We have learnt to-day to be sceptical of allegories. And we have learnt to look for ultimate reality in something outside both time and eternity. A poet of our time, as Eliot would no doubt be the first to acknowledge, must start from the assumptions of our time. He cannot make a show of knowledge 'by any concitation of the backward devils'. Nor has Eliot deliberately tried to conjure up or copy states of ecstasy to exploit them for poetic purposes (a behaviour which he reprehends in *After Strange Gods*). He has had experiences, differing probably in degree but not necessarily in kind, from those of St John of the Cross and Julian of Norwich. And he uses them as a poet. But he has also followed the more intellectual approach of Thomas Aquinas. Mr Raymond Preston rightly calls attention to the following passage from the work of a man whom Eliot called 'as great and lovely as Dante himself':[1]

> By means of the ordering of all things, which has been as it were projected out of Him and which bears certain images and likenesses of its divine patterning, we ascend in ordered degrees so far as we are able to that which is above all things, by the ways of negation and transcendence, and the conception of a universal cause.[2]

This short passage from Aquinas sums up some of the most important themes of Eliot's poetry.

[1] 'Shakespeare and the Stoicism of Seneca', *SE*, p. 136.
[2] *The Book of the Blessed Dionysius concerning the Divine Names*, vii, lecture 4; quoted from Preston, '*Four Quartets' Rehearsed*, p. 16.

Eliot's references to and images of the Divine Persons generally do not occur in his moments of ecstasy. They elude his supreme visions just as the hooded figure in 'What the Thunder Said' eludes his sight:

> Who is the third who walks always beside you?
> When I count, there are only you and I together

The Divine Persons, when they appear, which is not very often, are seen in the abstraction of dogma, and in a more matter-of-fact mood than that which produces 'the wild thyme unseen, or the winter lightning'. But there is still the vision in the sense of the 'higher dream', which Eliot found in so much medieval poetry and misses in our own.[1]

The 'higher dream', as I interpret it, is a vision of the sublime and the divine which is aesthetic rather than mystical. In this vision, the Father and the Holy Spirit appear under such ancient symbols as the eye and the dove. The eye (or eyes) from being entirely human in *The Love Song* become semi-divine in *The Hollow Men*, and finally completely divine in *The Family Reunion*, *Burnt Norton* and elsewhere. Christ appears as 'the tiger' of *Gerontion* and 'the wounded surgeon' of *East Coker*. And the Virgin, to whom prayers are addressed, is 'the rose' of many poems.[2] She is also the mysterious Lady of *Ash-Wednesday*, as well as the Lady of *The Dry Salvages*. There further seems to be a Beatrice in a number of the poems, who tends on the one hand to be identified with 'la figlia', and on the other hand with the Virgin. The role which is played by this figure suggests the intercession of saints in Catholic devotions.

The symbol of the garden or orchard, is a direct reference to the Garden of Eden (and occasionally to the Garden of Olives), but also represents a persistent longing of humanity for perfection here and now, and for a heaven of bliss to come. This longing is one that the poet feels acutely. But I think it would be wrong to see it merely as a nostalgic mood. It is something more: a mood of adoration, in which the object of adoration is a beautiful dream. Even before it became an article of faith, the dream was there. It is noticeable in *The Love Song*, which contains not only *spleen* but also

---

[1] Cf. 'Dante', *SE*, p. 262; and cp. *Ash-Wednesday*, IV.

[2] E.g. *The Hollow Men*, IV, *Ash-Wednesday*, II, and all the *Quartets*. Of course, the rose symbolises other things besides the Virgin Mary.

idéal, in the vision of a garden which is there submarine. It is visible in the fourth *Prelude*, in *La Figlia* and in the gardens of *The Waste Land*. We have considered Eliot's negative mood of doubt and despondency. But we must not forget that right from the beginning there were also this positive mood and this positive vision, even if they were almost submerged for a long time, partly because of the poet's literary prejudices.[1] It can hardly be doubted that the longing for a Paradise and the adoration of ideal perfection have been powerful inspirations in Eliot's poetry. However they were symbolised, in ancient myths or his own, in the beauty of roses in a sunlit garden or the blissful innocence of children in an apple-tree, by a return to past ages, or to childhood, or an advance into mysticism, this longing and this adoration have nourished the vital flame in his work.

The Biblical conception of heaven is that of a feast, in other words a beatitude shared by all. And one of the chief things that Eliot sought in the Church and its doctrine of immortal bliss, was clearly a sense of communion. Among the seven Catholic sacraments, that of Penance is most frequently alluded to in his work; but next comes that of the Holy Communion. We find it most conspicuously in *Gerontion* and *East Coker*. And, characteristically, the poet says in the ninth Chorus of *The Rock*:

> Let us mourn in a private chamber, learning the way of penitence,
> And then let us learn the joyful communion of saints.

In the second Chorus the need of community is emphasised very strongly:

> What life have you if you have not life together?
> There is no life that is not in community,
> And no community not lived in praise of GOD.
> Even the anchorite who meditates alone,
> For whom the days and nights repeat the praise of GOD,
> Prays for the Church, the Body of Christ incarnate,
> And now you live dispersed on ribbon roads,
> And no man knows or cares who is his neighbour

The life of the Church is still the solution of the problem of isolation, intensified in modern civilisation. In the Church, tradition is a living thing, which can make Communion actual. Here,

[1] Cf. 'Dante', *SE*, p. 262.

by annihilation of the self, one's isolation can be broken and even God can be communed with. For a long time there remains a sense of frustration in the poet's attempts to achieve fellowship with human beings. There remains a lack of warmth in the description of human relations. Even in the moments of ecstasy of which he tells us there is nothing comparable to the experience of the two souls who are united in Donne's *The Extasie*.[1] But Eliot's efforts to break down the spiritual barriers between himself and others were energetic, and have not been vain. We may find some significance in the growing use of the pronouns 'we' and 'us' in a real plural sense where earlier the first person singular was used or at least intended. An intermediate stage may be discovered in *Ash-Wednesday*, where 'I' alternates with 'we', and where, 'at its peaks and climaxes the poetry passes into the anonymous language of the Church.'[2] In the Monchensey family there is no real 'reunion', but Harry and Agatha really find each other, and Harry and Mary almost do. Harry seeks the life of the desert, not only for his own sake, but to meet God, and so vicariously to benefit his whole family. Something similar happens in *The Cocktail Party*, where Celia is the vicarious sufferer, while Edward and Lavinia find at least a measure of mutual understanding and happiness. In *The Confidential Clerk* the spiritual communion of the two young people is denied fulfilment by the discovery of their consanguinity, but in *The Elder Statesman* the communion of love is complete and perfect:

> Age and decrepitude can have no terrors for me,
> Loss and vicissitude cannot appal me,
> Not even death can dismay or amaze me
> Fixed in the certainty of love unchanging.

There is, then, a development in Eliot's poetry, as in his prose, from individualism by way of Christianity to a search for social unity and an acceptance of social obligations. But from an irreligious point of view he possibly appears to be as individualistic as ever. He tends to make Christianity a religion of spiritual discipline, and the social benefits which accrue from perfecting the individual in a life of disciplined devotion would obviously be

---

[1] There are obvious reminiscences of this poem in *Burnt Norton*.
[2] Mrs Duncan Jones in Rajan's symposium, p. 37.

doubted by the irreligious. A passage in *The Dry Salvages* seems to me to sum up Eliot's position quite well:

> 'on whatever sphere of being
> The mind of a man may be intent
> At the time of death'—that is the one action
> (And the time of death is every moment)
> Which shall fructify in the lives of others:

Only from a religious point of view can such a statement be appreciated. In this case poetic imagination alone can hardly help one to believe.

Catholic individualism and Protestant individualism are two different things. Catholicism, in spite of (or perhaps because of) the importance it attaches to the Church and the community, stresses the need and the right of the individual to perfect his own soul, even if this entails physical isolation from the society of men and devotion to a seemingly inactive life of contemplation. Protestantism tends to reject such religious cloistering, but teaches the need and right of the individual to receive and understand the word of God direct in his own heart and in his own way. Eliot here takes the Catholic position. If meditation is rightly practised it will not really be an individual affair and there will be no really separate and particular ways of understanding divine truths. To determine Eliot's poetry as Catholic or Protestant, however, is hardly of any interest except as indicating which aspects of Christianity he is particularly occupied with and which he more or less ignores. He leans to Catholicism in stressing the dogma of Incarnation rather than that of Atonement; the perfection of the will and religious discipline rather than the intensity of faith; penance, confession and purgation rather than judgment; communal rather than private worship. Such things as the adoration of the Virgin and the belief in the intercession of saints are more superficial Catholic elements of his poetry.

It is remarkable that it is only in his Christian poetry that certain hedonistic tendencies have manifested themselves, as if Omar and Lucretius had to wait for a Catholic acceptance of asceticism to come into their own. As a matter of fact Eliot's asceticism is not so much that of austere practices as that of severe thought. 'You must not deny the body,' he reminds us in the ninth Chorus of *The Rock*. He has not the Puritan distrust of pleasure. He has, however, the Puritan sense of the corruption of the world. And it may be worth remarking that the doctrine of original sin would hardly have received so central a place in his poetry without the emphasis given to it by generations of Puritans.

On the more definitely Puritan traits in his make-up there is no need to dwell. They consist rather in emotional attitudes than in points of doctrine. Eliot's eschatology is much concerned with the need for the individual to be constantly prepared for the end. 'The time of death is every moment,' he says in *The Dry Salvages*, and this idea underlies much of his vision. On the other hand, we rarely find him preoccupied with the general termination of all things. The apocalyptic phantasmagoria so beloved of many poets has little appeal to Eliot. It is 'a worn-out poetical fashion'. And so the common Puritan eschatology of a final destruction and judgment in connection with the second coming of Christ, gives place in his poetry to an individual eschatology, in which, as I have shown, the images of Heaven, Hell and Purgatory play an important part.

Eliot's Christianity is strongly tinged with a monist philosophy. We have seen how Bradleyan ideas constantly occur in his poetry. He seems to regard time and timelessness as distinct spheres, but the world of time is merely appearance and illusion. And good and evil are both subsumed in a higher purpose. No doubt his monism, from a religious point of view, is as much an extension of the Unitarianism in which he was brought up, as it is a remnant of his purely philosophical enthusiasms. He traced his mother's spiritual descent from Schleiermacher by way of Channing, Emerson and Herbert Spencer. And the philosophy of Schleiermacher is a meeting-ground of Absolute Idealism and Unitarianism, just as Harvard University in the last century was a meeting-ground of these two closely-related schools of thought. It may quite well have been in reaction against Unitarianism that Eliot has insisted so urgently on such doctrines as the Incarnation of God in Jesus Christ and the sacramental nature of the Eucharist. But in his tendency to see salvation in attaining to the divine union rather than in a divine atonement and forgiveness, his old Unitarianism, supported by a monistic idealism, may be found to be still alive.

During one period of his life he does seem to have preferred a dualistic view. Perhaps here again he followed the attraction of Bergson, whose 'matter' and 'memory' are radically distinct. In

1916 Eliot criticised Leibniz's philosophy, and by implication that of Bradley, in the following terms:

> It is really an attempt to preserve the reality of the external world at the same time that it is denied, which is perhaps the attempt of all pan-psychism: to substitute for two concepts which have at least a relative validity in practice—consciousness and matter—one which is less useful and consequently less significant, animated matter.[1]

The dualist attitude is plain. And in 1929 he defended Paul Elmer More's Christian dualism in the *Times Literary Supplement*.[2] This dualism was right, he thought, in maintaining the idea of a gap between the material and the spiritual, between science and religion, as opposed to the merging of these things in the writings of Whitehead and others.

In 1946, however, Eliot gave a broadcast talk in which he spoke of Charles Williams as 'a man who was always able to live in the material and the spiritual world at once, a man to whom the two worlds were equally real because they are one world'.[3] Eliot seems to have returned to the Bradleyan view, which is also, in the main, that of the *Four Quartets*. 'No cheap and easy Monism can stand before an enquiry into logic,' says Bradley. But 'the desire to comprehend our Universe as the double outgrowth and revelation of a single principle, depends on a genuine impulse of philosophy'.[4] This 'single principle' is of paramount importance in Eliot's later work.

Monism can be many things, and it is not necessarily hostile to perfectly orthodox Christianity. But on the whole it tends to regard the Christian conception of God as falling short of the Absolute, and the teachings of Christianity as failing to give a final interpretation of the universe. It is natural that Catholics should regard it with a certain amount of suspicion. In *The Catholic Encyclopedia* published in New York in 1911 I found the following comments on monism and dualism:

> Monism, which is not content with the partial synthesis of Dualism, but aims at an ideal completeness, often results in failure. Dualism leaves room for faith, and hands over to faith many of the

---

[1] *Monist*, Oct. 1916, p. 575. [2] Feb. 21, 1929.
[3] *Listener*, Dec. 19, 1946.
[4] Bradley, *The Principles of Logic*, p. 591.

problems which philosophy cannot solve. Monism leaves no room
for faith. The only mysticism which is compatible with it is rationalistic, and very different from that 'vision' in which, for the Christian
mystic, all the limitations, imperfections, and other shortcomings of
our feeble efforts are removed by the light of faith.

No doubt this article is a little partial. Surely many mystics
recognised by the Church could fairly be designated as monists.
But the general view expressed in the article does show by its
contrast with Eliot's general attitude that the poet has followed
his individual philosophical bent. It seems that he found in his
poetry (the statements of which do not, as we have seen, require
strict belief), an outlet for monistic and even Unitarian ideas to
which he otherwise denied a full expression. His poetry includes
more than his prose.

FOUR QUARTETS

'Rational assent may arrive late, intellectual conviction may
come slowly, but they come inevitably without violence to honesty
and nature. To put the sentiments in order is a later, and an im-
mensely difficult task.'[1] This statement, which so much resembles
a confession, is illustrated in the *Four Quartets*. The *Quartets* are
personal and emotional, perhaps more than those people realise
who like to call them intellectual. And the ideas which the emotions bring forward are probably not in the perfect order of
orthodoxy which we find in Eliot's criticism. Moreover, we cannot expect, nor perhaps should we hope, that such intellectual
order will ever be established in his poetry. But the emotions have
an order of their own, and a synthesising power, which are equally
valuable.

The deeper we go into the *Four Quartets* the more complicated
do the strains and counter-strains which constitute it appear.
They do form a unified outlook, but in any case it is an outlook
which comprehends considerably more than the Christian view,
and which at the same time is refined almost beyond Christianity.
There is nothing very dogmatic about the *Quartets*. Apart from
East Coker, perhaps, they are less specifically Christian than, for
instance, *Ash-Wednesday* or *Murder in the Cathedral*. Mr Richard
Lea wrote a somewhat over-excited review of the *Quartets* but was

[1] 'Second Thoughts about Humanism', *SE*, p. 453.

perfectly right when he found that, compared with *Murder in the Cathedral*, there is 'greater depth, greater intensity, and greater beauty in these quartets, but less Christianity. Is it possible,' he asked, 'that the level reached here is beyond Christianity? A non-Christian mystic can feel just as much at home here as a Christian.'[1]

The poems are the work of a man who has not only found a faith, but who has had to make a faith for himself by integrating all that he has believed in or been attached to or even strongly interested in. In the *Quartets* the 'primitive terror' and the primitive gods have been recognised in the modern world as something more than symbols. And Emerson, Bradley, Bergson, Patanjali and St John of the Cross are incorporated in an all-embracing, if rather diffuse, Christianity.

Since interpretation of the *Quartets* is generally considered to be particularly difficult, I may as well place my own reading of it on record, while affirming my belief that the main thought structure of the poems is much more definite and intelligible than is often assumed. If *The Waste Land* is the North Pole of Eliot's lyrical work and the summit of his achievement in his 'appearance' phase, the *Four Quartets* are the South Pole, and it is natural to stop for a brief exploration of them on the background of the philosophical and religious influxes which we have considered under the heading of 'Reality'. This will perforce have to be somewhat schematic; but recognising all the hazards of paraphrasing I still think that something may be gained from an interpretative review of the 'argument' of the *Quartets*, proceeding from movement to movement of each of the poems.

I should point out first of all, perhaps, that I fail to understand any other explanation of the word 'quartets' as used in the joint title than one which refers to the different attitudes, or moods, or styles, which are harmonised in each of the poems and which bear an analogical resemblance to the sounds of the different instruments in a musical quartet. The most obvious differences are between the 'poetic' and the 'prosaic' parts, but there are also descriptive, symbolical, meditative and ecstatic voices which would loosely fit the musical analogy. There is here no getting past Eliot's pronouncement in *The Music of Poetry* that 'There are possibilities for verse which bear some analogy to the develop-

---

[1] *Adelphi*, July/Sept. 1945.

ment of a theme by different groups of instruments; there are possibilities of transitions in a poem comparable to the different movements of a symphony or a quartet; there are possibilities of contrapuntal arrangement of subject-matter.' *The Music of Poetry* was written in 1942, when the last of the *Quartets* was being composed.

Burnt Norton begins with the reflection that if time is always 'present', i.e. always *here* or always with us, it is 'unredeemable'. The past and the future are equally meaningless and it is futile to wish that things had been different. The word 'echo' is used to suggest the hollow deceptiveness of such wishes for the might-have-been. There are 'other echoes' which may be equally deceptive, like the belief in 'our first world', the Garden of Eden. But in the garden of Burnt Norton, as if invited by the call of a thrush, in the autumn heat, the poet has a moment of mystic illumination, a sense of reality and completeness. It cannot last, but while it lasts it seems an experience out of time.

This experience now becomes a touchstone of reality and a goal to be sought in all the endeavours of life. In the two following movements of the poem the author describes the two ways to this goal indicated in the quotation from Heraclitus which originally served as an epigraph to *Burnt Norton* alone: 'The way up and the way down is one and the same.' The way up is by ascent and '*Erhebung*' towards the light of the sun; the way down leads to the darkness below the ground. In both cases a point of movement and stillness is reached: the sun as the still centre of the dance of the universe; the centre of the earth as the point round which our inhabited globe revolves. In other words, the experience of reality can be reached either in ecstatic happiness or in ascetic discipline. As Agatha says in *The Family Reunion*:

> There are hours when there seems to be no past or future,
> Only a present moment of pointed light
> . . . Perhaps there is another kind,
> I believe, across a whole Thibet of broken stones
> That lie, fang up, a lifetime's march.

The beginning of the second movement of *Burnt Norton*, in particular, has been the object of much guesswork and a certain amount of controversy. Whatever the literary derivations may be, I take the 'garlic and sapphires in the mud' to symbolise various aspects of the objective, sensuous world which surrounds us: organic, crystalline and amorphous. We have to start from our awareness of this sensuous world and its patterns and of the cycles of history and nature if we wish to move upwards 'above the moving tree' to a light in which we may see the eternal pattern even of temporal violence ('the boarhound and the boar' are 'reconciled among the stars').

In the third movement the way down starts from awareness of human life and modern civilisation typified by the London Underground. This seems at first a descent into complete meaninglessness. There is no pattern—not even regular cycles and relationships as in nature—until complete deprivation of the temporal is reached.

The fourth movement takes us back to the garden after the vision is over and when the light begins to fail. It is really a prayer for grace and permanence, that belief in the vision may remain. The sunflower and the clematis suggest Christ and the Virgin, and perhaps even the Father may be hinted at in the image of the yew.

The final movement of *Burnt Norton* contrasts motion and stillness. Motion belongs to the world of time, just as poetry and music move in time. But the complete pattern, in which the whole of a poetical or musical composition is contemplated at once in the mind, so that 'the end precedes the beginning, / And the end and the beginning were always there'—is timeless. Similarly, through desire and action, or movement, we attain to the stillness of absolute love and pure illumination. Thus 'Only through time time is conquered'. The 'all is always now' of the final movement has a quite different ring from the 'all time is eternally present' of the first movement. The vision of a meaningful pattern lies between them. Yet there is a pessimistic note in the very last two lines of *Burnt Norton*, which would have damaged the poem if it had not been followed by the other *Quartets*. For although our efforts to achieve illumination must take place in time, time itself—'the waste sad time / Stretching before and after'—is called merely ridiculous. Which means that time is not yet fully redeemed after all.

Eliot has revealed that *Burton Norton* partly had its origin in lines left over from the composition of *Murder in the Cathedral*.[1]

[1] See Mr Donald Hall's interview with Mr Eliot in the *Paris Review*, No. 21 (1959), p. 57.

This seems to be fairly characteristic of one aspect of his technique and would seem to reduce the importance of the momentary impulse or the single autobiographical event in the creative process of his poetry. What is more interesting than the left-overs from *Murder in the Cathedral*, however, is the close similarity of *Burnt Norton* to the fourth and fifth parts of *Ash-Wednesday*. The first movement of *Burnt Norton*, the vision in the garden, corresponds very closely to the fourth part of *Ash-Wednesday*, the main difference being that the earlier poem is centred about a female apparition which is absent or only implied in the later poem. The fifth section of *Ash-Wednesday* begins with meditations on the Word, the still point and the light shining in darkness, which are the main themes of *Burnt Norton*, II; it then considers 'those who walk in darkness', which is also the subject of *Burnt Norton*, III; and it ends with a prayer in the garden, as in *Burnt Norton*, IV. These sections of *Ash-Wednesday*, then, might almost be considered as a first draft of the later poem. This reveals something about the permanent patterns of Eliot's poetic thought, and also reinforces both the religious and the erotic associations which are present in *Burnt Norton* but subdued by its more abstract reflections.

While *Burnt Norton* contrasts the way up with the way down, *East Coker* is concerned with the antithesis of pattern and chaos and with a further exploration of the way down through renunciation, suffering and darkness. The first movement describes the patterns which may be found in the natural processes of growth and decay and the unforced observance of seasons and traditions. Such ordered life in itself partakes of the nature of 'a dignified and commodious sacrament'. The second movement, on the other hand, describes the chaos and frustration, the lack of a meaningful pattern, which were vividly demonstrated at the outbreak of the Second World War. The evolutionists and believers in progress had promised something better; but one cannot base one's beliefs on empirical knowledge or on theories which are artificially imposed on life, for the pattern of the *whole* keeps on changing and understanding of it is a revelation to be hoped for and accepted in humility.

In the right spirit of humility even darkness and deprivation may be turned into a source of enlightenment. This is the theme of the third movement, in which it appears that the garden is a garden of agony as well as of ecstasy:

> The laughter in the garden, echoed ecstasy
> Not lost, but requiring, pointing to the agony
> Of death and birth.

The fourth movement shows that not only must renunciation of self be complete, but Christ's passion, too, must be accepted if we are to be healed. In His passion, suffering is shown to be potentially meaningful, to be related to pattern and not to chaos. His love ordains a purgatory for our benefit. This leads to the conclusion in the final movement, which also provides an answer to the pessimistic ending of *Burnt Norton* and thus shows a development from the first of the *Quartets*: it is not just the isolated moment that counts, as the poet has now discovered, but the perpetual struggle and exploration. 'We must be still and still moving', not abstaining from movement as *Burnt Norton* advised us. The last words of *East Coker*, 'In my end is my beginning', mean not only that death is followed by rebirth, but also that in my goal (my 'end', absolute Love) lies the impulse of my striving.

In *The Dry Salvages* the poet has taken the wisdom arrived at in the previous *Quartet* to his heart. The poem is informed by the modesty of his aspirations and his realisation that, although sainthood may be within the reach of human beings, most of us are not saints and our moments of illumination are hardly more than distraction fits, 'hints followed by guesses'.

The first movement again describes the relative order of human life in the image of the river, which symbolises the succession or flow of seasons and ages, life and death. This is time, which is 'within us'. The sea, on the other hand, which is 'all about us', symbolises all time in limitless and patternless extension, without direction or meaning, end or beginning.

The sea is more dangerous than the river. And yet, as we see in the second movement, human beings continue their cyclic activities on this ocean of limitless time, because we are afraid to think that our toil is really useless or that the future may lead to an absolute destination, a final judgment. (I take 'the calamitous annunciation', 'the last annunciation' and 'the one Annunciation' to represent the Fall, the Last Judgment and the Incarnation respectively.) Only despair keeps a flicker of hope and the flicker of a prayer alive in us.

The poet, however, has learnt to see the past as more than a mere sequence of events and activities and more than an evolutionary development. It has a meaning given by the moments of timelessness, which includes history and pre-history right back to the Fall and the Creation. He realises even more fully than in *East Coker* that agony as well as ecstasy may be permanent and revealing, and that even 'the agony of others' may lead to a fuller understanding.

Having dealt with the past in the first two movements, the poet turns mainly to the future in the remainder of the poem, so that the structural polarity of *The Dry Salvages* may be said to be that of past and future. He shows that the future is not, any more than the past, a sequence or development, in fact past and future as such merge in the vast expanse of the ocean of time. Whatever aim or meaning there is must be found in our minds ('on whatever sphere of being / The mind of man may be intent . . .') and it is the present moment ('the time of death') that counts.

The characteristic prayer of the fourth movement, this time for all voyagers on the directionless sea, is followed by a rejection of all attempts to foretell the future and an affirmation of belief in 'The point of intersection of the timeless / With time', which is interpreted as the Incarnation of God in the temporal world.

The structure of *Little Gidding* is not determined by the same simple dichotomy that we have found in the other *Quartets*, but there does seem to be an alternation of two themes: history and the purifying fire. What they have in common is the fact that history, like the life of individuals, contains sin, violence and crime: therefore the fire of destruction may also be regarded as a punishment and purgation in the life of a nation.

In the first movement of *Little Gidding* a sacred place is found in present-day England, which, because of its hallowed associations, will give meaning to a journey whenever one arrives, at whatever time and for whatever reason. There is an exhortation to prayer, and the whole idea is that of a discipline, a ritual and a sanctuary which may enshrine the timeless in time. One might say that the poet points to the importance of the Church.

The second movement describes the destruction of and by the

four elements, i.e. of everything belonging merely to this world; then it introduces the now famous night scene in the London of the blitz. The poet meets a ghostly stranger who tells him of the futility of all mortal life and of the necessity of accepting the loss of everything as the source of a new, purified being. There is little doubt in my mind that the 'familiar compound ghost' is Robert Browning, and there is no advantage, poetic or otherwise, in leaving him unidentified—except, of course, that he merges with all the dramatis personae that he created, which I take to be the main reason why he is called a 'compound ghost' and why Eliot, too, assumes 'a double part'. Browning was a Londoner who died 'on a distant shore'. His very name reminds one of Brunetto Latini in the passage of Dante's *Inferno* which Eliot imitates, and it is punned on in the description of his 'brown baked features'. Eliot must at one time have taken an interest in Browning's 'thought and theory' concerning God, eternity and evolution, and would naturally introduce the author of *Rabbi Ben Ezra* to 'disclose the gifts reserved for age'. According to John Lehmann, Eliot was worried at the time of writing the wartime *Quartets* lest he should go on and on doing what he had already done well, as he felt that Browning did in old age.[1] Eliot's criticism is full of references to Browning's efforts to work out a new poetic idiom, or 'To purify the dialect of the tribe'.[2] And finally, it may be presumed that Browning, in Eliot's opinion, would be a more likely inmate of Purgatory than many of Eliot's other masters. Personally I am very much taken with the idea of Browning and Eliot treading the London pavement together.

The third movement of *Little Gidding* deals with the purification and expanding of love beyond desire. This is a love which includes love of one's country. We inherit both the victories and the defeats of the past, and if we contemplate struggles of faith like the Civil War we can now love both factions in the conflict equally.

In images of exploding bombs, the fourth section emphatically repeats the idea that suffering is ordained by Love and may lead to redemption. And in the final movement death is seen as a new

[1] John Lehmann, 'The Other T. S. Eliot', talk in the BBC Third Programme.
[2] See e.g. *The Sacred Wood*, p. 62; *Listener*, April 16, 1930; *New English Weekly*, October 31, 1946.

beginning and a reconciliation of all things. The dead of the nation provide new beginnings or starting-points for the living. Since death is a timeless moment, the story of the dead, history, is made up of a pattern of such timeless moments. History is meaningful. And so time, with its past and future, is at last fully redeemed. *Little Gidding* connects the timeless with objective things: a tradition, a nation, a period in time, and makes it independent of chance moments or solitary efforts in the life of the individual. And at the end of the poem the dualism and struggle which have been the burden of the *Quartets* is overcome in a great monistic credo:

> And all shall be well and
> All manner of thing shall be well
> When the tongues of flame are in-folded
> Into the crowned knot of fire
> And the fire and the rose are one.

The *Four Quartets* were not planned all at once, but perhaps for that very reason they contain something more than a music of ideas or a weaving and cross-weaving of poetical themes. They also contain a clear development of thought from poem to poem. The poetic magic of *Burnt Norton* may be greater than that of *Little Gidding*, but the greatest philosophical wisdom and detachment is to be found in the last of the *Quartets*.

At this point I may remark that although a poet must always believe in what he writes at the moment of writing, he may obviously outgrow the relevance of his poetic beliefs to his life. Thus the ecstatic moments of the *Four Quartets*, whatever they may have actually meant to the poet, seem to possess a finality of illumination beyond which he cannot pass. Yet in *The Cocktail Party* comparable moments experienced by Celia are regarded by her as a dream, and as insufficient to satisfy her completely. In *The Confidential Clerk* this dream is distrusted all along. And then in *The Elder Statesman* a new illumination occurs, in the love of Monica and Charles, but based this time in temporal reality. To Eliot the man, the vision of *The Elder Statesman* may have superseded that of the *Four Quartets*. But the *Four Quartets* have nevertheless objectified emotions and beliefs which he once felt, and have recorded them in the permanence of art to be re-experienced by any reader (including, now, the poet) who has the imagination to respond with poetic assent.

IX

ELIOT'S SYNTHESIS

THE thought structure of Eliot's poetry is obviously very complex, and if uniformity of ideas were to be demanded of a work of art he would be hard beset by his critics. But fortunately poetry, by its emotional quality, has a power of gathering even logically inconsistent elements into a synthesis. To quote Santayana: 'it is an old maxim with me that many ideas may be convergent as poetry which would be divergent as dogmas.'[1] Bergson expressed practically the same opinion in his *Essai sur les données immédiates de la conscience*:

> si . . . nous pénétrons dans les profondeurs de l'intelligence organisée et vivante, nous assisterons à la superposition ou plutôt à la fusion intime de bien des idées qui, une fois dissociées, paraissent s'exclure sous forme de termes logiquement contradictoires.[2]

And Eliot himself left no doubt as to his opinion when, in a lecture given at the Centre Universitaire Méditerranéen in March 1952, he spoke very self-revealingly of the philosophy of a poem and of the poet 'qui a fait des études philosophiques' and who has perhaps even constructed his own philosophical theories. He continued:

> Ces théories ont joué un rôle important dans sa formation, et donc paraîtront dans sa poésie, mais dans une forme dans laquelle elles ne sont plus proposées en tant que théorie mais présentées comme des faits d'expérience. . . . Des philosophies différentes, des opinions philosophiques opposées qui ne peuvent pas dans le domaine de la

---

[1] 'A Brief History of My Opinions', *The Philosophy of Santayana*, p. 18.
[2] Op. cit., p. 110.

Eliot's Synthesis

discussion philosophique être maintenues simultanément, peuvent être ainsi unies et réconciliés sur le plan poétique.[1]

No voice, in fact, is wholly lost. In effecting a synthesis of all the voices, the poetry directs our attention to what they have in common. And if there is no basic incongruity, the poetic synthesis may even suggest a rational one.

If we view the attitudes and ideas of Eliot's poetry as a whole, we do find a striking correspondence and inter-relationship between those of the seemingly most disparate derivations. And where there are discrepancies they have mostly been overcome in various ways. By trying to describe in poetry what it *feels* like to believe in something rather than to make statements of belief, Eliot has managed to integrate belief with art to a surprising extent, persuading each to fulfil the conditions of the other. Thus Christianity becomes a vision, a certain way of seeing and feeling things rather than a system of theology. 'The trouble of the modern age,' Eliot wrote in 1943, 'is not merely the inability to believe certain things about God and man which our forefathers believed, but the inability to *feel* towards God and man as they did.'[2] He would like to make religion a matter not of sentiment or emotional effervescence, but of emotional response.

This is not to say that he is uninterested in systematic theology. Even in his role of Eeldrop, as far back as 1917, he professed an interest in this subject. And it is well known that after he joined the Church of England he has taken a keen interest in its doctrine and policies. Occasionally he has come out as a champion of strict orthodoxy and an opponent of any measure of religious syncretism, as in his pamphlet *Reunion by Destruction*, in which he finds the Church of England already too latitudinarian and warns against the attempt that was being made in 1943 to form an amalgamation of Christian churches in South India. On the other hand, his recognition of other religions is very liberal. In 1945 he gave it as his opinion that 'any religion, while it lasts, and on its own level, gives a meaning to life, and preserves the mass of humanity from that boredom which ends in despair'.[3] And he actually

---

[1] Eliot, 'Charybde et Scylla', *Annales du Centre Universitaire Méditerranéen*, Vol. V (1951–2), p. 79.

[2] 'The Social Function of Poetry', *Norseman*, Nov. 1943.

[3] 'Cultural Forces in the Human Order' in M. B. Reckitt (ed.), *Prospect for Christendom* (1945), p. 69.

welcomes a degree of religious universalism if we may trust the introductions he has written for two anthologies of excerpts from scriptural and contemplative writings. In one of these[1] he commends 'the fusion of Eastern and Western culture in the anthologist's mind and heart'. In the other[2] he criticises both those readers who 'regard Asiatic literature as the sole repository of religious understanding' and those who 'refuse to venture further than a narrow Christian tradition'. He then continues:

> For both kinds of reader, it is salutary to learn that the Truth is not 'occult', and that it is not wholly confined to their own religious tradition. . . . With these thoughts in mind, I attach a special value to an anthology which places side by side passages from Christian, Jewish, Moslem, Hindu and Buddhist scriptures and devotional writings.

It is curious to think that Eliot once registered concern at the interest in Chinese philosophy shown by I. A. Richards, Irving Babbitt and Ezra Pound. This interest indicated, he feared, 'a deracination from the Christian tradition'.[3] If it did, Eliot, with his similar interests, would now be equally uprooted. Not only does he admit to such interests in his prose writings, but his poetry, in which he presents the emotional aspects of his beliefs, clearly depends very strongly on elements from religions other than Christianity to which he has responded emotionally. His early pessimism, connected with the general disillusionment of our epoch, found support both in a certain aspect of Christianity and in the philosophies of Hinduism and Buddhism. His later acceptance of suffering and askesis as ways to blissful perfection is in agreement both with Protestant and Catholic Christianity and with the religions of the East. His idea of divine union might be that of either Christian or Oriental mysticism. In fact it belongs to both. That the difference between them can be made negligible may be illustrated by a short passage from Thomas Aquinas:

> Thus God is known in all things and yet apart from all things; and He is known through knowledge and through ignorance. On the one hand, He is apprehended by intuition, reason, understanding, touch, sense, opinion, imagination, name, and so on; while on the

---

[1] N. G., *The Testament of Immortality* (1940).

[2] N. Gangulee, *Thoughts for Meditation* (1951).

[3] *UPC*, p. 132, note.

other hand He cannot be grasped by intuition nor can He be uttered or named, and He is not anything in the world, nor is He known in any existent thing.[1]

This passage might almost have been an excerpt from the *Bhagavad-Gita*. Hegel and Bradley, Schleiermacher and Emerson would sanction most of it, and even Aristotle would recognise some of his own principles.

Eliot's conception of divine union also appears to have borrowed more than one would think from higher Nature cults and esoteric mysteries. The identification of the 'I' of *The Waste Land* with the Fisher King is more than a whim, and Christ is deliberately associated with the Vegetation God. We have only to notice the part played by the seasons and the prominence of the ideas of fertility in Eliot's poetry to realise the importance he attaches to the divine symbolism inherent in nature and primitive life. In some respects Eliot's position is that of the Gnostics of early Christian times, of whom G. R. S. Mead wrote: 'The claim of these Gnostics was practically that Christianity, or rather the Good News of The Christ, was precisely the consummation of the inner doctrine of the Mystery-institutions of all the nations: the end of them all was the revelation of the Mystery of Man.'[2]

Among the elements of Eliot's poetry that derive from 'the primitive terror', there is one of pagan superstition pure and simple. He resorts from time to time to magic and incantation, despite his contempt for Madame Sosostris and her sisterhood and his condemnation of magic practices in the fifth movement of *The Dry Salvages*. This element appears clearly in Agatha's conjuring in *The Family Reunion*:

> Round and round the circle
> Completing the charm
> So the knot be unknotted
> The crossed be uncrossed
> The crooked be made straight
> And the curse be ended

It would be impossible to tell to what extent magic is woven into the poetry as a whole. In one way, of course, all poetry has

---

[1] From *The Book of the Blessed Dionysius concerning the Divine Names*, vii, lecture 4; quoted from R. Preston, '*Four Quartets*' *Rehearsed*, p. 16.

[2] Quoted by Jessie Weston, *From Ritual to Romance* (1920), p. 145.

an incantatory purpose, or at least an incantatory effect, even at its 'freest'; otherwise it would not be poetry. But Eliot frequently seems to emphasise the effect, for instance in the close of *The Waste Land* ,and *The Hollow Men* and the beginning of *Ash-Wednesday*:

> Because I do not hope to turn again
> Because I do not hope
> Because I do not hope to turn

The problem of reality is generally approached by the poet both from a Christian point of view and from that of a rationalistic monist philosophy. Both points of view may be simultaneously present, as in the statement of the final Chorus of *Murder in the Cathedral* that 'Those who deny Thee could not deny, if Thou didst not exist.' This is an argument taken straight out of the phenomenology of Meinong and Bradley and used to express a religious truth.

The view of history which corresponds to such a view of reality is, in Bradleyan terms, that of a sequence of timeless moments, or 'a pattern of timeless moments' in Eliot's words. There is a feeling of the Absolute, or alternatively of God, in history, vivifying tradition, which would otherwise have been dead and waste, and providing a teleology for all development. Time and timelessness are dealt with according to the theories of modern philosophers combined with the intimations of mystics of various religions, including Christianity, and memories of personal experiences.

Perhaps the most fascinating aspect of Eliot's synthesis is the way in which he seems to identify the Platonic and Christian ideal of Love with the Platonic and Bradleyan idea of timelessness. He finds similar patterns in our experience of love and our experience of time. Just as the time which is measured by hours and minutes is the moving image of eternity, so, as Eliot wrote in a book review, 'the love of two human beings is only made perfect in the love of God'.[1] The world of Appearance is characterised both by being chained to time and by possessing desire without love. It is the world in which the timid lover is reduced to measuring out his life with coffee spoons. But Prufrock is really attracted to something higher than human love, something of which Eliot

---

[1] *CR*, July 1931, p. 773.

said in later life that 'The final cause is the attraction towards God.'[1] There is, as we have seen, a gradual ascent in Eliot's poetry, through the stages of *Prufrock*, *La Figlia*, *The Waste Land*, *Ash-Wednesday*, *Burnt Norton* and the modern plays to the final bliss of earthly and heavenly love in *The Elder Statesman*.

The world of Reality is characterised in its emotional aspect by love and in its intellectual aspect by timelessness (so that the synthesis is also one of thought and feeling). Thus the vision in the hyacinth garden of the *Waste Land*, and in all the other gardens of Eliot's poetry, is a vision at once of absolute love and of absolute being. The formula of this synthesis is given beautifully and concisely at the end of *Burnt Norton*:

> Love is itself unmoving,
> Only the cause and end of movement,
> Timeless, and undesiring

Or in *Little Gidding*:

> . . . This is the use of memory:
> For liberation—not less of love but expanding
> Of love beyond desire, and so liberation
> From the future as well as the past.

Or in the words of Monica in *The Elder Statesman*:

> Before you and I were born, the love was always there
> That brought us together.

One might even say there is a certain eroticism in Eliot's philosophical mysticism, though perhaps not of the kind which he has found vaguely reprehensible in the Spanish mystics of the seventeenth century.[2] He has certainly produced a happy synthesis of the lyrical and the philosophical.

Eliot achieves a very comprehensive synthesis. Yet I think it may be confidently said that his interest in Eastern mysticism and various non-Christian philosophies neither indicates nor causes a deracination from Christianity. He ranges far from Christian dogma at times, but his synthesis of ideas is still ordered and dominated by his religious beliefs.

Whether or not his later works should be called 'religious

[1] 'Dante', *SE*, p. 274.
[2] See 'Thinking in Verse', *Listener*, March 12, 1930

poetry' is a matter of definition. *The Rock* and *Murder in the Cathedral*, which were written for special Church occasions, have a more direct devotional character than most of the other writings, and this character is shared to some extent by the Good Friday poem *East Coker*. In the remainder of his works he strives, generally with great success, to avoid a didactic attitude and to express merely his personal religious feelings. But if his poetry is not religious in the sense of devotional verse, it is certainly not just lyrical effusion into which religion enters as more or less fortuitous material. In Donne's poetry Eliot found only 'a vast jumble of incoherent erudition on which he [Donne] drew for purely poetic effect'. A malicious critic might say the same of Eliot's poetry. But he would be wrong, just as Eliot was probably wrong about Donne. In our discussion of poetic belief we concluded that belief is emotional attachment, and such attachment cannot be absent from poetry if the poetry is at all moving. The suggestions of Eliot's poetry (as of Donne's) certainly call for belief just as they are inspired by belief.

I think most readers would agree that Eliot makes his synthesis without doing violence to Christian orthodoxy. But he does take up Christian positions which in many respects are extreme, while he more or less ignores others. And in so doing he has helped to change Christianity, if ever so slightly. We remember his words about Christianity having to be constantly adapted into something that can be believed in (which, he said, had nothing to do with liberal theology). By his own work he has contributed to the adaptation of Christianity to the consciousness of our age. To illustrate this we need only consider the way in which he repeatedly suggests the redemption of mankind, not by 'the blood of the Lamb', but through the realisation of timelessness. Miss Helen Gardner objects to the introduction of Krishna in *The Dry Salvages* on the ground that 'there is an unbridgeable gap between a religion that despairs of the material world and a religion that is built upon faith in an event by which the material world was not condemned but saved'.[1] But Eliot envisages redemption *from* history *and* redemption *of* history. By leaning towards the doctrine of the Incarnation ('the intersection of the timeless with time') rather than towards that of the Atonement, he finds it possible to believe in redemption through the realisation of a timeless fulfil-

[1] Rajan's symposium, p. 69, note.

ment of the temporal and manages to reconcile Christianity and Hinduism without offending against either. As Brother George Every says: 'Saint Augustine's City of God "that does all to the glory of God" may legitimately receive an even wider acceptation [than the Church Universal in *The Rock*], that would put Arjuna among its citizens, with other saints, sages and statesmen, known and unknown, who have in their own office and ministry obeyed the will of God.'[1]

Our response to Eliot's poetry is facilitated by its being, in general, closely relevant to the thought of our time. Whether or not he took the cue from Arnold his work is a good illustration of Arnold's views concerning the subject-matter and aim of literature, as set forth in 'The Function of Criticism':

> In literature . . . the elements with which the creative power works are ideas; the best ideas on every matter which literature touches, current at the time. . . . And I say *current* at the time, not merely accessible at the time; for creative literary genius does not principally show itself in discovering new ideas, that is rather the business of the philosopher. The grand work of literary genius is a work of synthesis and exposition, not of analysis and discovery.

Eliot employs current ideas rather than special and recondite theories. Speculations regarding the nature of time, for instance, have been very common in English literature since the nineteen-twenties. Often they are little more than a game. Priestley may have taken J. W. Dunne's ideas seriously, but he serves us his 'Split Time, Serial Time and Circular Time' as so many fancy dishes. Wells and Shaw, in their experiments with time, are only half in earnest; but Joyce, Huxley and Virginia Woolf all have a background of real thinking for their imaginative treatment of time. That Eliot himself regards a vague awareness of modern ideas on this subject as common property, is shown amusingly in *The Rock*, in which one of the workmen is made to declare: 'There's some new notion about time, what says that the past—what's be'ind you—is what's goin' to 'appen in the future, bein' as the future 'as already 'appened. I 'aven't 'ad time to get the 'ang of it yet; but——'

Mysticism—Christian and Oriental—has also become a widespread interest among writers. When Somerset Maugham briefly

---

[1] March and Tambimuttu's symposium, pp. 186–7.

introduced the thoughts of St John of the Cross into *Of Human Bondage*, he was probably acting on an original impulse. But when, in *The Razor's Edge*, he introduced yoga it seemed a tribute to the fashion of the moment. Aldous Huxley's has probably been the strongest influence in our time to popularise the mysticism of the East. But Eliot's influence has been far from negligible.

Both Freud and Frazer with other pioneers in the sciences of the human mind and human conduct are accepted in Eliot's poetry. And since they are united there with the teachers of religion, it is demonstrated—as clearly as poetry can demonstrate anything—that neither psychoanalysis nor anthropology is incompatible with Christianity. Rather the points of contact between them come to the fore: the psychoanalyst's demonstration of the imperfection, or the sinfulness, of human nature; the anthropologist's demonstration of the perennial urge towards religious belief and community in life and tradition.

Politics also contribute to the general 'ideology', though I have not thought it necessary to mention the political element before: it is not so important as some critics of Eliot would have it. In *Coriolan*, the aristocratic ideal is held up to reflect unfavourably on the bureaucratic clumsiness of a falsely democratic society, and on the mob mentality which Eliot so much detests. His political and social ideals are not those of American, or French, or Russian equalitarianism, but spring in the last analysis from Plato, Aristotle, Brahmanism, Confucianism and the Schoolmen. In *The Rock*, the author turns equally against redshirts, blackshirts and plutocrats:

> There is no help in parties, none in interests,
> There is no help in those whose souls are choked and swaddled
> In the old winding-sheets of place and power
> Or the new winding-sheets of mass-made thought.
> O world! forget your glories and your quarrels,
> Forget your groups and your misplaced ambitions,
> We speak to you as individual men;
> As individuals alone with GOD.

Writing in 1924, Eliot saluted T. E. Hulme as 'the forerunner of a new attitude of mind, which should be the twentieth-century mind, if the twentieth century is to have a mind of its own. Hulme,' he said, 'is classical, reactionary, and revolutionary; he is the antipodes of the eclectic, tolerant, and democratic mind of the end of the last century.' Hulme's closest affinities he found in France, with Charles Maurras, Albert Sorel and Pierre Lasserre.[1] Eliot, however, does not give his allegiance to any party. He envisages a state of things in which the Church, 'the Rock', shall be our guide in temporal as well as in spiritual affairs. His interest in King Charles I in *Little Gidding* is dictated by Anglican as much as by royalist sympathies, and he sees Charles with his opponents 'folded in a single party' by the reconciliation of history. In the same way, it is suggested, present controversies will be reconciled. Meanwhile he advises us to take sensible policies where we can find them. In *The Rock* he advocates the principles of Credit Reform and the economic theories of J. M. Keynes. *The Rock*, however, is something of a propaganda play, so that its preoccupation with practical questions of politics and economics cannot be regarded as typical of Eliot's poetry as a whole.

In modern philosophy Eliot exhibits such varied tastes that it is easiest to define him by negatives. He dislikes Utilitarianism, Pragmatism, Behaviourism and the New Realism, as well as secular Humanism, his inclination being against the schools of thought which tend to emphasise the practical and contingent. His tastes in philosophy, as in literature, are definitely classical. But he has not escaped the impress of individualistic thought, such as that of Schleiermacher and Emerson.

Poetry does not have to worry about contradictions, and Eliot reconciles very many. Whether an actual compromise takes place or a balance of opposites is established, the effect is usually that of moderation, of the avoidance of extremes, of what is so very characteristic of Eliot both as a critic and as a poet: the *via media*.

'During the past twenty years the chief or average complaint against the almost reverend Eliot has been that he exaggerated his moderations.' The words are Ezra Pound's and were written in 1937.[2] They may not be quite true as the statement of an average complaint, but they do put something of the essential Eliot in a nutshell. It was no accident that made him choose the *via media* of the Church of England[3] and a political Toryism that was neither conservative nor liberal; that brought him to England rather than

---

[1] *CR*, Commentary, April 24, 1924.   [2] *Polite Essays*, p. 98.
[3] 'the bastard, schismatic and provincial if genteel kind of Catholicism that, for the time being, at any rate, he has, somewhat New Englishly stopped at'! (McGreevy).

to France, and to a classicism that was almost absorbed into modern romanticism. It was not for nothing that he applied for guidance to the philosophers of the golden mean, Aristotle and Buddha, or that he wrote in praise of Machiavelli: 'For Machiavelli is a doctor of the mean, and the mean is always insupportable to partisans of the extreme.'[1] In another connection he declared that 'there must always be a middle way, though sometimes a devious way when natural obstacles have to be circumvented; and this middle way will, I think, be found to be the way of orthodoxy; a way of mediation, but never, in those matters which permanently matter, a way of compromise'.[2]

Thus the middle way represents no mere pruning and abandonment of extreme or absolute ideas. Eliot revolted (e.g. in 'Tradition and the Individual Talent') against the individualism of the Imagists, but did not drop it; instead he brought it, by a kind of transcendence, into a wider whole. Both the personal and the objective were to count in poetry: the personal as brute matter, the objective as the finished product. And similarly his Puritanism, his Unitarianism, his Absolute Idealism remained very actively with him to mingle with his Catholicism. For this reason he has always been abused by somebody or other. But the trouble with Eliot is not his own extremes, for in his early phase there was much Christianity mingled with his scepticism, and in his later phase there is much scepticism and unorthodoxy mingled with his Christianity. The trouble is the extremes of the belligerents who surround him. Eliot, in fact, has proved to be, what he admired Hulme for not being, eclectic and tolerant.

As to the literary problems that have concerned us in this book, these, too, are solved in Eliot's typical mediating fashion. In theory as well as in practice, he tries to reconcile the demands of thought with the demands of form. The following passages from his criticism sum up his views on this point very clearly:

> The one extreme is to like poetry merely for what it has to say. . . . The other extreme is to like the poetry because the poet has manipulated his material into perfect art. . . . But between these extremes occurs a continuous range of appreciations, each of which has its limited validity.[3]

---

[1] *For Lancelot Andrewes*, p. 63. [2] *EAM*, pp. 134–5.
[3] 'Poetry and Propaganda', *Literary Opinion in America*, p. 33.

. . . we must avoid being seduced into one or the other of two extreme opinions. The first is, that it is simply the value of the *ideas* expressed in a poem which gives the value to the poetry; or that it is the *truth* of his view of life—by which we ordinarily mean its congruity with our own view—that matters. The other is, that the ideas, the beliefs of the poet do not matter at all; that they are rather like some alloy, necessary for the poet in order to manipulate his true material, which is refined out of the poetry in the course of time.[1]

The moral and educational value of poetry is regarded as positive but limited. In Eliot's words, 'between the motive which Rivière attributed to Molière and Racine [distraire les honnêtes gens] and the motive of Matthew Arnold bearing on shoulders immense what he thought to be the orb of the poet's fate, there is a serious *via media*.'[2]

In poetic form and imagery Eliot avoids all kinds of overloading, unless he is out for very special effects. Generally he finds a middle way between intellectualism and lyricism, or he balances the two in alternate lines and stanzas. The difficult and involved is continually set off by the simple and translucent, a fact which immediately emerges if his poetry is compared with the far opaquer medium of W. H. Auden. And Eliot's symbolism is supported and made accessible by naturalistic imagery, as a comparison with Yeats will bring out.

Eliot is not the arch-intellectualist in poetry that many people think. But, of course, his intellectual habits are mirrored in his poetry, so that the latter presents the attitudes of one accustomed to reflection. He may have had good reasons for the anti-emotionalism expressed in 'Tradition and the Individual Talent', but it is impossible to refine emotion out of poetry altogether; and this Eliot has recognised, for he has told us repeatedly that his poetry expresses what it *feels* like to believe in something.

We may reasonably ask in what lies the greatest beauty of poetry in general and of Eliot's in particular. Are not the most beautiful passages of Eliot's work the emotional ones, and the intellectual sections rather like intervening prose commentaries? And is his poetry 'poetic' in the same measure as it is 'traditional'? That this may be so seems to be testified by the admiration to which many

[1] 'The Social Function of Poetry', *Adelphi*, July/Sept. 1945.
[2] *UPC*, p. 137.

critics are moved by the musical evocativeness of *Marina* or the poignant emotions of *Journey of the Magi*, or the rich, Pre-Raphaelite picturesqueness of *Ash-Wednesday*. It might even be asked whether, for real beauty, it is not necessary to use images from nature, like Eliot's orchards and thrushes and New England coastline. Are not his streets and smoke and fog made poetically beautiful, as far as they *are* poetically beautiful, by being compared with natural objects and living beings? Spender calls an aeroplane 'more beautiful and soft than any moth'; yet it is precisely the image of the moth that lends it its beauty. Beauty, like humour, feeds on comparison.

It is true that poetry which seems to vibrate with emotion, and poetry which uses natural imagery or picturesque substitutes for it moves us more immediately with a sense of beauty than other kinds. *La Figlia* moves us in this way, while *Sweeney Erect* moves us primarily with a sense of the ludicrous. If beauty is the soul of poetry and wit-writing another thing altogether, then, one might say, *La Figlia* is poetry and *Sweeney* or *A Cooking Egg* is mere verse. But that is not to say that the poetry which stirs our emotions most deeply embodies the deepest or most original feelings of the poet. *La Figlia* may contain much personal matter, but it certainly contains much pasticcio, ranging from Drummond's *Madrigal* to Rossetti's *Blessed Damozel* and Laforgue's *Pétition* and *Sur une défunte*. Even the prosiest parts of *Gerontion*, on the other hand, may spring from very intense feelings indeed. It is all a matter of how we read. If we are capable of being moved by the same things as the poet, we shall find that the outward shows may be least themselves; and that even the grotesque and ribald may hide a pathos that gives it poetic dignity. Eliot's cat poems are no more than comic verse, for they are void of pathos. But everything that he has submitted as poetry has a good right to that name. And this right is not impaired by his sparing use of 'beautiful' effects, because this is only one of his ways of showing moderation. We are not required to call ugliness beautiful; but we are required 'to see beneath both beauty and ugliness; to see the boredom, and the horror, and the glory'. These things Eliot can make us see, and there is an amazing power in the imagery, the associations and the sequences by which he makes them visible to us.

Because of the balance of his effects, it is necessary for his readers to develop a sense of counterpoint. And this must not only embrace the style, so that one obtains, for instance, a systematic accompaniment to the actual rhythm; but it must also embrace descriptions, ideas and feelings. Thus ugliness will set off beauty and both together will point to something beneath or beyond them. And the intellect and the emotions will be constantly united, realising Eliot's great ideal, the sensuous apprehension of thought and the fusion of ideas with feelings.

Eliot's message to our divided age, and his importance in our spiritual situation, lie chiefly in these two things together: synthesis and compromise. These things have nothing to do with petty bourgeois timidity, and are not despicable, but wise and sane. There exists a sort of fortuitous synthesis which is due to lack of critical ability, and there exists a sort of compromise which is due to lack of moral fibre and moral standards. But rightly understood the ideals of synthesis and compromise can only be realised in any degree by understanding and imagination, by critical intelligence and daring passion. They need, in fact, the imagination and the daring of a poet.

'Our age is an age of moderate virtue / And of moderate vice.'[1] We need no further moderation at least in virtue. But we need moderation in intellectual and materialistic aspirations, in political allegiances, in mass consciousness. The doctrine of the mean must not be applied indiscriminately. Eliot on the whole applies it rightly. In our contemporary situation, the importance of his visionary and philosophical approach to poetry must not be underestimated.

Altogether, Eliot's synthesis may not be very original in its details, as some critics have pointed out. But it is original and great in the final combination which it effects. There are inconsistencies, but they appear rather as different facets of one body of philosophy than as contradictory fragments of various philosophies. This combination has been possible because the thoughts of the age have been deeply experienced by a poet who has not been deterred by doctrines or prejudices from creating a unity of his experiences. Perhaps it was a boon that Eliot came late to Christianity: he assimilated more ideas than he might have done if he had come to anchor at an earlier date.

'A great poet, in writing himself, writes his time,' said Eliot.

[1] *The Rock*, Chorus VIII.

He himself not only writes his time, or he no longer does only that. He is also instrumental in *creating* the outlook of his time by amalgamating its scattered ideas. Eliot praised Joyce for trying to do something like this. The structure of *Ulysses*, he said, 'is simply a way of controlling, of ordering, of giving a shape and a significance to the immense panorama of futility and anarchy which is contemporary history'.[1] Joyce, however, imposed an artificial significance on his world for the purposes of art only. Eliot in some measure does the same thing, as when he uses the four elements as a scaffolding for the *Quartets*. But both Joyce and Eliot, particularly the latter, are saved from artificiality by their awareness of and their loyalty to the unifying experience. Eliot finds the union of scepticism and faith, hedonism and asceticism significant because it has been significant to him. And his poetry is 'the expression of a totality of unified interests',[2] to use his description of Wordsworth's and Coleridge's work.

No voice is wholly lost if it has once sounded with authority or charm in Eliot's ears. Of a poet's development it may indeed be said that *il n'abandonne rien en route*. Thus we see that tradition operates on the level of individuals as well as on that of general culture. The whole past history of a man composes an ideal order, and the sense of this order compels a man to write with his whole past in his bones. One's allegiance can change, as Eliot's changed in respect of Babbitt or Bradley, but one's views and attitudes can hardly change so completely that the old ideas lose all their appeal and do not present themselves in moments of doubt as the only tenable ones. The hovering between two or more worlds is not only a personal affliction, but the affliction of our time, and we must be grateful to the poet who can help us to find a pattern of belief. I do not subscribe more than Eliot to the Arnold–Richards view that poetry can save us, ultimately, but at least it can help us over a difficult crossing. It is the difficulty to-day of integrating theories of life into a view of life that makes the work of poets significant from a philosophical point of view.

Eliot has not only given our age a poetic idiom, as has sufficiently been recognised, but has also shown the way to an integral philosophy. My calling it integral does not mean that it accepts all tendencies of our time or takes cognisance of all its spiritual

[1] 'Ulysses, order, and myth', *Dial*, Nov. 1923.
[2] *UPC*, p. 81.

features. It repudiates mechanism[1] and materialistic determinism. It repudiates equalitarianism and all sorts of mass loyalties. It also has little to do with the exact sciences and has not caught up with atomic physics. But there is enough left, as I have endeavoured to show. And what is left out is generally left out because it is incompatible with the *Primat des Spiritualen*. For Eliot's synthesis, human *ratio* and all, is based on the recognition of the supernatural. And 'to believe in the supernatural', he said in an address to Unitarian clergymen, 'is not simply to believe that after living a successful, material, and fairly virtuous life here one will continue to exist in the best-possible substitute for this world, or that after living a starved and stunted life here one will be compensated with all the good things one has gone without: it is to believe that the supernatural is the greatest reality here and now'.[2] A supernatural, or shall we call it an irrational, principle is at work in the combination of the very elements of Eliot's outlook: it is not for nothing that this outlook is expressed in poetry and could hardly have been expressed otherwise without being mutilated.

Mr Delmore Schwartz regards Eliot as 'a culture hero', chiefly because experience in the modern world has become international, 'the true causes of many of the things in our lives are worldwide', and Eliot has been able to interpret this internationalism. 'Since the future is bound to be international . . .' concludes Mr Schwartz, 'we are all the bankrupt heirs of the ages, and the moments of the crisis expressed in Eliot's work are a prophecy of the crises of our own future in regard to love, religious belief, good and evil, the good life and the nature of the just society. *The Waste Land* will soon be as good as new.'[3]

Mr Schwartz's arguments are sometimes fanciful, but his main conclusions stand. Eliot is a cosmopolitan, and apparently wants to be, for he addresses himself to readers who have a cosmopolitan culture. I would add that if Eliot is to be regarded as an international prophet it is not only because he has stated the dilemma of the modern *déraciné*, the international man, but because he has

---

[1] Strangely enough, it has little to say of the outward mechanisation of life and still less of the value of country life. Mechanisation is reflected in the characters portrayed, and it is dealt with in *The Rock*, but otherwise these things do not seem to have interested Eliot very much as a poet.

[2] *Christian Register*, Oct. 19, 1933.

[3] See Unger's *Selected Critique*, pp. 43–50.

brought together in his work cultures widely separated in time and space—Phrygian, Indian, Roman, nineteenth-century American and modern European.

'Britain is the bridge between Latin culture and Germanic culture in both of which she shares,' wrote Eliot in 1928. He added that Britain, because of the Empire, was also 'the connection between Europe and the rest of the world'.[1] And almost twenty years later, in his reflections on 'The Unity of European Culture', he declared that 'the variety of the elements of which English is made up' makes it, 'of all the languages of modern Europe, the richest for the purposes of writing poetry'.[2] These opinions help to explain the comprehensiveness of tradition, both philosophical and linguistic, that we find in his work. He is steeped in the English heritage on the one hand, and on the other hand he acknowledges his debt to such remote literatures as those of ancient India and China.[3]

The Elizabethan inheritance, itself a composite affair, is conspicuous in his work. Its thefts and borrowings, echoes and re-echoes, its baroque phrasing penetrated by thrusts of startling simplicity, its subtlety of sensual and emotional effect, its feeling for the horrible and grotesque, even the perverse, its metaphysical curiosity, are all present in Eliot. From Webster, Chapman and Drummond, by way of Donne, Marvell and Browning, there is an unbroken line to the contemporary poet. Nor has Eliot remained unaffected by the poets of this succession or of collateral lines whom he finds less congenial: Spenser, Shelley, Tennyson, Rossetti, Swinburne. To point to specific debts to all of these poets would be simple but supererogatory.

The French Symbolist succession, which may be said to start with Baudelaire, is related to the English line. And it would not be out of place to mention the New England tradition, especially the novelists Hawthorne, Melville and Henry James, in the same breath, for there are distinct similarities. The Symbolist movement was in part a reaction against naturalism, and by its belief in a transcendent reality it had strong affinities with Christian and philosophical idealism, though its connection with neo-Thomism is a later phenomenon and to a great extent due to Eliot.

---

[1] Commentary, *CR*, March 1928.
[2] *Notes towards the Definition of Culture*, pp. 110–11.
[3] Vide ibid., p. 113.

A line of religious and mystical poetry cuts across national and denominational boundaries, and connects Dante with Herbert, Milton and Blake. Of these Dante has exerted incomparably the greatest influence on Eliot's poetry, from first to last. We should also mention St John of the Cross, Pascal and other great men and women of faith and illumination, whose prose writings have appealed strongly to many modern poets.

Right faith is associated in Eliot's mind with Toryism and classicism, and the combination of these elements seems to him to represent the summit of what the cultured mind should aspire to. From Homer and Virgil and their countrymen comes a legacy of maturity and poise, from the Old and New Testaments a sense of the infinite, which meet in the theology of St Thomas, of Hooker and Andrewes, in the poetry of Dryden and the criticism of Johnson.

A tradition that runs counter to the religious, if not to the classical strain of his poetry is that of worldly-wise scepticism and disrespectful satire. Richard Aldington calls it 'the secular tradition of "poètes contumaces" or "poètes libertins", which runs from the poets of to-day to Laforgue and Verlaine, to Rimbaud and Corbière, to Aloysius Bertrand, to Saint-Amant, to Théophile, back to Villon, and beyond him to a shadowy host of mediaeval "pinces-sans-rire", "goliards" and satiric "goguenards", whose sharp tongues spared neither the Church nor the rich nor the pretty ladies.'[1] We find a good deal of this in James Joyce, and we are not surprised to find the author of *Mr. Eliot's Sunday Morning Service* expressing the liveliest admiration for the author of *Ulysses*.

His importance in our literary situation is even greater than in our spiritual situation. I do not think it is true that modern poets must be difficult, or that there is any reason why ideas connected with a complex civilisation must be expressed in complex terms. But Eliot fortunately does not practise these principles to the extent that might be feared. And he is more important in other respects than as a representative of difficult poetry. Mr Michael Roberts, in his preface to *New Signatures* (1932), wrote: 'The poems in this book represent a clear reaction against esoteric poetry in which it is necessary for the reader to catch each recondite allusion.' And Louis MacNeice, who quotes this preface,

[1] Unger's *Selected Critique*, p. 7.

adds: 'These new poets, in fact, were boiling down Eliot's "variety and complexity" and finding that it left them with certain comparatively clear-cut issues.'[1] Thus in spite of all the imitation of Eliot's complexity of form and matter which undoubtedly has taken place, it was not this aspect that young poets found most stimulating. And many of them found it a hindrance.

But Eliot has realised, in his own way, MacNeice's wish for '*impure* poetry, that is, for poetry conditioned by the poet's life and the world around him', adding the metaphysical element which MacNeice did not include in his wish. 'Poetry to-day', says MacNeice, 'should steer a middle course between pure entertainment ("escape poetry") and propaganda. . . . The writer to-day should be not so much the mouthpiece of a community (for then he will only tell it what it knows already) as its conscience, its critical faculty, its generous instinct. . . . Others can tell lies more efficiently; no one except the poet can give us poetic truth.'[2] These conditions Eliot has fulfilled most admirably; and it is a literary as well as a spiritual achievement.

While allowing the application of art for useful purposes, Eliot has been one of the staunchest upholders of its integrity, and has thus done it an inestimable service in an age when propaganda is seeking whom it may devour. He has helped to save it from the indignity to which psychoanalytic, marxist and other theories (including religious ones) might have reduced it. He has earned the gratitude of the aestheticists, particularly Edith Sitwell, while he has exercised a considerable ascendancy over such writers as Day Lewis and Henry Treece. The latter's 'Apocalypse' was not much more than a different name for Eliot's synthesis of experience and ideas, and his 'Anarchism' differs only slightly from Eliot's Toryism.[3]

Modern poets have been greatly occupied with symbols and images, and a good deal of critical writing on these subjects has been produced. Symbolism and allegory as means of stating difficult thoughts in 'clear visual imagery' owe much of their popularity (which has extended even to fiction) to Eliot's theory and practice. The break with surface realism with which Eliot was associated and which he has more and more come to stand for, was a break both with Georgian descriptive prettiness and late

---

[1] MacNeice, *Modern Poetry* (1938), p. 15. [2] Ibid., Preface.
[3] Cf. Treece: *How I See Apocalypse* (1946), pp. 21, 76 and *passim*.

Victorian narrative and picturesque poetry. Symbolism, as it has been *practised* by Eliot (and not the 'dislocation' of language or verbal conceits) is the best means of grappling with a complex civilisation, for it gives an amazing penetration and power to the poet's vision, and enables him to combine concepts which ordinary language has no way of combining.

Many people would say that Eliot's greatest contribution to literature is a modern poetic idiom. His adaptation of contemporary speech to poetic uses gave his diction an air of sophisticated crudity at first; but it has become more and more fluent and un-selfconscious with time. He has generally kept clear of slang and technical jargons but otherwise he has won acceptance in poetry for the whole vocabulary of cultivated speech and for common conversational style at its best. At the same time his careful use of words and his deliberate archaisms have reminded us more forcibly than most linguists have been able to, of the urgent need for word-consciousness and precise expression. As for his metrical achievements, not many of his imitators have fully appreciated his discreet use of 'free verse'. But it is constantly there as an example.

It is no doubt Eliot's technique and imagery that have attracted the largest number of disciples to his poetry. Young poets, as Edmund Wilson says, 'took to inhabiting exclusively barren beaches, cactus-grown deserts, and dusty attics overrun with rats'[1] in imitation of the author of *The Waste Land*, and Eliot's visionary concepts often became mere technical props in the hands of his admirers. But sometimes they were more than an affectation. 'No one,' wrote Archibald MacLeish in 1938, 'has made his language, his rhythms, more nearly a part of our own lives, our own experience [than Eliot]—so that there are streets, houses, windows, people, cities in our past which recall only his poems'.[2]

In Anne Ridler's opinion, 'Eliot provides the necessary standard of perfection', but for that very reason she thinks it is difficult to learn from him. 'For the generations following Eliot,' she declares, 'it was a more voluble poet who loosened their tongues . . . It was Auden's use of stanza and stress which proved the easier for the novice to handle.'[3] Auden himself, however, transmitted

---

[1] *Axel's Castle*, p. 114.
[2] *Harvard Advocate*, Dec. 1938, p. 18.
[3] Rajan's symposium, pp. 118, 109.

much of Eliot's influence indirectly;[1] and, by whatever channels it has penetrated, Eliot's manner is discernible in the work of most contemporary poets writing in English. It has not always been beneficial, but this will usually be found to be due to a lack of just estimation on the part of his imitators. Few have achieved his balance in the use of free verse. Many have found their chief inspiration in his modernistic conceits—and Auden is not entirely innocent of exaggerating effects such as these. Some, like Dylan Thomas, have gone to extremes in obscure symbolism. Others have over-reached themselves in experimenting with discontinuity in their thematic variations.

Perhaps the most generally successful (or the least frequently unsuccessful) influence of Eliot's form has been the establishment of the long–short poem of the type of *The Waste Land* or the *Quartets*. These varied, descriptive-philosophical poems have obviously meant much to Edith Sitwell. Her *Song of the Cold*, for instance, plainly owes a great deal to *The Waste Land*, as well as to St.-J. Perse's *Anabase*. (The latter poem Eliot has helped to make known to English readers by his translation of it.)

Such similarities with Eliot as we find in *The Song of the Cold* and *The Shadow of Cain*, are similarities of content as well as of form. And this is all to the good. There is an intimate correspondence between matter and manner in Eliot's poetry, as I have tried to show, and many of his imitators have probably gone astray in indiscriminately admiring his technique whilst rejecting his thought. On the other hand, though Eliot's influence has been primarily technical, the influence of his thought has been far from negligible. It looks as if the enormous interest in poetic technique which dominated the decade from 1912 to 1922 began to wane among poets after the latter date,[2] and their attention was turned more to ideas. It was fortunate for Eliot's growing ascendancy that he could stimulate thought as well as formal invention, and though many poets refused to follow him into the Christian camp, he may yet have been instrumental in bringing them to realise the need of an ordered vision.

In conclusion, the value of the poetry is largely a matter of taste and circumstance—of individual readers and of the generations to which they belong. Few people would be as unapprecia-

[1] Cf. G. M. O'Donnell, *Harvard Advocate*, Dec. 1938, p. 18.
[2] Cf. Malcolm Cowley in Unger's *Selected Critique*, p. 32.

tive as the London bookseller who, on being asked for a book called *The Achievement of T. S. Eliot*, indignantly demanded, 'What achievement?' And not everybody would rapturously compare Eliot's work to the Grand Canyon in Colorado, as does the author of *T. S. Eliot and the Lay Reader*. But between these extremes there is still room for many gradations, from admiration through indifference or bewilderment to vexation. And again, among the many admirers of Eliot's poetry, some will be found who admire it for this reason and some for that. It has assumed importance in our generation because it appeared at a time when a bold lead in a new direction was badly needed. But T. S. Eliot would be the first to recognise how differently his works may be treated in the future.

GENERAL INDEX

General Index

Objectification, 41, 98, 150, 197, 221

Objective correlative, 34, 41, 43, 110, 137, 150

Obscurity, 81, 93, 95f, 242

O'Donnell, G. M., 242n

Old age, 183, 192f, 209, 220

Omar Khayyám, 8, 68, 210

Optimism, 11, 30, 162

Order, 15, 129, 213, 236

Order of Merit, 31

Oriental mysticism, philosophy, 13f, 18, 143f, 163, 182–9, 195, 224, 227, 230

Original sin, 23, 178, 194–7, 211

Orthodoxy (Christian), 13, 52, 59, 138, 189, 193n, 212f, 223, 228

Ouspensky, P. D., 181

Oxford, 19f

Paganism, 225

Pain, *see* Suffering

Pali, 18

Paradise, Eden, 197, 202, 205, 207f, 215

Paris, 17ff, 26, 134

Pascal, 138, 239

Passion (of Christ), 179, 218

Passivity, 187ff, 203

Patanjali, 18, 186ff, 214

Pater, *The Renaissance*, 174

Pattern, 16, 55, 57, 100ff, 160f, 164, 167, 175–9, 191, 198, 217

Penance, 200f, 208, 210

Perry, R. B., 17n

Perse, St.-J., *Anabase*, 242

Personality, 42, 44, 86, 123f, 193, 201

Pervigilium Veneris, 127

Pessimism, 9, 134, 144, 146, 149, 186, 193, 216, 224

Phenomenology, 20, 72, 129, 160, 226

Philippe, C.-L., *Bubu de Montparnasse*, 19, 134

Philosophy, 11–19, 38f, 50f, 60–9 and passim

Pitkin, W. B., 17n

Plato, Platonism, 13f, 16, 118, 153, 158, 163f, 171, 181, 191, 226, 230

Poetic belief, assent, 61, 66, 68, 73ff, 80, 116, 221, 228

Poetry, 21

Point of view, 38, 80–95

Politics, 12f, 27, 29, 230f, 235

Pound, Ezra, 1, 20–4, 26f, 30, 61, 92, 98, 133, 150, 224; *Exultations*, 21; *Personae*, 21, 92; *Polite Essays*, 231; 'Vorticism', 24

Prabhavananda and Isherwood (tr.), *Bhagavad-Gita*, 183–8

Pragmatism, 14, 231

Predestination, 198

Prejudice, 35, 39, 67f

Pre-Raphaelites, 11, 98, 234

Presentation, 23, 38, 44, 222

Preston, R., *'Four Quartets' Rehearsed*, 185n, 204, 206n, 225n

Priestley, J. B., 229

Primitive myth, ritual, tabus, 18, 61, 106, 189ff, 214, 225

Prince, Morton, 18

Propaganda, 59, 115, 231, 240

Prosody, 8, 10, 82, 104ff

Protestantism, 2, 54, 205, 210, 224

Proust, Marcel, 27

Provençal literature, 22

Psalms, 89

Pseudo-statements, 66, 69f

Psychoanalysis, 132, 230, 240

Psychology, 15, 18, 111, 131ff

Purgatory, Purification, 187, 202ff, 210ff, 218ff

Puritanism, 4, 6, 54f, 210f, 232

Quartet, 214f

Racine, 51, 58f, 233

Rajan, B. (ed.), *T. S. Eliot . . .*, 36n, 139n, 187n, 209n, 228n, 241n

Ransom, J. C., *The New Criticism*, 34

Rationalism, 2, 74, 226

Read, H., 117

Reader's response(s), xii, 49, 65, 71, 75, 150, 221

Reality, 15f, 153, 157–63 and passim

General Index

INDEX OF WORKS BY
T. S. ELIOT

Note: For complete bibliographical information the reader should consult D. Gallup, *T. S. Eliot: A Bibliography* (1952).

A. CRITICISM

Index of Works by T. S. Eliot

Index of Works by T. S. Eliot

B. POEMS